EXPERIENCES
IN
ENTREPRENEURSHIP
AND
SMALL BUSINESS
MANAGEMENT

EXPERIENCES IN ENTREPRENEURSHIP AND SMALL BUSINESS MANAGEMENT

DONALD L. SEXTON
Caruth Professor of Entrepreneurship
Center for Private Enterprise and Entrepreneurship
Baylor University

PHILIP M. VAN AUKEN
Center for Private Enterprise and Entrepreneurship
Baylor University

Prentice-Hall, Inc., *Englewood Cliffs, New Jersey 07632*

Library of Congress Cataloging in Publication Data

Sexton, Donald L.
    Experiences in entrepreneurship and small business management.

    1.-Small business—Management—Case studies.
2.-Entrepreneur—Case studies.   I.-Van Auken,
Philip M.   II.-Title.
HD62.7.S45   658'.022   81-13803
ISBN 0-13-294884-2   AACR2

HD
62.7
.S45

BLACKWELL LIBRARY
SALISBURY STATE COLLEGE
SALISBURY, MARYLAND

WITHDRAWN

Editorial/production supervision and
  interior design by Alice Erdman
Cover design by Carol Zawislak
Manufacturing buyer: Ed O'Dougherty

©1982 by Prentice-Hall, Inc., Englewood Cliffs, N.J. 07632

All rights reserved. No part of this book
may be reproduced in any form or
by any means without permission in writing
from the publisher.

Printed in the United States of America

10 9 8 7 6 5 4 3 2 1

ISBN 0-13-294884-2

Prentice-Hall International, Inc., *London*
Prentice-Hall of Australia Pty. Limited, *Sydney*
Prentice-Hall of Canada, Ltd., *Toronto*
Prentice-Hall of India Private Limited, *New Delhi*
Prentice-Hall of Japan, Inc., *Tokyo*
Prentice-Hall of Southeast Asia Pte. Ltd., *Singapore*
Whitehall Books Limited, *Wellington, New Zealand*

to CAROL and CAROLYN

contents

Preface xv

Introduction xvii

EXPERIENCE PHASE I: Venture Initiation 1

1

Wicker Designs 3
situational management challenges associated with each stage of the company growth cycle

2

The Klothes Korner 7
assessment of alternative pro forma financial plans

3

Pharr Composing Service   13
early venture growth and financing; relationship with a banker; business buyout offer; female entrepreneur

4

Aspheric Enterprises   23
difficulties of new venture initiation; forming the venture team

5

Peppy's Pizza   26
business plan evaluation

6

Craig Nichols and Gary Harwell   44
new venture strategy and competitive edge

7

Exploration Graphics   46
new venture financing; timing of growth; characteristics of entrepreneurs

8

Waterhaus Aqua Slide   55
assessment of new venture potential

9

S & S Farms   58
financial assessment of an agricultural venture; farmers as entrepreneurs

contents ix

EXPERIENCE PHASE II: Venture Management   65

10

Cumberland Crafts   67
management of growth; operations management

11

The Millionaire   **80**
venture investment strategy; assessment of personal entrepreneurial style

12

Polymar Manufacturing   **81**
small business planning

13

Sun City Delivery   **83**
management of growth and expansion; dependence on key customers; business buyout; female entrepreneur

14

Big Sky Western Store   **93**
design of computerized inventory system; competitive strategy focused on pricing

15

Telguard Services   **100**
business growth; strategy evolution; entrepreneurial leadership; role of entrepreneurs in larger companies

16

Emergency Mobile Garage 108
promotional strategy

17

Vessel Apparel Shop 110
entrepreneurial planning; operations planning

18

Sonics Systems-Audio Arts 115
growth strategy; assessing a small company's performance capability

19

Atkins Machining 122
small business managerial responsibilities and roles

20

Magic Carpet Travel Agency 124
response to threatening governmental legislation

21

OMNI Ski Productions 126
business forecasting

22

Colonial American Kitchens 128
production management; getting new venture through the keyhole; product innovation

23

Infomatics Corporation   **140**
business ethics

24

Chama Steelworks   **142**
small business social responsibility; public relations

25

Midwest Municipal Airport   **145**
growth planning; organization survival

26

Eberhardt Products, Inc.   **148**
marketing research

27

Kath Surgical Equipment   **150**
cash flow planning

28

Fantasia Music Company   **152**
profit management; managerial philosophy

29

People Providers   **160**
strategic planning; competitive edge

30

Cameron Mobile Homes   167
response to attempted unionization

EXPERIENCE PHASE III: Venture Transition   171

31

Janeck Furniture   173
planning for expansion

32

Prudhoe Bay Oilfield Servicing   179
key partner death; strategic realignment

33

Philmark Productions   183
making the transition from entrepreneurial management to professional

34

Iron Kettle Restaurant   185
buyout decision; strategic realignment

35

Casner Filtration Systems   189
family transition in a small business; preparation for small company management

36

Animator Toys   **191**
business relocation decision; retail competition in malls; competitive strategy

37

Sicorski and Associates   **202**
determining the financial worth of a company; techniques for buying and selling businesses

38

Nardis Creations   **206**
business turnaround; strategic realignment

39

Goodbuy Grocery   **212**
strategic realignment; relocation decision

EXPERIENCE PHASE IV: The Entrepreneurial Lifestyle   **217**

40

An Entrepreneur's Diary   **219**
The daily experiences and lifestyle of an entrepreneur

41

New Generation Software, Inc. **226**
Minority entrepreneurship

42

McGowan Realty **231**
enterpreneurial lifestyle; female entrepreneur

43

The Keys to Entrepreneurial Success: A Roundtable Discussion **236**
a practitioner's discussion of entrepreneurial success factors

44

Damon Electric **241**
the personal and family side of entrepreneurship

45

What's Your Entrepreneurial Potential? **247**
self assessment questionnaire

preface

Experiences in Entrepreneurship and Small Business Management is aimed at enriching the student's learning experience in courses concerned with initiating and managing small business ventures. Courses in entrepreneurship and small business management are flourishing in business schools as never before, yet there is a noticeable gap in learning resources designed to enrich small business curricula.

In the quest to prepare themselves for future entrepreneurial activities, today's students need, and want, more than standard textbook coverage of small business managerial issues. Cognitive learning must be creatively applied and emotionally experienced to provide a well-rounded educational experience.

Although there is ultimately no substitute for actually operating a business venture, a pragmatic, applications-oriented, educational background can equip the student to make the successful transition from classroom to "real world." *Experiences in Entrepreneurship and Small Business Management* is designed to assist both undergraduate and graduate students in making this pivotal transition.

The book contains a well-balanced variety of learning experiences including comprehensive cases, focused incidents, interviews, experiential exercises and structured problems. All have been classroom tested. A glance at the annotated Table of Contents will reveal the book's thorough coverage of entrepreneurial and small business management issues, both quantitative and qualitative.

The authors have sought to make the book unique in several respects. First of all, the material is organized around a small business life-cycle format consisting of four experiential phases: venture initiation (Phase I), venture strategy and management (Phase II), venture transition (Phase III), and the entrepreneurial lifestyle (Phase IV). Thus the book covers small business strategy as well as operating issues.

A second distinguishing feature of the book is its here-and-now writing style featuring the entrepreneur's own "lingo". The various learning experiences are written in realistic, conversational style to enable students to get into the situation and relate to personalities involved. All of the material is up-to-date and much of it is written in the present, rather than in the past tense, to increase the sense of immediacy and current relevance.

A third unique feature involves the book's mix of industries and varieties of small businesses. Additionally, female and minority entrepreneurs are featured. The geographical coverage is also well-balanced.

A final feature concerns the range of analytical sophistication within the book. The various learning exercises vary in their capacity to challenge students and stretch their skills. However, the exercises are all similar in two important respects: relevance and realism. Questions for analysis and learning are included throughout the book in a stop-action format as a stimulus to student preparation and learning.

All of the material in the book is based on actual, real-world situations, although names and geographic locations have been disguised.

One final mention: *Experiences in Entrepreneurship and Small Business Management* is a flexible book which can be easily adapted to the instructor's own teaching style. The book can be used as a stimulating supplement to small business and entrepreneurship texts or it can be used in conjunction with instructor lectures.

The authors are greatly indebted to a number of individuals who generously devoted their time to us as we prepared this book. We thank the following people for contributing cases or exercises: Helen Ligon of Baylor University, *Big Sky Western Store*, James Weir of Southern Illinois University-Edwardsville; *Colonial American Kitchens*, and Herbert Kierulff of Seattle Pacific University, *Kath Surgical Equipment*.

We want to thank a number of our colleagues at Baylor for their assistance in preparing content material: Dale Allen, Lowell Broom, Terry Frame, Justin Longenecker, Terry Maness, Kris Moore, Richard Scott, and Mike Umble.

We also extend our gratitude to the following friends and associates who assisted in preparing material for the book: Robert Bradford, Jr., Lenelle Campbell, William Cardin, Nancy Carpenter, Vicki Downing, Harold Fletcher, Marie Tarvin Garland, Marcia Grad, Robert Horton, A. J. Hutson, Timothy Jeffery, Jerry Manseur, Darrell Massey, William McCartney, Fred Newman, David Newcomb, Brent Rickels, John Schoen, Charles Synder, Jamie Thompson, Platt Turner, Charles Van Auken, Betty Willis, and Tom Wooten. Thank you, Pat Carroll and Sandy Tighe, for typing the manuscript. Finally, a word of sincere appreciation to W. W Caruth, Jr. who provided, through the Hillcrest Foundation, the Caruth Chair in Entrepreneurship.

Donald L. Sexton

Philip M. Van Auken

introduction

This book has one basic purpose: to help you become better acquainted with the realities of starting and managing small business ventures. The book's many-faceted learning experiences focus on what entrepreneurs do, the problems and challenges they face, their frustrations and satisfactions, and on how entrepreneurs think, feel, and act.

The book is organized into four interrelated learning sections to increase your understanding of the evolving business challenges associated with each stage of the small company lifecycle. Phase I is concerned with venture initiation activities, including such topics as growth financing, business plan development, forming the venture team, and strategic planning.

Phase II deals with how to manage effectively the going-growing concern. Learning experiences in this section of the book focus on both strategic and operating issues: small business planning, inventory management, pricing strategy, forecasting, advertising, marketing research, and cash-flow analysis. In addition, Phase II focuses on the more philosophical issues of small business ethics and social responsibility.

Phase III deals with the small company in transition; the byword is *change*. Specific issues include business buyouts, turnaround strategy, family transition, business relocation, key partner death, and realignment of competitive strategy.

The entrepreneurial lifestyle is explored in Phase IV. The focus here is on what enterpreneurs do and how they feel about their work. Both the personal and family side of entrepreneurship are explored.

The book was written with you, the student, specifically in mind. The authors have not sought to write just another academic volume. Rather they have tried to stress realism and relevance throughout. The book is narrated from the entrepreneur's point of view, using an informal, lively, conversational style. We hope you find it a fresh change of pace.

A Word about Case Analysis

As you tackle the *questions for analysis* found in the stop-action format throughout the book, remember that clearcut, simple answers to managerial problems rarely exist in the real world. Rather than searching in vain for right-versus-wrong answers to questions, focus instead on formulating recommendations that can be persuasively defended in light of the facts at hand.

Strive to make your recommendations specific, clear, and action-oriented. Would a practicing manager be able to take action on the basis of what you have said? Could you successfully defend your action recommendations to an experienced, "bottom line" decision-maker?

Interject your own personal, individual point of view in the way you respond to questions. Entrepreneurship is the domain for individualism and personal creativity. Commit yourself in an articulate way on the book's issues and decisions—know where you stand and why!

Above all else, strive to make your recommendations for specific questions tailor-made for the business situation at hand and your interpretation of it. Consider the size of the company, the capabilities of the management team, the past-performance track record, the competitive environment, and so on. Situational thinking is the key to profitable small business management.

The book ultimately provides you with an opportunity to learn from the pragmatic business experiences of others. The authors hope these experiences in entrepreneurship and small business management are the next best thing to being there!

EXPERIENCES IN ENTREPRENEURSHIP AND SMALL BUSINESS MANAGEMENT

EXPERIENCE PHASE I
venture initiation

wicker designs

1

Wicker Designs, Inc., located in Eau Claire, Wisconsin, manufactures a variety of fashionable wicker and rattan furniture. Started eighteen months ago by Ramond Palacio, production facilities are housed in a medium-size, reconverted garage on the outskirts of Eau Claire. Besides Ramond and his brother Vincent, the company employs a crew of twelve. Gross sales for the first twelve months of operation exceeded $124,000.

Although the company is solvent and on the verge of generating a profit for the first time, the Palacio brothers have expressed concern about the company's future. They recently shared their thoughts with Jay Caststevens, a mutual friend and certified public accountant in Milwaukee.

Caststevens—Wicker Designs has certainly come a long way since I visited you last time. Looks to me like you have gotten off to a fine start both financially and competitively. How many states do you now distribute your furniture in?

Ramond Palacio—Besides most of Wisconsin, we've penetrated southern Minnesota, all of Iowa, and the northern portion of Illinois—Chicago especially. We're working on a new retail chain prospect in St. Louis at the moment.

Caststevens—I'm genuinely impressed with your business know how. I guess you both must feel pretty optimistic about the future.

Vincent Palacio—Actually, Ramond and I are beginning to get cold feet.

Caststevens—Why do you say that? I've just gone over your latest statements and the company is really in pretty solid shape financially. You're due to break out of the red next quarter aren't you?

Ramond Palacio—Oh, we're basically pleased with the company's financial situation. I think what Vince meant by getting cold feet pertained to our readiness to take Wicker Designs through all of the managerial changes that loom ahead.

Vincent Palacio—Like forecasting our sales, adding on to the plant, borrowing money, starting to advertise our furniture line. We're worried about our ability to manage the company's growth.

Caststevens—Boy, I know a lot of struggling businessmen who would love to have those kinds of worries!

Vincent Palacio—Maybe challenges is a better word than worries. Every month confronts Ramond and me with new business challenges that we've never faced before.

Ramond Palacio—Yes, and the bigger Wicker Designs becomes, the more important daily decisions become. When we first opened last year, we could recover from our mistakes with ease. But as the business expands, the mistakes become magnified and harder to rebound from. It's frightening to contemplate what decisions made today may do to us tomorrow.

Caststevens—All businessmen have to take risks. Tomorrow is always a risk, especially in running a small company. You just have to do the best you can every day and trust that things will eventually come out all right. Your capacity for making sound business decisions depends on your ability to anticipate future problems.

Ramond Palacio—You've hit the nail on the head with that last statement. The key to decision making is definitely tied to anticipation of future problems. That's what Vince and I want to talk with you about.

Vincent Palacio—Exactly, Jay, you have specialized your accounting practice in the small venture area. You've seen hundreds of companies grow and die. In our opinion, you are superbly qualified to offer us some guidance for the future.

Caststevens—I appreciate your confidence in me and will be glad to help you out any way that I can. Specifically how can I be of assistance?

Vincent Palacio—Explain to us how small companies typically grow—the stages they evolve through and the management and operations challenges that come with each stage.

Ramond Palacio—In other words, map out for us how you think Wicker Designs is likely to expand and alert us to obstacles we're likely to encounter along the way. With this knowledge we can anticipate future problems and gear up before they sneak up on us.

Caststevens—You've got a pretty tall order there, but I think I can at least draw you a sketch of venture growth patterns. It's really not all that complicated.

Companies typically progress through four major growth phases: start-up, fast growth, maturation, and then stability. After this the company will either decline and eventually go under or start on a new growth curve, perhaps via the merger route.

I would say that Wicker Designs is in the latter stages of start-up and about to move through the key hole. That's an expression that means a company has made it through its initial survival test and is poised to take off along the bell-shaped growth curve.

How fast you progress along the four-stage curve depends on the nature of the product, how competitive and regulated the industry is, the rate of technological obsolescence, and so on. Some companies zoom along the growth curve while others poke along. As you have perceptively noted, the key to business success is not trying to rush through the curve but rather taking situationally appropriate action along the way.

Vincent Palacio—Exactly what do you mean when you say "taking situationally appropriate action"?

Caststevens—Just that you calibrate your operational decisions to fit where you are on the curve. For instance, the financial needs of a company, access to capital, cash flow, use of leverage, and forecasting ability, all change along with growth.

In the area of personnel growth, key growth challenges would include adding line managers, hiring staff people (clerical, technical, sales, and maintenance), and formalizing the training process. Among marketing related variables which evolve along the growth curve are such things as sales volume, extensiveness and content of advertising, and the role of R & D.

Manufacturing concerns revolve around plant expansion, process layout and engineering, and achieving economies of scale. Growth variables keyed to organizational and managerial issues include use of external consultants, proliferation of formal policies and procedures, going public with the sale of stock, involvement with acquisitions and merger, dealing with unions, and making the transition from entrepreneurial (owner-based) management to professional.

Finally, and most importantly, the small firm's competitive strategy evolves along the growth cycle. The company may select different market niches, modify its competitive edge, and vacillate between being a proactive leader in the industry or a reactive follower.

Ramond Palacio—See why we have cold feet, Jay? Managing growth is obviously no simple affair.

Caststevens—But entrepreneurship wouldn't be fun if it were easy! Situational growth management is not really as complicated as I've made it sound. To a large extent, it's just a matter of common sense. The operating challenges along the growth curve are actually quite predictable.

Vincent Palacio—Glad to hear you say that Jay! Would you do us one more favor? Take each of the operating variables that you mentioned a minute ago relating to finance, personnel, marketing, manufacturing, organizational management, and

6 *Experience Phase I: Venture Initiation*

competitive strategy and outline for us the situational challenges that exist in each operating area for every growth phase: start-up, fast growth, maturation, and stability.

In other words, describe for us how operating problems and challenges change as the company continues to grow. With this understanding, Ramond and I can gain a much better feel for where Wicker Designs is headed. Problems won't sneak up on us that way!

Analysis: Respond to Vincent Palacio's request as thoroughly as you can. Using the situational operating variables mentioned by Jay Caststevens, discuss how managerial problems and challenges evolve along with company growth. Use illustrative examples where possible.

the klothes korner

2

The Klothes Korner, located in Providence, Rhode Island, is a specialty clothing store for children. Owned and operated by Marlene Conlee, the Klothes Korner sells new and previously owned children's clothing from newborn through early teens. Approximately 30 percent of sales are of previously owned merchandise, and clothing for girls outsells boy's clothing two to one. Ten percent of sales accrue from custom-made dresses sold on commission. Repeat business accounts for 75 to 80 percent of sales.

Marlene Conlee is thirty-four years old and holds a college degree in secondary education. She taught high school for two years before opening the Klothes Korner in March 1977. Her husband Duane is a junior-high-school assistant principal and helps with the business on weekends. The 1000 square foot store is located in a mini shopping mall that caters to small crafts stores, candle shops, and boutiques.

The primary new clothing lines carried include Polly Flinders clothes for girls, Play Pals togs for boys, Baby Bliss baby wear, and Shirley pajamas. Custom-made dresses sell for $6.50 to $12.50; girls' dresses from $16.50 to $18.50; girls' play sets from $6.50 to $10.50; boys' pants and jeans from $7.50 to $9.50; and baby clothes range from $7.50 to $15.00. All sales are by cash, although major credit cards are used for about 15 percent of sales.

During December of 1980, Marlene developed her pro forma business projection for the coming year. She generated three sets of data based upon a pessimistic projection, a realistic projection, and an optimistic projection. Plan A, the

8 Experience Phase I: Venture Initiation

pessimistic projection, assumes a no-growth position for sales after the store moved into the new building in March, 1979, and before the impact of the recession was felt in April 1980. This plan also assumes that Marlene would continue to operate with a 37 percent gross margin on selling price, which is below the industry average of 48 to 52 percent. Plan B assumes a 25 percent increase in sales, with roughly 15 percent of this coming from inflation, and the balance coming from a higher gross margin and increased sales. In Plan B, the gross margin on selling price is increased to 42 percent. Plan C assumes an increase in sales of 40 percent, and a gross margin of 45 percent. These are shown in the following series of exhibits along with the financial data for 1979 and the first eleven months of 1980.

Analysis: Analyze each of the business plans from the standpoint of assumptions apparently made. Do you question any of these assumptions?

If you were managing The Klothes Korner, which business plan would you accept for 1981?

Compare projected financial ratios for The Klothes Korner with industry averages for retailers of children's clothing.

If you were Marlene Conlee's banker, would you lend her $20,000 for working capital?

If the store were put up for sale, what would be a fair negotiating price range?

EXHIBIT 2-1

1981 BUSINESS PLAN "A": PESSIMISTIC

	Jan.	Feb.	March	April	May	June	July	Aug.	Sept.	Oct.	Nov.	Dec.	Total
Gross Sales	3300	4700	5800	5000	3700	3900	4200	7300	6500	6300	7200	5200	67100
Sales tax (5%)	165	235	290	290	185	195	210	365	325	315	360	460	3355
Net Sales	3135	4465	5510	4750	3515	3705	3990	6935	6175	5985	6840	8740	63745
Cost of goods sold (63%)	1975	2813	3471	2992	2214	2334	2514	4369	3890	3770	4309	5506	40151
Net Income from Sales	1160	1652	2039	1758	1301	1371	1476	2566	2285	2215	2531	3234	23588
Expenses													
Advertising	250	250	250	250	250	250	250	250	250	250	250	250	3000
Rent	445	445	445	445	445	445	445	445	445	445	445	445	5340
Property taxes	13	13	13	13	13	13	13	13	13	13	13	13	156
Telephone	50	50	50	50	50	50	50	50	50	50	50	50	600
Utilities	80	80	80	80	80	80	80	80	80	80	80	80	960
Supplies	70	70	70	70	70	70	70	70	70	70	70	70	840
Auto expense	60	60	60	60	60	60	60	60	60	60	60	60	720
Miscellaneous expense	70	70	70	70	70	70	70	70	70	70	70	70	840
Insurance expense			140										
Wages (part-time help)	550	550	550	550	550	550	550	550	550	550	550	550	6600
Wages (bookkeeper)	40	40	40	40	40	40	40	40	40	40	40	40	480
Wages (contract labor)							70	70	70				210
TOTAL EXPENSES	1628	1628	1768	1628	1628	1698	1698	1698	1628	1628	1628	1628	19886
Income Before Debt Service	(468)	24	271	130	(327)	(327)	(222)	868	657	587	903	1606	3702
Debt Service	345	345	345	345	345	345	345	345	345	345	345	345	4140
NET INCOME	(813)	(321)	(74)	(215)	(672)	(672)	(567)	523	312	242	558	1261	(438)
CUMULATIVE CASH FLOW	(813)	(1134)	(1208)	(1423)	(2095)	(2767)	(3334)	(2811)	(2499)	(2257)	(1699)	(438)	

EXHIBIT 2-2

1981 BUSINESS PLAN "B": REALISTIC

	Jan.	Feb.	March	April	May	June	July	Aug.	Sept.	Oct.	Nov.	Dec.	Total
Gross Sales	4125	5875	7250	6250	4625	4875	5250	9125	8125	7875	9000	11500	83875
Sales tax (5%)	206	294	362	312	232	244	262	457	406	394	450	575	4194
Net Sales	3919	5581	6888	5938	4393	4631	4988	8668	7719	7481	8550	10925	79681
Cost of goods sold (58%)	2273	3237	3995	3444	2548	2686	2893	5027	4477	4339	4959	6336	46214
Net Income From Sales	1646	2344	2893	3444	1845	1945	2095	3641	3242	3142	3591	4589	33467
TOTAL EXPENSES	1628	1628	1768	1628	1628	1698	1698	1698	1628	1628	1628	1628	19886
Income Before Debt Service	18	716	1125	866	217	247	397	1943	1614	1514	1963	2961	13581
Debt Service	345	345	345	345	345	345	345	345	345	345	345	345	4140
NET INCOME	(327)	371	780	521	(128)	(98)	52	1598	1269	1169	1618	2616	9441
CUMULATIVE CASH FLOW	(327)	44	824	1345	1217	1119	1171	2769	4038	5207	6825	9441	

EXHIBIT 2-3

1981 BUSINESS PLAN "C": OPTIMISTIC

	Jan.	Feb.	March	April	May	June	July	Aug.	Sept.	Oct.	Nov.	Dec.	Total
Gross Sales	4620	6580	8120	7000	5180	5460	5880	10220	9100	8820	10080	12880	93940
Sales tax (5%)	231	329	406	350	259	273	294	511	455	441	504	644	4697
Net Sales	4389	6551	7714	6650	4921	5187	5586	9709	8645	8379	9576	12236	89243
Cost of goods sold (55%)	2414	3438	4243	3657	2707	1853	3072	5340	4755	4608	5267	6730	49084
Net Income from Sales	1975	2813	3471	2993	2214	2334	2514	4369	3890	3771	4309	5506	40159
TOTAL EXPENSES	1628	1628	1768	1628	1628	1698	1698	1698	1628	1628	1628	1628	19886
Income Before Debt Service	347	1185	1703	1365	586	636	816	2671	2262	2143	2681	3878	20273
Debt Service	345	345	345	345	345	345	345	345	345	345	345	345	4140
NET INCOME	2	840	1358	1020	241	291	471	2326	1917	1798	2336	3533	16133
CUMULATIVE CASH FLOW	2	842	2200	3220	3461	3752	4223	6549	8466	10264	12600	16133	

EXHIBIT 2-4

MONTHLY GROSS SALES FOR 1979 AND 1980

	1979	1980
January	1360	3210
February	1800	4460
March	4700	5460
April	4990	3700
May	3690	4130
June	3900	2690
July	4250	3890
August	7300	6690
September	6550	5210
October	6350	6730
November	7200	6910
December	9300	—

pharr composing service

3

Cynthia Pharr is president and founder of Pharr Composing Service in Memphis, Tennessee. Since its inception in May 1967, the company has grown steadily showing a net income of $39,000 on sales of $357,000 during 1979. Cynthia has won several civic awards in Memphis, including the city's Business Woman of the Year award. She holds a B.B.A. degree from Memphis State University.

Cindy, tell us how you got into this business.

I started it about thirteen years ago when I went looking for a part-time job that wouldn't take me away for long periods from my three junior-high age kids. I was very involved with football practices and ballet lessons and didn't want to work full-time.

I started working part-time for an appraisal service, putting together an in-house publication. I'd write the copy and then have to get it produced. I had to have one hundred copies of the publication printed each time, and I was very surprised to learn how expensive the process was. It also struck me as strange that when I would go to get the negatives set, the printers and typesetters were often rude and indifferent.

Then I heard about a woman in town who did typesetting in her own home, so I looked her up and found that she was less expensive and much nicer to customers. The only problem, though, was that she was very slow and usually would not make my deadline, so I was back in trouble again.

It occured to me that I had always liked to type and that the small typesetting machines shouldn't be all that difficult to operate. I decided to try it out, so I got a lease on a machine for about $300. Although I found that there were many things that I didn't know how to do on the machine, I soon caught on to the typesetting process. Before I knew it, people were asking me if I would do odd jobs for them.

I quit my job and stayed at home for about six months working on small jobs for other people. They came to me strictly by word-of-mouth. I soon got busier and knew that I was going to have to make a decision about whether to expand my operation.

I decided to go ahead and rent an office with one small room located near my house. It rented for about $100 a month. I had some friends in the office down the hall who had opened a business and were needing a part-time secretary. They said to me, "Look, if you're worried about your space and making the rent on it, we'll let you do a little typing for us and that will help pay your bills. That way you can minimize your risk." I took them up on the deal. I rented this little room and did some work for them and then met Connie Brenners.

Connie had small children of her own but wanted part-time work just like I had wanted in the beginning, so I talked her into coming on board with me. Connie had the typing aptitude and was willing to learn about the typesetting business. Fortunately, I had the good sense to let Connie pretty much set her own schedule around her kids and their needs. Over the years, I have done this with most of my employees and have found it to be a competitive edge. It has allowed me to keep some great people on board who couldn't work strictly on an 8:00 to 5:00 basis.

With Connie around, things continued to get busier and busier so that we quickly needed another person to help us out. Connie knew Susan Kelly, who was a student majoring in accounting at Memphis State. Susan worked with us one summer on a part-time basis and really began to enjoy what we were doing. When Susan graduated, she was so enthusiastic about our business that she decided to stay in typesetting rather than start a career in accounting.

We were quite a team. Not only were we women who did not have a long apprenticeship in the printing industry, but we also had new equipment which most of the old-line typesetters made fun of and said was of doubtful quality. I think they really resented the fact that we were women, so they ended up criticizing our machines. They just couldn't believe that women could be successful in typesetting. They couldn't understand that typesetting was very much like typewriting work.

But we showed the male profession that we could be very successful at what we were doing. I think what really made the difference was that we treated our customers very well. This was a lesson that I had learned at the start of my business, and it's one that I have never forgotten. I think our customers saw that we enjoyed our work and wanted to serve them in the very best possible way.

Over time, we kept getting the better customers and the bigger jobs, so we decided to go to some automated equipment. This decision brought us to another cross-roads in the business, because the automated equipment called for an investment of at least $15,000. Compared with the little machine that we had been leasing, this was a giant step for us. We knew that we would have to get a lot more business in order to pay for the automated equipment.

We progressively got more and more automated, and it seemed that for two or three days after we'd get a new piece of equipment, our volume wasn't going to be large enough to pay for it. But the new customers would always manage to come, and we soon found the need to add even more equipment. It got to be a predictable cycle. The big problem with all of this success was that we had to work harder and harder because getting highly qualified people to work at night was very difficult. We had to work at night to avoid buying more equipment which would be used only during the day.

Success meant growth problems for us. We soon outgrew the first room that we had been renting, so we leased another office next door. This new office doubled our rent, but it gave us considerably more room. We ended up staying there about five years.

Those years saw an awful lot of growth in the business. We expanded with more and more equipment and added about fifteen employees. But the overgrowth problems came back to haunt us again. We knew that we were either going to need more room, or that we were going to have to do some major redesign work on our leased facilities. The landlord offered to sell me the building, and it was at that point that I realized we needed to borrow some money. We just didn't have the volume of operations to warrant making a major purchase like the building through retained earnings. The need for credit brought up a problem because up to this point, we had never needed to borrow money. We had always leased our equipment from IBM. I had never had to go to a banker.

Analysis: In what ways can growth pose problems for a business? How should these problems be counteracted?

What are the signs that a business is growing too fast? Too slow?

Tell us about your first experience at borrowing money.

I can tell you, for sure, that it wasn't an easy decision. However, it had been apparent for quite some time that our cash flow needed to be supplemented with some outside funds. I hate to admit this, but our cash was so tight that each month we could not pay off both of our major accounts, which were IBM for machine leasing and the IRS for tax installments. So on some months we would pay IBM and ignore the taxes and do just the opposite the next month. Thank goodness

IBM was very, very decent to us and flexible regarding their monthly payments, or I don't know how we would have made it during this liquidity crisis. But the handwriting was on the wall that we were going to need some extra money. I decided on asking for a loan of $500.

That's all you asked for?

That's all I asked for; just $500. I was scared to borrow much money. With our tight working capital I figured I probably shouldn't be borrowing at all. Anyway, I worked up my courage and went to visit the bank.

Well, it didn't take long. The loan officer looked me in the eye and said flat out, "I can't loan you the money."

I said, "Why? How do you know?"

He said, "Because you're a woman. We can't loan you any money; it's just that simple."

And I said, "You're not even going to look at my situation and see what my business can do?"

He answered, "I'm sorry; we just can't loan you the money."

So I just picked up my portfolio and left. I came back to the business and did the only thing I could—I just worked hard. The expanding volume of business finally caught up with me, and I had to work around the clock almost literally. I'd go home, fool with the kids, do what I had to do, and then it was back to work. I didn't have the revenue coming in to expand the payroll, so I had to do more and more work myself.

In retrospect, though, I don't feel bad about that period and our lack of financing. Perhaps if I had had the supply of money coming in from the bank, I might have gotten careless and not worked as hard as I did. That might have hurt the company's overall success.

Before long, Connie and Susan were also working days and nights along with me. For the next several years we worked practically constantly, the longest hours— no one would believe it. We had to do it to make up for not having enough money.

Then in 1973, the friend that I had originally shared an office with saw our potential. He had gone on to bigger and better things and realized that our business should have been growing more than it was. He said, "You're just crazy not to go down to the bank and get the money that you need for equipment and employees."

Analysis: Do you feel the problems experienced by Cynthia in borrowing money are typical for female entrepreneurs?

In your opinion, did the banker have any justification for rejecting the $500 loan to Cynthia?

Tell us what you did at this point.

As you can imagine, I wasn't too excited about going back to visit with bankers who had turned me down cold just a couple of years before. I hadn't really thought that much would have changed in the meantime. My friend, however, assured me that he knew a good banker down at First National and that I would have no hassle getting the money.

I went down there and the banker couldn't have been nicer. I couldn't believe it. I borrowed $500 and paid it back in a couple of months. Then I think I bought a car next. Of course, one thing that had helped in getting the credit line was the fact that, by this point, I had incorporated my business. That seems to have made a large difference in the banker's mind.

Now that I had solved my funds-flow problem, at least for the time being, I still had to do something about the lack of room in our building. We decided that we needed to expand to another location once again. The landlord, however, liked us and gave us a very strong inducement to stay. He said he would let us stay in the building if we bought it from him. No down payment was required and he offered us an 8 percent loan. That would make our payments about $500 a month. It was a very inviting offer. However, the building just wouldn't suit our needs over the long-run.

Then one of my artists noticed two buildings in Memphis which seemed to fit our needs quite well. So I went down to First National again and asked if I could have the money to buy both of the buildings.

How much did you ask for this time, Cindy?

Sixty thousand dollars. That was in 1975. The banker was very nice, but he said that he could give me only a five-year loan. After I multiplied that out, I decided that I couldn't repay it. I couldn't afford the payment over so short a period. So I talked to my accountant, who seemed very much against buying the buildings. He said that I should lease for tax purposes. I told him that there was something in me that went against perpetual renting. I guess it's just the old necessity instinct, but I like to think that I'm getting equity in something. I had gone through the whole renting-versus-owning question with our equipment purchasers. I had decided with them that buying was the way to go once we got to the point we could afford it. I have not ever regretted that decision, because now I have a lot of paid-for equipment that is still very productive.

As it turned out, the reason my accountant was so much in favor of leasing was that he had some spare office space that he wanted to unload on us. Well, I saw through that in a hurry and decided that we had better get a new accountant. I was acquainted with a young man who had just left a CPA firm to go into business for himself. He very much wanted my account. I told him we would be glad to sign on with him because we would be happy to have someone who would pay close attention to our financial needs. He's been one of our biggest assets. He genuinely cares about us and is interested in how the business is doing.

The new accountant advised us that getting an SBA loan would be no problem and that he would love to help guide us through the process. He said that there was a suburban bank that granted the loans and that we ought to look into the possibility as soon as possible. It turned out to be the bank that had denied me the $500 several years before. I said, "No way will I go back to that bank."

He said, "They've got new personnel, a whole new management team. You'll be treated differently."

I said, "O.K., Chris, but I'm telling you, if they aren't decent to me, I'm not dealing with them for five minutes."

Chris and I put together a very simple proposal along with my financial statements. I went right into the bank and in so many words said, "This is who I am; I have an office around the corner. I do this. I've been in business seven years, and I doubt that you'll loan me this money; but I want to buy a building, I need $60,000, and I have to go through the SBA. Do you want to handle it or not?"

To my surprise the banker said, "Oh, I think we might be very interested."

I said, "Look, I don't want to waste my time here. If you're going to turn me down I want you to do it quickly because I don't have much time. The buildings are going to be sold quickly and I need to say, 'yes' or 'no'. Do you understand?"

So he asked me all about what I did and then said, "Do you mind if I come over and look around your business this afternoon?"

Well, I went back to the office that afternoon and forgot about it. I became very, very busy. Before I knew it, he was there to look around. I didn't really pay any attention to him. But what do you know, the next morning he called and said, "Well, we have approved your loan."

I said "What?"

"We've approved your loan."

I said, "You can't be serious—you haven't taken enough time yet. Don't you have to go before a board or something?"

He said, "No. Do you want me to sign the loan?"

So we borrowed the money. We didn't even have to put anything down. Since that day, the bank has been wonderful to us. Now I can go and say that I need $10,000 for jobs I'm working on, and I get the money with no questions asked. It's easy to get money, but I certainly don't abuse my credit line. I never borrow anything that I don't really need.

Analysis: Provide guidelines for a small business to follow in developing a supportive, long-term relationship with a bank.

Cynthia, tell us how your business is doing at present.

I'm glad to say that at the end of 1979, we were very happy and making a profit. I think we are making a very nice percentage for the printing industry. We are continuing to get bigger customers all the time, and we are tackling quite sophisticated assignments. However, we have now reached another crossroads in the business.

What do you mean?

I guess to a certain extent we're victims of our own success. We have reached the stage where future rapid growth is going to depend on getting a whole new generation of sophisticated equipment in here. I'm talking about word processing equipment and electronic automated equipment. We're looking at somewhere in the neighborhood of $120,000 in new investments to advance our business another major step forward. We're on the threshold of becoming a whole new kind of company, offering services to entirely new types of customers than we have in the past. The other real big challenge that we're currently facing has to do with a recent offer to buy us out.

Tell us about that offer.

This all happened in early 1979. In April of 1979, I was approached by Fred Lindsey of Stagecraft Industries. They were very interested in acquiring us because of our big-customer clientele. They offered me ten times earnings, which in the previous year had run about $37,000. So they were making me a buyout offer of around $370,000.

I am very flattered, of course, to receive the attention of Stagecraft but I'm having a tough time deciding whether or not to continue growing on our own. To make matters even more complicated, one of our largest graphics customers, headed up by Clifford Jason, absolutely doesn't want us to sell out. Jason is worried about breaking his long-time relationship with us because we have done some very sophisticated things for them and I guess they are pretty dependent on us. I don't mean to make it sound like there is no other person in town who could handle the Jason account, but we have jobs in progress for him and have built up certain relationships with his company that would be hard to replace overnight.

Analysis: Is $370,000 a good offer for the business?

What other reasonable terms of purchase might also be offered?

EXHIBIT 3-1

Pharr Composing Service, Inc.

INCOME STATEMENT

for the fiscal year ended September 30, 1979

Sales		$357,131
Less Operating Expenses		
Materials	$ 71,123	
Wages and salaries	215,570	
Utilities	3,847	
Interest	6,137	
Depreciation	4,170	
Other	5,261	
Total Operating Expense		306,108
Income Before Taxes		51,023
Corporate Income Tax Expense		11,727
NET INCOME		$ 39,296

Do you want to continue working as hard in the future as you have in the past, Cindy?

Now that is a very good question. You see, I'm nearly 50 years old and I do wonder how many more years I can put in going full-blast. There are so many daily problems and hassles to put up with. Sometimes the idea of selling out at a good profit and then, maybe, either retiring early or going to work for the new company at a nice salary is mighty tempting.

Can you tell us about your immediate plans and priorities?

I sure can. Right now, I'm sweating blood over an audit by the IRS. Can you believe it; I went on vacation a few months ago for the first time in many years and that's when the IRS decided to audit us. While I was in Europe they sent a notice in the mail which Susan and Connie didn't pay any attention to, thinking it was just something routine about taxes. Before they knew what was happening, the IRS representative got hold of them and said that she would be down in the next couple of days for an audit. Susan and Connie told her that the owner was out of town and asked if the audit could wait? The IRS lady said, "We contacted you some weeks ago about this, so you should be ready." Connie and Susan explained that they hadn't opened the mail since I was out of town. The woman wouldn't believe it. It seems that she was new in the IRS office and on her first case, so she wanted to make a good impression with her boss. Well, Connie and Susan finally managed to contact

EXHIBIT 3-2

Pharr Composing Service, Inc.

BALANCE SHEET

September 30, 1979

Assets			
Current Assets			
Cash	$ 59,647		
Accounts receivable	28,696		
Supplies and materials	26,378		
Prepaid insurance	1,500		
Total Current Assets			$116,221
Plant and Equipment			
Building	60,000		
Less: accumulated depreciation	8,000	54,000	
Equipment and fixtures	101,200		
Less: accumulated depreciation	34,500	66,700	
Total Plant and Equipment			120,700
TOTAL ASSETS			$236,921

Liabilities and Stockholder's Equity			
Current Liabilities			
Trade accounts payroll	$ 16,394		
Other	5,126		
Total Current Liabilities			$ 21,520
Long-term liabilities			
SBA notes payable			54,000
Total Liabilities			75,520
Stockholder's Equity			
Paid-Capital	40,073		
Retained earnings	121,328		
Total Stockholder's Equity			161,401
TOTAL LIABILITIES AND STOCKHOLDER'S EQUITY			$236,921

me in Europe, apologized for ruining my vacation, and explained the situation to me.

I came back frantically to prepare for the audit. It scared me to death—made me physically ill. We dealt with the IRS lady for several weeks, but the investigation is not through. I've still got that hassle hanging over my head. That's just an example of some of the daily headaches that I encounter, although I feel quite confident that we'll eventually work things out satisfactorily.

As for now, I have the IRS on my mind along with the big decision about whether to expand the business into electronic services or sell out to Stagecraft. I can tell you, it's not going to be easy to make up my mind.

How do you feel about the buyout offer?

As you can see, I have mixed feelings about it. I believe our business has an awful lot of potential, but the Stagecraft offer is attractive. But then, I don't wish to alienate any of my big customers or cause a break in any trusted relationships built up over the years. I'm also not convinced that I can't continue to guide our business to new heights on our own, using retained earnings as our primary source of financing. At this point, I'm not really sure what I want to do. A lot more thinking is going to have to go into it.

Analysis: What do you think Cynthia Pharr should do?

What do you predict she will do?

---

aspheric enterprises

4

Aspheric Enterprises was formed in 1978 by Y. L. Chung, an immigrant from Taiwan, who invented a revolutionary procedure for making aspheric optical lenses. Based outside of Chicago in Evanston, Illinois, the corporation was funded under private stock placement by five investors led by Sidney Blackmon, a Chicago investment counselor. Two of the investors were university professors, one was a dentist, the other a member of Chung's family.

In 1968, Dr. Chung received dual doctorates in physics and mathematics from a prestigious American university. He was a research scientist for a large multinational corporation at the time he patented the aspheric technology under his own name. He subsequently left his corporate position to form Aspheric Enterprises.

Dr. Chung's aspheric process produces lenses with a uniform focal point. Unlike regular spherical lenses, such as those typically used for prescription eyewear, all points on an aspheric lens have the same optical acuity. No optical distortion occurs at any point on the lens. Potential applications exist for cameras, microscopes, and general purpose optical equipment.

Backed by $125,000 of seed equity, Dr. Chung patented the aspheric manufacturing process in 1979 and set about marketing his invention. He initially approached several high technology companies near Palo Alto, California, using his patent-application blueprints and working papers as marketing documents. Although several firms congratulated him for technical brilliance, Chung found no backers for his invention.

He then approached a venture capital partnership in Boston, Venture Search, which initially expressed an interest in the project but eventually declined to became involved. The explanatory letter from the senior partner, L. Haynes Sinclair, is contained in Exhibit 4-1.

With capital beginning to run low in the summer of 1980, Dr. Chung contacted Re-Search Patents, a private marketing firm headquartered in Philadelphia. Re-Search Patents worked closely with universities and government-sponsored laboratories in marketing technical products to the private sector for 30 percent of the royalty rights.

Chung and his five stockholders agreed that their venture suffered from inadequate marketing and saw the need for expert guidance in this area. However, they were reluctant to turn over such a large royalty share to Re-Search Patents, especially so early in their venture history. For its part, Re-search agreed to design a marketing strategy for Aspheric Enterprises upon signing of royalty agreement contracts.

Before taking further action of any kind, Dr. Chung decided to call a stockholder's meeting in September of 1980. After six and one-half hours of sometimes heated discussion, the meeting adjourned with no definitive decision reached regarding the Re-Search offer.

Two stockholders with 29 percent ownership favored turning over the entire project to Re-Search Patents due to the limited marketing expertise of Aspheric. Majority holder Sidney Blackmon (40 percent ownership) opposed the tie-in and suggested that Aspheric continue to go it alone. Blackmon expressed his willingness to invest an additional $50,000 in the company.

Aspheric's two other investors expressed ambivalence about future strategy and declined to contribute more equity. Dr. Chung offered to return to work for his former corporate employer until all five stockholders could reach accord on Aspheric's future strategy.

Analysis: As you see it, why has Aspheric Enterprises failed to gel?

If you had already invested $25,000 in the company, would you contribute more?

If Dr. Chung receives another $50,000 from Mr. Blackmon, how should the money be spent?

Where should Aspheric Enterprises go from here?

EXHIBIT 4-1

LETTER FROM VENTURE SEARCH

Dr. Y. L. Chung
10094 Mayhill Estates Drive
Suite B
Evanston, Illinois 60611

Dear Dr. Chung:

Since talking with you last month, my associates and I have had the opportunity to discuss your aspheric lens project thoroughly. While we are genuinely intrigued with your invention, we must turn down your request for financial support. This was a difficult decision for us to reach, because the aspheric process appears to have some merit.

Unfortunately, we were unable to do adequate forecasting work on your product due to the sketchy nature of the business proposal sent to us. We would have much preferred a complete business plan with pro forma statements and concrete marketing guidelines. While your patent report data were informative, they still did not enable us to gauge overall profit and market potential adequately.

One of our consultants, Dr. A. Barry Witten, professor of physics, was familiar with your work and vouched for its technical merits. However, he was not conversant with potential markets for aspheric optics.

In closing, let me strongly encourage you to spend more time formulating your business plan. Your probability of eventual success will be greatly enhanced when you can generate some "numbers" to sell your project.

My associates and I wish you every future success. Thank you for considering our firm in your project's plans.

Sincerely,

L. Haynes Sinclair
Senior Partner
Venture Search
Boston, Massachusetts

peppy's pizza

5

The following business plan was developed by Ted Latham and Leon Haliburton, recent business graduates of Indiana State University in Terre Haute. They are seriously committed to opening Peppy's Pizza outlets in Terre Haute and plan to submit the business plan to local bankers in the near future.

Competitive Strategy

Peppy's Pizza can succeed in the carry-out pizza business by differentiating itself from the competition in several ways:

1. Lower cost
2. Better product
3. Faster service
4. Reliable delivery
5. Very accessible location

Lower Cost. The marketing survey we conducted here in Terre Haute (see Exhibit 5-1 ahead) showed that price is very important to customers. Peppy's significantly lower overhead will enable us to undercut our competition and still offer a better-tasting pizza.

Better Product. We firmly believe, after tasting various pizzas in Terre Haute, that our recipe is one of the best available. It is significantly better than any of the chains, and customers will definitely be able to taste the difference. Being able to provide a better product is a key advantage as "good pizza," "better quality," "the best," and "better ingredients" accounted for 79 percent of the survey respondents' patronizing local pizza restaurants.

Faster Service. The desire for fast food and fast service is increasing, so being the fastest and most reliable pizza restaurant in town definitely will be an advantage. We are confident that Peppy's can easily have pizzas ready faster than pizza restaurants which place their primary emphasis on dining customers. Typically, the local competition is slow in filling take-out orders, and they do not advertise their carry-out service.

Reliable Delivery. Pizza restaurants are notorious for not having take-out orders ready when they say they will and for having slow delivery to homes (for those that do make home deliveries). Every minute beyond the promised time that a customer waits is a minute that he or she wishes the order had been placed elsewhere. By having the pizza ready when we promise it, we will become that somewhere else. Since Peppy's Pizza is strictly carry-out and free from other distractions, we will have no problem with prompt service and delivery.

Our delivery service will be a very important part of Peppy's operation, so it deserves special attention. We will have at least two vehicles and two employees with drivers licenses on every shift. This combination is more than enough to guarantee excellent home delivery of Peppy's Pizza. We will charge one dollar for delivery service in order to encourage pick-up at Peppy's. To avoid problems with gas and vehicle wear and tear, the employee making a delivery will keep the dollar in addition to any tips. The delivery income will be in addition to regular wages. Most Peppy's Pizza customers will pick up their food at the restaurant, but for those who don't, we plan to have a delivery service which will be friendly, reliable, and as fast as possible. No business can operate without customers, so we plan to make ours happy.

Very Accessible Location. Most pizza restaurants are not conveniently located for residential customers. This is in keeping with their emphasis on sit-down business, because people are willing to drive a bit further for a sit-down meal. Peppy's will locate close to residential areas to make it quicker and easier for customers to pick up pizzas while they're still hot.

In conclusion, our competitive edge will help to make Peppy's Pizza a successful and welcome addition to Terre Haute. When a family would like to eat prepared food at home, pizza will be more appealing than a hamburger and fries and much less expensive than chicken or fish. Buying frozen pizza from a store is also less appealing than stopping by Peppy's for a freshly-made pizza that will be nice and hot when it is put on the dining-room table. In addition, the menu will be rounded out with submarine sandwiches, spaghetti, and ravioli to please everybody in the family.

As Peppy's Pizza becomes successful, it is possible that the national chains will begin to stress carry-out service in an attempt to force us out of the market. If they do indeed try this, we believe that Peppy's will prevail, because our five competitive advantages will still exist. Also by the time we are recognized as a threat in the market place, Peppy's will be well-established as a quality company that is here to stay.

Other pizza restaurants will not be concerned with Peppy's Pizza at the start, because they seem to believe either that the carry-out market is not large enough to support a business, or that they don't need carry-out given their present success with the sit-down market. We believe that the national chains will not attempt to develop carry-out as a major part of their business unless they are significantly hurt by Peppy's. Even if this were to occur, they would still be unlikely to vary strategies because of their sizable investment in the dine-in market. Consumer confusion resulting from such a switch in pizza restaurant strategy would only benefit Peppy's Pizza.

Peppy's Location

From our discussions with survey respondents it was apparent that, for Peppy's Pizza to be as competitive as possible, a prime site location will be necessary. This is not to say that we will need an expensive site with lots of elaborate surroundings. What Peppy's needs is a high-traffic area close to residential housing. A 600 square-foot area is more than enough room for Peppy's to operate efficiently without feeling cramped. In addition, there will be no need to have more than a few parking spaces in front of Peppy's because customers will simply walk in, get their pizza, and leave.

After careful consideration, we have concluded that the two best locations for a Peppy's Pizza would be northern Mills Drive (or within one block of it) or near the Indiana State campus. A location near ISU would have the disadvantage of having very slow business during the summer months because of the small number of students who attend summer school.

Therefore, we would want to open up the initial Peppy's Pizza operation on northern Mills. Once this location prospers, we think it would be a good idea to open a second near the campus, which would close during the summer months. The ISU location of Peppy's would most certainly generate enough business to justify its existence during the school year, so closing it for the summer is simply another positive point in the already excellent Peppy's Pizza scheme.

While we were in the process of considering various locations for Peppy's initial operation, a real estate salesman was consulted for cost figures. After we explained the type of operation that we expected to start, we were told that the probable monthly rent per square-foot would be 50 cents. At our optimal 600 square-foot location, this translates into $300 per month for rent. We also inquired as to the problems we were likely to encounter in finding a location that suits our needs. The real estate agent told us that there would definitely be no problem, since there is an abundance of shops of that size available.

Another factor to be considered, when looking for specific sites, would obviously be the competition. One would intuitively think that the national and regional chains would provide formidable competition, since they have the advantages of sophisticated advertising, attractive and comfortable dining areas, choice of thin and thick pizza, and salad bars. However, we feel that there is a basic difference in philosophy between Peppy's Pizza and the dine-in restaurants. Peppy's doesn't need elaborate advertising, nice dining areas, or a salad bar. We simply want to provide the best pizza in town, in such a way that Terre Haute consumers can enjoy it in their homes. In light of the above facts, we want a location that is not right next door to a pizza restaurant, but it could be within a block of one.

Analysis of Survey

One of the questions we asked survey respondents was whether they more often ate pizza in a restaurant or took it home. The answers were skewed toward the "eat at the restaurant" end of the scale. This could be, on the surface, an indicator that people simply don't want to eat pizza at home. However, in discussions with the respondents after they had completed the questionnaire, we discovered that they based their response on the fact that no pizza restaurant properly catered to the carry-out market. As discussed earlier, local pizza restaurants are less than enthusiastic toward carry-out orders. In our post-survey discussions, we were delighted to find an overwhelming positive response to the Peppy's Pizza concept. Most people said that they would be overjoyed if an operation like Peppy's would open in Terre Haute.

A related question in our survey asked whether a carry-out pizza restaurant was a good idea. We were quite surprised to find that only 36.7 percent of the respondents said that they thought it was a good idea. Again, in our post-survey discussions we found out why the respondents answered the way they did. In this particular instance, there were two reasons why people tended to dislike the carry-out-only concept. The first stemmed from the fact that poor service has been associated with carry-out pizzas. People tended to think that poor service was an inherent part of this type of operation, and thus, they thought it would not succeed. After we explained Peppy's competitive advantages, the respondents almost universally endorsed the idea. They thought that it would be great to have good service on the occasions when they wanted to eat pizza at home as opposed to dining in a restaurant. In fact, about half of the respondents suggested that they would always eat their pizza at home if they could get proper service.

The respondents also doubted that a carry-out pizza place would be able to generate enough business. There seemed to be some mystique that surrounds a restaurant that has an elaborate dining room. When we began to explain the concepts of lower overhead and how this would allow lower prices to be charged, most people changed their minds.

In actuality, we simply had people fill out the survey as a basis for a short discussion. The percentages we have presented were taken from answers given before the discussions took place. From a time perspective, we felt it would be too much to ask respondents to fill out another survey, so we decided to present the results we had and clarify them.

The final question that requires clarification concerns competitors. In response to why they favored a particular restaurant, 44.2 percent of the respondents said "good pizza," 11.6 percent said it was the "best," 11.6 percent said "better quality," and 11.6 percent said "better ingredients." That's a total of 79 percent saying they preferred their favorite restaurant because of the good pizza. This particular question excited us more than any other, because we are quite confident that Peppy's Pizza makes a pizza superior to any found in Terre Haute.

Cost and Financial Data for Peppy's Pizza

Much of the information compiled thus far in our report resulted from interviews with pizza restaurant owners and managers in Terre Haute. An additional source was the owner of Hungry Howie's pizza operation in Livonia, Michigan. We feel this is the appropriate place to discuss these interviews, because the current section of our report is based almost entirely upon data compiled during these interviews. The financial exhibits found ahead reflect a conservative average of all the personal interviews conducted. We would like to emphasize that, even though the information may appear to be very optimistic, it falls below the averages of our interviews. In other words, we feel we have drawn pessimistic financial estimates. With an effective and efficient operation, we are confident that Peppy's Pizza could do even better.

Peppy's Products

Peppy's Pizza will definitely offer several different sizes of pizza in addition to a wide variety of toppings. Our main question in developing the product mix was whether we should offer other items to complement the pizza business. In the survey, respondents were asked if they thought it was a good idea to serve only pizza. Of the total, 71.8 percent said they thought it was a good idea to also serve items other than pizza. However, only 3.6 percent of the respondents listed "variety" in answering why they liked their favorite pizza restaurant. This apparent contradiction could be the result of people not necessarily wanting other items but believing that other foods would be required for a pizza restaurant to be successful.

Interviews with several pizza restaurant owners and managers gave us another reason why we might want to serve several choices of food. Serving submarine sandwiches offers a good way to make use of food stocks that might otherwise spoil. Due to the fact that large quantities of most of the items must be purchased in order to get a reasonable price, there sometimes is too much stock on hand. Selling subs (we feel thirty-five a day is a conservative projection) would allow us to keep food stocks fresher and at the same time have variety in the menu. After careful consideration of all relevant items, we think the menu and price list shown in Exhibit 5-14 is an excellent one.

Peppy's Pizza Promotion

Price is definitely a factor that can be used in establishing Peppy's Pizza in the marketplace. Sixty-three percent of our survey respondents said that they do pay attention to price when they go out for pizza or take it home. Initial promotion of Peppy's should put emphasis on lower-priced pizza to attract what appears to be a very price-conscious public. Then the question that arises is how to go about attracting business with the lower prices. We decided to explore two different alternatives, both of which consist of not lowering prices directly but using other means to effectively lower costs to consumers.

The first of these consists of offering a free quart of soda pop with every pizza purchased. Secondly, we like the idea of giving with every purchase, Peppy's tokens good toward a free pizza when four are collected. Responses to both of these ideas were extremely positive, as "yes" answers made up 82.1 percent and 89.7 percent respectively. The slightly lower percentage for free soda pop is probably due to some people not wanting soda pop with their pizza, for example, beer drinkers.

In trying to determine further the effectiveness of discount coupons, respondents were asked how often they used pizza coupons found in local newspapers. Of the total, 23.1 percent said they always use them, 66.7 percent said they sometimes use them (forgetting the coupons at home was a common problem), and 10.2 percent said they never use them. This adds additional credence to the price consciousness of consumers.

After examining the above responses and their implications, we have decided to adopt the following initial strategy: The cost of the tokens (31 cents each in lots of 2000) makes their use feasible only if Peppy's needs an additional boost to increase sales. We feel strongly that this boost will not be needed due to our other competitive advantages. Therefore, we will stick with the coupon system, discounting at the outset. On Peppy's Pizza handbills, which will be distributed throughout the local area, will be a complete menu and price list along with the following coupons:

- Free small pizza with purchase of an extra large
- Monday only: buy a medium pizza and get the same size pizza free
- 2 quarts soda pop free with large or extra large pizza
- 1 quart soda pop free with medium pizza
- $1.25 off extra large pizza
- $1.00 off large pizza
- $.75 off medium pizza
- One order of ravioli or spaghetti free with purchase of the same

The variety of coupons offered will undoubtedly appeal to all pizza lovers. We are confident that the use of coupons in conjunction with regular newspaper advertising will be sufficient to attract significant initial business. This initial business will lead to referral business thanks to the friendly and speedy service, and great pizza at Peppy's.

Expansion Plans

As discussed earlier, once Peppy's Pizza has become successful with its first outlet, we will expand to a second location near the Indiana State campus. After both locations are operating smoothly, we will give consideration to opening other company-owned stores throughout Indiana. This would obviously be dependent on finding capable and trustworthy managers to run the individual locations. Peppy's initial period of slow, controlled, growth will allow us to build up the necessary capital for a possible franchise system. It will also allow us to perfect the logistics of opening and operating new units.

It should be emphasized at this point that our main concern is getting started in Terre Haute, not franchising. We could conceivably be very content with our local operations and not expand, or only open a limited number of company-owned Peppy's around Indiana. The costs of starting a franchise system are very large. Entrepreneurs who have started franchise systems estimate that a minimum of $250,000 is needed. The franchisor must pay a $4,000 registration fee and file a disclosure statement to satisfy government requirements, with legal fees for this alone amounting to approximately $26,000. The franchisor must also develop training programs, promotional campaigns, a system operations guide, and other related items to insure that a franchisee can profitably run the unit even if he has had no experience in business. In conclusion, Peppy's Pizza will first concentrate on its Terre Haute units, which may lead to company expansion through owned units or franchises after their successful start-up. We are very confident that Peppy's will soon become a welcome addition to the Terre Haute community.

Analysis: Is the preceding document with subsequent exhibits an adequate business plan? Do you feel Latham and Haliburton have capably planned for their prospective new venture? How can the document be improved?

Evaluate the marketing research conducted by the entrepreneurs from the standpoint of validity, completeness, and objectivity. In what ways could it have been improved?

As a banker, would you loan seed capital to Peppy's Pizza? If so, how much?

EXHIBIT 5-1

RESEARCH SURVEY QUESTIONNAIRE

1. What percentage of the people in your family like pizza? _____
2. How many times a month does your family get pizza from a pizza place?
       1   2   3   4   5   6   or more
3. When you have pizza, which do you do most often?
       carry out for home   carry out for work   eat at restaurant
4. In your opinion, is a pizza restaurant that is strictly carry-out a good idea?
       Y   N
5. In your opinion, is it better for a pizza restaurant to serve only pizza, or to serve other items as well, such as submarine sandwiches, spaghetti, and ravioli?
       Y   N
6. When you go out for pizza, do you pay any attention to the price?
       Y   N
7. Do you use the pizza coupons found in local newspapers when you buy pizza from a restaurant?
       never   sometimes   always
8. Do you like the idea of a pizza place giving a free quart of soda pop with every pizza bought?
       Y   N
9. Do you like the idea of a pizza restaurant offering a free pizza with the redemption of four tokens (one given each time you purchased a pizza)?
       Y   N
10. Overall, what are your two favorite pizza restaurants in Terre Haute? _____ _____
    Why?
11. Do you always go to one of your two favorite pizza restaurants?
        Y   N

EXHIBIT 5-1 Continued

12. What is your age range?
    - 10-19
    - 20-29
    - 30-39
    - 40-49
    - 50-59
    - 60_____
13. What is your family income range?
    - $10,000 or under
    - 11,000-19,000
    - 20,000-29,000
    - 30,000-39,000
    - 40,000-49,000
    - 50,000 and up

EXHIBIT 5-2

SURVEY RESULTS

	All	ISU Only
Question 1		
10	1.7%	—
20	3.3	—
25	1.7	—
30	1.7	—
40	1.7	—
50	10.0	—
70	1.7	—
75	10.0	3.8
80	6.7	—
83	5.0	11.5
90	1.7	—
100	55.0	84.6
Question 2		
1	15.0%	26.9
2	21.7	38.5
3	23.3	15.4
4	20.0	15.4
5	8.3	—
6	11.7	3.8
Question 3		
1	25.5%	8.0
2	44.0	12.0
3	30 5	8.0
Question 4		
Yes	36.7%	34.6
No	63.3	65.4

EXHIBIT 5-2 Continued

	All	ISU Only
Question 5		
Yes	71.8	56.0
No	28.2	44.0
Question 6		
Yes	63.3%	69.2
No	36.7	30.8
Question 7		
Never	10.0%	7.7
Sometimes	68.3	76.9
Always	21.7	15.4
Question 8		
Yes	86.7%	92.3
No	13.3	7.7
Question 9		
Yes	88.3%	84.6
No	11.7	15.4

	First Favorite		Second Favorite	
	All	ISU	All	ISU
Question 10				
Pappa Rollo's	15.0%	30.8	11.9%	24.0
Mr. Gatti's	26.7	38.5	35.6	48.0
Giovanni's	6.7	—	5.1	—
Pizza Planet	21.7	23.1	11.9	16.0
Pizza Hut	13.3	3.8	23.7	8.0
Pizza Inn	16.7	3.8	11.9	4.0

	All	ISU Only
Question 10 – Why?		
Better Quality	11.6%	5.0
Good Pizza	44.2	40.0
Atmosphere	7.0	10.0
The Best	11.6	—
Variety	2.3	—
Big TV	7.0	15.0
Better Ingredients	11.6	25.0
Where Friends Go	2.3	5.0
Guys	2.3	5.0
Question 11		
Yes	61.0%	68.0
No	39.0	32.0

EXHIBIT 5-2 Continued

	All	ISU Only
Question 12		
10-19	11.9%	24.0
20-29	74.6	76.0
30-39	13.6	—
40-49	—	—
50-59	—	—
60+	—	—
Question 13		
10 + under	33.3%	63.6
11-19	9.3	—
20-29	29.6	9.1
30-39	11.1	—
40-49	3.7	4.5
50+	13.0	22.7

EXHIBIT 5-3
COST AND FINANCIAL DATA ON PEPPY'S PIZZA

	Items Subject To Depreciation	
Ovens:	10 year life $4,000 original cost Straight-line depreciation $400/year depreciation = ($33.33/month)	$4,000.00
Mixer:	5 year life $2,000 original cost Straight-line depreciation $400/year depreciation = ($33.33/month)	$2,000.00
Retarder:	10 year life $3,000 cost Straight-line depreciation $300/year depreciation = ($25/month)	$3,000.00
Cooler:	10 year life $2,500 cost Straight-line depreciation $250/year depreciation = ($20.83/month)	$2,500.00
	TOTAL	$11,500.00

EXHIBIT 5-4

INITIAL SUPPLIES NEEDED

100 lbs flour	$ 34.00
2 cases pizza sauce	43.08
40 lbs. mozzarella I	38.40
40 lbs. mozzarella II	38.40
25 lbs. pepperoni	57.00
56 lbs. imported ham	117.60
10 lbs. Italian sausage	15.50
20 lbs. hamburger	34.78
15 lbs. steak	37.50
2 boxes mushrooms	25.00
2 cans anchovies	16.58
4 cans yeast	17.96
1 case lettuce	9.99
2 cases mild peppers	25.98
2 cases hot peppers	25.98
2 boxes tomatoes	12.90
40 lbs. American cheese	32.00
2 jars black olives	13.50
2 dozen green peppers	3.92
2 dozen onions	4.68
10 lbs. bacon	19.60
10 boxes spaghetti	8.90
2 cases canned ravioli	45.65
2000 pizza boxes	250.00
1000 quart containers for pop	95.00
1000 straws	2.98
Stapler and staples	9.98
50 large sub buns	20.84
500 bags	11.75
40 gal. pop (Dr. Pepper, Coke, etc.)	64.96
10 screens to cook pizza on	40.00
2 checkbooks	30.00
Kitchen utensils	50.00
Stainless steel storage pans	100.00
2 oil (cases)	48.00
25 lbs. salt	7.00
25 lbs. sugar	7.00
12 oregano (can)	20.40
12 basil (cans)	12.72
12 parsley (cans)	11.45
24 pepper (cans)	19.50
12 crushed red pepper	12.12
12 cans garlic	30.00
24 grated Parmesan cheese (large shakers)	36.00
50 garbage liners	5.50

EXHIBIT 5-4 Continued

2 mops	5.98
2 bleach (cases)	6.72
12 ammonia (quarts)	5.16
Miscellaneous and/or forgotten items	50.00
	$1,649.00

EXHIBIT 5-5

START-UP COSTS

Food handling permit @ 5.00 per person	$ 5.00
Tile for floor (already provided)	—
Restroom facilities for employees (already provided)	—
Counter to work on and serve customers	150.00
Cash register	499.00
Store-front sign	562.00
Stainless steel tables (4 @ $300 each)	1,200.00
Stainless steel sink	500.00
Chairs for customers who are waiting (4)	40.00
Plants to make it look nice	50.00
	$ 3,006.00
Ovens, mixer, retarder, cooler (described earlier)	11,500.00
Initial supplies needed (described earlier)	1,649.92
	$16,155.92

EXHIBIT 5-6

FINANCING REQUIRED

36 month loan
Assuming a loan at 20% for $17,500:

Monthly payments	=	$	650.36
Total payments	=		23,413.06
Less: principal	=		17,000.00
Total interest	=	$	6,413.06
Monthly interest payment	=		6,413.06
			36
	=	$	178.14

EXHIBIT 5-7

AVERAGE INGREDIENTS COST PER PIZZA

Cost of dough:				
	Water	—		
	Yeast	$ 0.132		
	Salt	0.140		
	Sugar	0.160		
	Flour	17.00		
		$17.43 ÷ 70	=	$0.25
Pizza sauce:			=	0.22
Cheeses:			=	0.23
Toppings:			=	0.53
Spices:			=	0.04
Box:			=	0.13
Spoilage, overcooking, mistake orders:			=	0.10
	TOTAL AVERAGE COST OF PIZZA		=	$1.50

EXHIBIT 5-8

EXPECTED PIZZA SALES PER DAY

Sunday		175
Monday		190
Tuesday		200
Wednesday		200
Thursday		200
Friday		300
Saturday		300
	Weekly	1,565

EXHIBIT 5-9

NUMBER OF EMPLOYEES NEEDED PER DAY

Sunday	3
Monday	3
Tuesday	3
Wednesday	3
Thursday	3
Friday	5
Saturday	5

EXHIBIT 5-10

PROJECTED MONTHLY COSTS

Cost of goods sold		$10,120.00
Wages (including manager's salary)		4,005.71
Advertising		500.00
Rent		300.00
Telephone		25.00
Utilities		120.00
Miscellaneous supplies		175.00
Depreciation		112.49
Interest		178.14
	TOTAL	$15,536.34
Fixed portion:		
Fixed wages	$ 3,560.00	
Advertising	500.00	
Rent	300.00	
Telephone	25.00	
Utilities	120.00	
Depreciation	112.49	
Interest	178.14	
	$ 4,795.63	
Variable portion:		
Cost of goods sold	$10,120.00	
Variable wages	445.71	
	$10,565.71	

EXHIBIT 5-11

MONTHLY BREAK-EVEN POINT

$$BE_{Units} = \frac{\text{fixed cost}}{\text{selling price} - \text{variable cost}}$$

Fixed cost = $ 4,795.63
Selling price = $ 5.50 average
Variable cost = $10,565.71 ÷ 6707 = $1.57 average

$$BE_{Units} = \frac{4,795.63}{5.50 - 1.57} = 1,220 \text{ pizzas}$$

$$BE_\$ = 5.50 \times 1,220 = 6,710.00$$

Note: We have assumed, for conservatism, that all revenue will be from pizzas. In actuality, the above figures are probably understated, because sales will be generated from other food. The variable costs include the estimated cost of goods sold for the other items, so breakdown would be lower. We feel that the variance is not significant.

EXHIBIT 5-12

MONTHLY INCOME STATEMENT

Revenues:			
	Pizza	$36,889.29	
	Subs and other items	2,517.75	
	TOTAL		$39,407.04
Expenses:			
	Cost of goods sold	$10,120.00	
	Wages (including manager's salary)	4,005.71	
	Advertising	500.00	
	Rent	300.00	
	Telephone	25.00	
	Utilities	120.00	
	Miscellaneous supplies	175.00	
	Depreciation	112.49	
	Interest	178.14	
	TOTAL		$15,536.34
	Income Before Taxes		$23,870.70

EXHIBIT 5-13

PEPPY'S MONTHLY CASH FLOW

Sources of Cash:			
	Sales revenue from pizza	$36,889.29	
	Sales revenue from subs (etc.)	2,517.75	
	TOTAL CASH GENERATED		$39,407.04
Uses of Cash:			
	Cost of goods sold	$10,120.00	
	Monthly wages (including manager)	4,005.71	
	Advertising	500.00	
	Rent	300.00	
	Telephone	25.00	
	Utilities	120.00	
	Miscellaneous supplies	175.00	
	Payment on note (including interest)	650.00	
	TOTAL CASH APPLIED		$15,896.07
Increase in cash during month before taxes			$25,510.97

EXHIBIT 5-14

PIZZA MENU

Pizzas	Junior 6 pc.	Small 8 pc.	Medium 10 pc.	Large 12 pc.	Extra Large 16 pc.
Cheese	1.95	2.75	3.95	5.05	5.90
Cheese and one item	2.45	3.40	4.85	5.95	7.15
Cheese and two items	2.70	4.15	5.50	6.85	7.85
Cheese and three items	3.05	4.55	6.05	7.40	8.45
Special	3.95	5.65	6.95	8.35	9.50
(pepperoni, mushrooms, ham, green pepper, onion, and bacon — anchovies on request)					
Pizzaburger	3.05	4.55	6.05	7.40	8.45
(cheese, hamburger, onion, and green pepper)					
Italian Delight	2.70	4.15	5.50	6.85	7.85
(cheese, Italian sausage, and mushrooms)					
The Peppy	3.05	4.55	6.05	7.40	8.45
(steak, cheese, and mushrooms)					
Extra items or double dough	.45	.55	.65	.75	.85
Taco Supreme Pizza	3.95	5.65	6.95	8.35	9.50
(taco meat, cheese, topped with lettuce, tomatoes, cheddar cheese, hot sauce on the side)					

Pizza Toppings To Choose From!!!

    Mushrooms, cheese, pepperoni, hamburger, black olives, Italian sausage, green onion, anchovies, ham, bacon.

Chef Salad

    Lettuce, tomato, onion, green pepper, mushrooms, black olives, ham and cheese
    Dressing: French, Italian, or Thousand Island   2.75

Pasta

Spaghetti with meat sauce	2.25
Ravioli with meat sauce	2.25
Meatballs .60 extra Mushrooms .35 extra	
Above orders served with bread and cheese	

Submarines

	Half	Whole
Deluxe combination	1.30	2.55
Ham, pepperoni, and cheese		
Steak sub	1.55	2.90
Steak and cheese	1.85	3.20
Steak and mushrooms	1.80	3.30

EXHIBIT 5-14 Continued

Steak, mushrooms, and cheese		2.10	3.60
Pizza sub		1.15	2.20
Pepperoni, ham, mushrooms, onion, green pepper, cheese, and pizza sauce			
Ham sub		1.45	2.60
Ham and cheese		1.55	2.70
Hamburger sub		1.45	2.60
Cheeseburger sub		1.55	2.70
Italian sausage sub		1.55	2.70
Italian sausage and cheese		1.65	2.80
Meatball sub		1.50	2.40
Spaghetti sauce and cheese			
Vegetarian sub		1.25	2.40
All submarines include lettuce, tomatoes, onions, and hot peppers, except Pizza subs			
Additional Items	.25 on any half sub		.40 on any whole sub

craig nichols and gary harwell

6

"We've got the merchandise and facilities; all we need now is a competitive edge."

Craig Nichols summed up the status of a new venture he just initiated with friend Gary Harwell. Craig and Gary reside in Eugene, Oregon, where they attended college and pursue their mutual hobby of science-fiction book collecting.

"Craig and I are really into science fiction," Harwell explains. "We have pooled our book collection and have over 4,000 volumes—Heinlein, Van Vogt, Asimov, Bester, Moorcock, Pohl. You name the book; it's somewhere in our collection."

"Not only that," Nichols adds, "we've got sci-fi magazines going back over twenty-five years. All neatly catalogued and indexed."

During the summer of 1980, both Nichols and Harwell decided to stay out of school to investigate the possibility of opening a used-book store in Eugene as a means of supplementing their income year round. Nichols and Harwell elaborate:

Nichols—Gary and I figured that we might as well try to capitalize on our love of books and reading. Both of us are familiar with used-book store operations because we have haunted them so regularly in building our collection.

Harwell—That's right. Going to bookstores all over the Northwest has been a hobby of ours. We've seen just about every used-paperback operation in this part of the country. A lot of them seem to be profiting.

Nichols—Gary's uncle owned a service station here in Eugene near the University of

Oregon campus. OPEC put the station under in 1978, and it's been vacant since. We made a deal with his uncle to convert the facility into a used-book store. He agreed to do it for 25 percent of our take for two years.

Harwell—Not a bad deal, actually, since the station was located near the campus and in a good state of repair. To say the least, there are hoards of avid readers at the University.

Nichols—Just three weeks after lining up the station, Gary and I lucked into a deal over in Portland. The owner of a pretty good-sized used-paperback outlet put his merchandise up for sale to raise quick cash to cover farming losses suffered in southern Washington. Can you believe his luck? He had 200 acres within 50 miles of Mount St. Helens!

Harwell—We swung a good deal with him—over 10,000 paperbacks, magazines, and comics for $3,500. That's about 35 cents apiece. We borrowed the money from some fraternity brothers, rented a U-Haul truck, and carted home our start-up inventory.

Nichols—It filled the service station about half way. We're currently in the process of cataloging the stuff. We definitely got a great deal. Most of the books are in good shape and have recent copyrights. We got a good mixture of fiction and nonfiction, including westerns, mysteries, gothics, biographies, and a few technical books.

Harwell—We're virtually ready to open the doors, but we still haven't decided on what competitive strategy to use.

Nichols—That's our problem. We don't want to be just another used-book store. Eugene already has a half-dozen of those. We want to be something different in our image and in the way we operate.

Harwell—We've kicked around a few ideas that might provide us with a competitive edge, but we haven't really settled on anything. We're ready to open but want to wait until we have crystalized our strategy.

Nichols—We want to be able to attract customers based on our differentiated image and unique style of operating. We're looking to be something a little different.

Harwell—And profitable!

Analysis: Design a competitive strategy and competitive edge for the new bookstore. Include a suggested name for the store. Strive to satisfy the criteria established by Nichols and Harwell, to be different and profitable.

exploration graphics

7

Jamie Thompson is president and manager of Exploration Graphics, Inc., a computer services company that prepares graphics and interprets geographical data for the oil and gas industry. The company is located in Midland, Texas, where Jamie was born and currently resides.

Jamie graduated from Midland High School in 1965 and has taken a variety of college courses since then. She was recently chosen by *Texas Business* magazine as one of the top ten women executives in Texas.

Jamie's interests range from reading various business periodicals to outdoor recreation including hunting, fishing, camping, and swimming. She is a member of the Permian Toastmasters, Midland Business and Professional Women's Club, West Texas Geological Society, the High Sky Bass Club, and the Midland Rifle and Pistol Club.

Jamie and her husband, Doyle, are the parents of two girls, ages seven and five.

Jamie, please tell us what Exploration Graphics does—what your company is all about, and the kinds of services you offer.

Basically, we apply computerization to oil-field-exploration analysis. This is a fancy way of saying that we provide our clients with computer assisted analytical services. We have a data file containing more than a decade's worth of information about oil and gas wells drilled in the Permian Basin region, which encompasses a large part of West Texas. We use this information to develop computer printouts or contour maps for many independent oil companies as well as the majors.

These computerized geographical maps show data such as which oil and gas wells are producing, what these wells have done historically, patterns of well production in the area, and related concerns. We use a variety of information inputs such as a base map, correlated electric logs, scout data, samples, cores, and so on. We take this information, process it by a computer, and merge it into convenient printouts for the busy geologist to use. In effect, we type, file, retrieve, draft, and process data which would be much too complex and cumbersome for practitioners to use.

These services boost the user's productivity by a minimum of 20 percent. Just imagine, the technician would have to spend days and perhaps weeks compiling and processing this geological information. Our computerization does this in a matter of a few seconds. Not only do we process the information, but we package it in a useful, convenient way for the geologist. I'm not bragging when I say that our business is really unique.

Tell us how you got into such a unique business.

In 1965, I began working for the Mobil Oil Corporation as soon as I finished school. I started out as a mail clerk but in a few months I was promoted to stenographer. I went to work during the day and took classes at the local junior college in the evening. I was taking data-processing courses and had a strong interest in computer science at the time.

The company noticed my interest in computers and encouraged me to take a series of in-company aptitude tests dealing with programming skills. I did very well on the tests and was selected to receive extensive training within the company. The training period was a tough time for me, because the friends I had made at work in my clerical positions evidently were jealous of my advancement. They gave me the cold shoulder and I was left to myself. They didn't even want to associate with me much during the coffee breaks, so I used this time for further study.

After awhile, the social isolation at work got to me, and I knew I was going to have to change jobs. I was being completely ignored by everyone. I was offered a job with the Midland Independent School District and quickly took it. This gave me my initial experience in doing data processing work.

In 1969, I was ready to do contract programming, so I established a firm called DecoData Processing. I took on a partner early in the business. The business did pretty well, but in 1975 my partner died. We had no survivor's agreement, so the partnership was automatically dissolved, and I was faced with striking out in a new commercial direction.

Tell us what options you were considering at this point.

Basically, I had three options. First of all, I could go to work for someone else. A second option would have been to stay home and spend all of my time

EXHIBIT 7-1

Exploration Graphics

INCOME AND EXPENSE LIST

Description	1979-80	1978-79	1977-78	1976-77	1975-76
Income	$446,179.86	$276,624.85	$264,338.30	$139,280.97	$56,501.36
Salaries and wages	94,976.82	68,860.62	71,761.14	52,405.61	20,152.52
Payroll taxes	5,278.57	3,542.05	4,502.85	2,907.73	1,173.74
Accounting expense fees	2,585.00	3,468.28	2,565.00	725.00	100.00
Accounting expense mach.	.00	.00	.00	.00	.00
Advance on wages	20.80	.00	.00	.00	4.51
Director's salary	3,050.00	.00	.00	1,000.00	1,250.00
Admin. overhead	.00	.00	.00	.00	.00
Advertising	6,062.29	3,555.23	2,042.99	1,349.51	.00
Sales commissions	.00	2,319.75	4,456.75	9,392.50	.00
All car expense	1,080.72	1,201.62	520.16	.00	.00
Contributions	125.00	1,150.00	1,000.00	3,028.00	.00
Drafting	.00	.00	.00	.00	.00
Dues & subscriptions		955.96	1,448.70	149.89	.00
Education – seminars	811.31	384.27	201.16	135.00	121.58
Employee benefits	680.74	867.74	475.00	200.00	50.00
Promotion & goodwill	2,089.11	535.26	375.77	100.00	203.88
Equipment expense	5,960.00	3,590.82	403.37	.00	.00
Equipment – rental	.00	431.03	120.96	651.00	.00
Equipment – rental	10,460.40	2,240.47	1,863.61	130.20	1,127.77
Equipment – rental	4,609.27	13,472.54	5,835.07	1,163.74	571.60
Equipment – rental	18,665.85	3,097.74	3,006.25	.00	.00
Equipment – rental	2,234.44	.00	.00	.00	.00
Insurance	5,857.19	5,329.85	3,753.81	2,202.62	1,167.78
Interest	2,936.23	2,618.17	2,843.40	2,112.85	2,981.62
Labor – contract	668.97	622.84	36.00	270.71	41.38
Outside D.P.	1,052.75	7,260.55	2,779.65	871.30	56.18
Maps & reproduction	9,260.80	8,276.41	7,623.33	7,901.20	1,464.00

EXHIBIT 7-1 Continued

Exploration Graphics

INCOME AND EXPENSE LIST

Description	1979-80	1978-79	1977-78	1976-77	1975-76
Materials & supplies	$ 23,284.33	$ 9,600.18	$ 4,329.04	$ 4,643.59	$ 2,240.36
Miscellaneous	1,416.51	2,209.71	1,357.39	413.38	703.96
Office supplies	2,321.40	4,110.55	1,500.07	1,651.39	736.89
Parking	.00	.00	123.27	280.00	201.95
Part-time labor cost	.00	.00	219.80	235.50	32.00
Post, freight, & ship	471.00	316.63	502.46	312.70	196.81
Legal	437.53	3,142.95	.00	.00	330.15
Geo-consult-fee	$ 20,053.48	$ 8,835.47	$ 21,474.00	$ 7,079.37	$ .00
Rent and/or lease	6,300.00	8,463.00	7,000.00	7,972.91	5,103.95
Repairs & maint.	6,833.74	10,992.70	4,600.24	4,459.25	3,307.38
Texas sales tax	1,179.24	15,471.87	253.92	0.00	73.61
Fed. unemployment tax	598.47	496.97	134.77	110.80	65.28
State emp sec com	52.60	44.80	44.92	510.25	354.54
Fed income tax-co.	5,250.00 cr	.00	.00	.00	.00
Taxes – other	6,846.55	4,924.29	688.89	700.55	398.46
St income tax-co	.00	.00	.00	.00	.00
Tele-communications	3,882.59	2,763.91	2,116.50	1,650.00	752.11
Travel expense	8,696.67	6,974.92	1,703.15	2,379.92	950.00
Utilities	1,556.96	1,079.86	.00	268.80	261.33
Xerox reproductions	1,231.90	10.95	103.20	26.50	141.80
Abandonment loss	.00	.00	.00	.00	.00
Royalties	.00	.00	.00	.00	.00
TOTAL EXPENSES	252,236.35	213,219.96	163,766.59	119,391.77	46,317.15
INCOME	446,179.86	276,624.85	264,338.30	139,280.97	56,501.36
	$193,943.53	$63,404.89	$10,057.71	$19,889.20	$10,184.21

rearing my children. The third option was the biggest challenge of all—to open my own business. I sat down and analyzed each alternative from the standpoint of pluses and minuses. I was having a very difficult time making up my mind exactly which way to go when I remembered someone I knew who was a vice-president in a Houston oil company. It occurred to me that he might be able to provide some sound advice given his perspective on the industry.

I phoned him and explained the situation. He was very gracious and said, "Please fly down any time. Just give me a day's notice and I'll meet with you."

I quickly took him up on the offer and within a week spent a half-day at his office in Houston going over my various options.

During the meeting, I told him of my great interest in trying to computerize geological data. I had what I thought were a lot of fairly innovative ideas, and I really wanted the opportunity to use my data processing knowledge in a new way. He was immediately interested and felt I could help his company a great deal if I could make the ideas pan out in practice.

One thing led to another, and before I knew it, he had made me an offer to do contract work for the company for a six-month period. They would cover my expenses during the time and help me to make some of my ideas ready to use. In order to expedite the contractual obligations, I formed Exploration Graphics. That is how my present company was born.

Did you have any second thoughts about going it alone in a new business?

Yes, I had a number of reservations about it, but I knew that I had an independent personality and would not be satisfied staying at home or working for someone else. I also knew that I didn't really want to establish a new relationship with another partner. Don't get me wrong, the previous partnership had worked out satisfactorily, but I had a strong desire, now, to do things on my own. I really wanted to accomplish something autonomously. Besides, I had a number of innovative ideas and I'm not sure anyone else would have appreciated them and their potential.

Analysis: Besides her technical expertise with computers, what additional skills and personal characteristics helped Jamie in successfully launching Exploration Graphics?

Tell us about your initial experiences in running Exploration Graphics.

I started the company and began working on the oil company contract in May of 1975. I had no financing or working capital whatsoever. The contract paid me on a month-by-month basis, so I had the benefit of being independent without the pressures of paying my own way. I knew that I could pay my bills month-to-month because I had the contract revenue coming in on a regular basis.

The half-year project turned out successfully and I was optimistic about the future. Rather than staying on with the company in a short-term, contractual relationship, which they had offered me, I decided to go beat the bushes for additional business. I had to go knocking on doors, and that's exactly what I did. I leased a small computer and was ready to go.

The next few months were very erratic because my work was strictly on a project basis. Money would come in for awhile and then dry up until I was able to land another contract for someone in the Permian Basin. I went out and rented an office—a very small one—and, along with my computer, this was my entire plant and equipment. During this time my husband helped me a whole lot through emotional support and by providing a steady income. Also my mother helped out in a number of ways by watching my kids during the day and offering me a lot of solid business advice.

After six months of hand-to-mouth existence, it became apparent that I needed someone to help me with the work. There was a need for one person to engage in sales and client contact work practically full-time, and there was another slot revolving around the technical computer work. The two responsibilities simply would not go together because of the time required in both areas.

I managed to hire someone who could help handle some of the paperwork and customer relationships. This freed up a lot of time for me to continue to plan and do the technical part of the business.

Securing a loan through the Small Business Administration was our next priority. This seemed to be the most logical source of financing because of the low interest rate. It seemed to me that the company required around $500,000 over a period of two or three years to do all of the things we needed. After the usual amount of red tape, hassles, and bureaucratic maneuvering, we were able to obtain $150,000 from the SBA. This was the financial nucleus to considerable growth for Exploration Graphics. From 1975 to 1979, the company grew very rapidly and our successes certainly outnumbered our failures.

Analysis: How can a fledgling company determine the amount and timing of growth-capital needed?

Are your current problems still financial in nature?

Exactly. The SBA loan was certainly a blessing, but it wasn't really enough. We still have a need for capital, but I'm not really sure how to go after it. We need a bigger computer, much more office space, and we have to hire still more technical personnel—especially more geological analysts. We definitely need money to grow on, and getting that money is currently my number one priority and problem.

EXHIBIT 7-2

Exploration Graphics

COMPARATIVE BALANCE SHEET

Assets	1979-80	78-79	77-78	76-77	75-76
Current Assets					
Cash	5,524.52	6,992.40	19,435.79	20,518.27	2,081.82
Accounts receivable	333,992.40**	208,378.81**	72,715.50	21,463.22	9,055.30
Notes receivable	.00	.00	.00	.00	.00
Materials & supplies inventory	10,054.87	3,103.35	1,507.66	800.00	800.00
Fixed Assets					
Office furniture, equipment, land	118,620.91	120,141.11	42,854.02	27,538.11	28,371.98
Sale of asset – warehoused or stored equipment	.00	.00	.00	.00	.00
Leasehold improvements and fixtures	.00	.00	.00	.00	.00
Other Assets					
Deposits	6,128.13	425.88	.00	.00	.00
TOTAL ASSETS	474,320.83	339,041.55	136,512.97	70,319.60	40,309.10

EXHIBIT 7-2 (continued)

Exploration Graphics

COMPARATIVE BALANCE SHEET

Liabilities					
Current Liabilities					
Notes payable	196,512.83	80,491.46	25,348.15	42,509.19	29,648.44
Accounts payable	42,211.48	13,045.92	10,000.00	.00	.00
Withheld taxes	1,179.00	7,250.54	530.19	363.40	222.18
FICA taxes	1,303.11	4,709.96	709.38	335.67	254.27
Option deposits and/or escrow	2,844.34	583.92	.00	.00	.00
Liabilities – deferred	.00	.00	.00	.00	.00
Net Worth					
Capital-equity	36,656.92	52,663.36	19,353.54	7,222.14	10,184.21
Net income	193,945.53	63,404.89	100,571.71	19,889.20	
TOTAL LIABILITIES & NET WORTH	474,320.83	339,041.55	136,512.97	70,319.60	40,309.10
April-December, 1979	214,815.82	87,268.38			
**Geological Data Files Costs Included as 1220					

Analysis: Analyze Exploration Graphics' current financial needs, both short-term and long-term.

Evaluate available financing options in terms of benefits and drawbacks.

Present concrete and specific recommendations for the company's future financing: amount of funding required, sources of funding, funds timing, and funds utilization.

waterhaus aqua slide

8

Mickey Gerrard is a successful swimming pool contractor in Yuma, Arizona (population 30,000). He is currently studying the possibility of building a water slide on commercial property he owns in Yuma. Mr. Gerrard is convinced of the slide's recreational appeal and profit potential but is concerned about its longevity as a viable commercial venture.

"Water slides are extremely popular nationwide today," Mr. Gerrard comments, "and Yuma has no facility of this sort. There's no question that these slides have strong profit potential for the near-term. Rental rates are very lucrative and construction costs are modest. My sole concern lies with whether or not the slide is strictly a fad item that will quickly run its course and then disappear from the scene—you know, like the giant metal slides fifteen years ago and trampoline centers in the 1950s.

"I'd be looking for a worthwile return on my investment, which I estimate would be in the neighborhood of $30,000. If I could recoup my investment and realize a decent return, I wouldn't really care if water slides were only a passing fad. I'd make my money and move on to other ventures. The payback period on the slide is what I'm most interested in."

Gerrard owns a large, developed land-tract in Yuma near a popular strip shopping center. His plan calls for construction of the water slide on that site under the name Waterhaus Aqua Slide. Mr. Gerrard outlines his venture idea as follows:

"I plan to have a complex of three water chutes emanating from a common access tower. The chutes would empty into a small swimming pool at the bottom of the tower's hill. Sliders would walk up one concrete sidewalk to reach the top. An unshaded observation deck would be constructed over the chutes mid-way up the hill.

"To minimize initial expenses, we would not have locker rooms for changing clothes. Customers would have to come in their bathing suits. The admission office area would resemble that typically found at public swimming pools. There would be a small building to house employees, the plastic slide-mats, and several lockers for checking valuables. We would have two soft-drink vending machines as well as machines for candy and chips.

"I would anticipate opening from May 15 through September 15 from 10:00 A.M. to midnight daily. Three minimum wage employees would work on each shift: one to work the admissions booth and the other two to provide assistance in the slide tower.

"I have a good friend in Tempe who operates a slide. He assures me that I can draw plenty of customer traffic at $3 per half-hour. I have also used his operating expenses as the basis for my financial planning (Exhibit 8-1).

"The Waterhaus slides would accommodate up to sixty people at any one time. The parking lot would hold forty-five to fifty cars. Our only other facilities would consist of a loudspeaker system and four poles of night lighting.

"Having looked at my friend's financial statements in Tempe, I know that water slides are big profit producers. What's more, there are no other slides here in Yuma. I'll have a corner on the market. My decision to go ahead will hinge on my analysis of payback period and return on investment. I plan to complete this soon."

Analysis: Analyze the short-run profit potential of Waterhaus Aqua Slide. Does the venture have sufficient potential even if water slides turn out to be a fad? On what assumptions does your analysis rest?

State conditions under which you (1) would, and (2) would not recommend that Mr. Gerrard build the slide.

EXHIBIT 8-1

PROJECTED EXPENSES

Construction Expenses	
Slide construction:	$215,000 (18 month loan at 12.55 percent)
Building construction:	$ 65,000 (24 month loan at 11.75 percent)

Monthly Expenses During Open Season	
Utilities:	$2,500
Payroll:	$4,500 (minimum wage at $3.50 per hr.)
Advertising:	$1,000
Insurance:	$ 850
Water purifiers:	$ 150
Miscellaneous administrative:	$ 250

s & s farms

9

"Well Don, what do you think? Do we take the deal or pass it up?" asked Bob.

"I don't know," replied Don. "It sounds good but there are so many variables. Farming is one of those businesses where the manager doesn't have much control over the outcome. It's bad enough that the weather can wipe out all your profits, but the federal government, which is supposed to be helping the farmers, does more damage than it does good. Look at last year—the retaliation against the Russians for invading Afghanistan was to stop corn shipments to Russia. As a result, ear corn dropped from about $2.50 a bushel to $2.00. We could have lost our pants."

Don Sanderson and his brother-in-law, Bob Schneider, were discussing a potential farming venture. Don is a school teacher in Eldon, Missouri, a small town close to the Bagnell Dam which forms the Lake of the Ozarks in south central Missouri. Bob, a general manager of a heating and air-conditioning firm in Jefferson City, grew up on a farm. He would provide the technical know-how for the business.

The arrangement looked pretty good. Bill Schneider, Bob's father and Don's father-in-law, was nearing retirement age. He had offered to lease his 300-acre farm to the two men. Bob and Don had agreed that if they entered into the plan, Bob would perform most of the labor associated with planting and harvesting the crops, while Don would provide the labor for repairing fences and maintaining the equipment. Don's teaching job would allow him plenty of free time during the summers and Christmas vacation period.

"Dad will keep us out of trouble" asserted Bob. "He knows the farming business and has spent his lifetime on the farm. He can advise us what to plant, when to fertilize, and so forth."

The two men had received an offer from Bill Schneider to lease his 300-acre farm. Under the agreement, the lease was to run for three years at $70 per acre annually. The lease would be renegotiated at the end of the three-year period but could also be terminated at the end of any year if desired by any two of the three parties involved. Like most of the hilly farms in the Ozark foothills, only one third of the Schneider farm could be used for farming. The remainder could be used for pasture.

The tentative agreement also specified that the men could purchase thirty cows with calves at $400 each and a registered Hereford bull for $500. Mr. Schneider had been developing his herd to breed Black Baldy calves. The Black Baldy is a cross between an Angus and a Hereford, yielding characteristics of both breeds of beef cattle. The face of the animal is white, like a Hereford, with the remainder of the body black, like an Angus. The Black Baldies normally bring about $4 more per hundred pounds at the central Missouri markets.

In addition to the purchase of the cattle, Mr. Schneider had offered the two men use of his existing equipment at no charge so long as they paid for all maintenance and repairs. The equipment consisted of a Farmall tractor with a three-point hydraulic lift; a four-row turning plow with disks and cultivator; a four-row corn picker; and an 1,800 bushel grain wagon.

"It does sound like a good deal Bob," agreed Don, "but let's put the numbers to it to find out if we can make any money. With our present jobs, it's not like the normal situation where we either make a profit or starve. However, I would like to find out if I can make more money farming during the summers than I could make at some other job."

"Let me check with Dad about the expenses, " said Bob, "and we'll figure it out the next time we get together."

Two weeks later, Bob provided the following information:

"Dad and I checked his records on the farm. The normal yield is between 70 and 80 bushels of corn to the acre. I also asked about crop failure during drought conditions. The last time he lost his corn crop was during the drought of 1934, so we can conservatively estimate a yield of 70 bushels for each acre. Ear corn lately has been selling for about $2.50 per bushel, except during the grain embargo when it dropped to about $2. We can plan on $2.50 per bushel.

"Our costs for a corn crop will run about $45 per acre for fertilizer, $5 an acre for seed corn, and around $5 per acre for weed killer. Our labor can be estimated on a 100-acre crop. For the 100 acres we can expect about ten days to plow, five days to disc, five days to plant, and ten days to cultivate after the corn is up. I can probably handle this if we don't have any rain delays.

We can also expect to use about 20 gallons of gasoline per day. Since we don't pay federal or state taxes on gasoline used on the farm, we can estimate gasoline costs at about 80 cents per gallon. During harvest we will need about five days to pick the corn, and we will need to hire one person to haul the wagons to the corn crib. We can pick up one of the local boys for this at about $3 an hour.

"We can also use the farm to raise beef," Bob continued. "We will need to add more cattle but we won't be able to buy them at the $400 price offered by Dad. We will probably have to pay $550 for cows with calves at the livestock market. We have 300 acres, and it takes about three acres to pasture one cow and calf. Of course we'll need hay for the winter, so we can't use the entire acreage for pasture.

"Assuming we sell our calves in the fall, we'll still need about one-and-a-half tons of hay to get each cow through the winter. If we plant alfalfa hay, the hay field will be good for three years. We can get three cuttings each summer from the field. The first cutting will be the best, about one-and-a-half tons of hay per acre. The yield from the second and third cuttings will be less, unless we get some good summer rains. Let's plan on a total of three tons of hay per acre overall. It will cost us about $12 per ton to get the hay cut and baled, since we don't have the equipment to do this.

"I got some estimates on the costs of putting in hay from the local Co-op. We will need to plant 12 pounds of seed per acre at a cost of $1.75 per pound. We will also need to lime the field when we first plant. We will need two tons of lime per acre at about $12 per ton. Our fertilizer costs will be $20 per acre. Fertilizing will have to be done each spring. Once the hay field has been planted, we can cut for three years off that field. After the first year, the only expenses will be for fertilizing, cutting, and baling. Our labor will be approximately the same as for planting corn—one day to plow and another day for discing and planting for every ten acres.

"If we sell our calves as feeder calves in October, they should weigh about 450 pounds and bring about $80 per hundred. This is a rough estimate and assumes that the cows will have their calves in March. Some will have calves earlier and some later, but we can use this figure as an average. We can always carry over the late calves and butcher some for our own use in December or sell them at market in the spring as yearlings. They won't bring $80, but they will be larger. I would rather not do this since feeding may be difficult when the weather gets bad.

"There may be another reason why we would want to sell calves, or corn for that matter, after the first of the year. For tax purposes, farming is done on what accountants call the cash method. This means that costs are expensed in the year in which they're incurred. For example, even though our hay field will last for three years, we can claim the total expense for tax purposes in the year we put in the hay field. In the same vein, we claim all the income from the sale of corn or beef in the year in which we receive our money. There may be some years when we may want to sell only part of the crop during the season and hold the balance for sale after the first of the year."

"There's another way we can save money too," added Don. "The federal government, for tax purposes, expects only 70 percent of the cows to have calves each year. Bill thinks we can plan on about 90 percent to have calves.

We could always butcher one or two calves a year for our own use. We wouldn't have to use income that we had paid income tax on to buy meat. Further, we wouldn't have to pay taxes on the beef we didn't sell. I don't want to pay the federal government any more taxes than I have to. If businesses were run as inefficiently as the government, they would go broke. All the government does is increase taxes."

"We could also employ our boys at minimum wage to work on the farm," said Bob. "They don't pay taxes until they make more than $3,500 per year. With my two boys and your two, we could shelter $14,000 of income each year."

"Aren't we putting the cart before the horse?" asked Don. "We don't even know if we can make a profit, yet we are already thinking about ways to save taxes."

"You're right, Don," Bob answered, "but I'm really excited about this. It's a real opportunity for us. If the numbers look good, I would certainly like to salt away $3,500 a year for future college expenses. I'm now in the 40 percent tax bracket, so I've got to make in excess of $5,000 in order to save $3,500. Also we eat two calves a year. At $375 apiece and in my income tax bracket, this amounts to about $1,050 a year in taxable income. Just for meat and college expenses, I could save about $11,000 a year by being involved with the farm."

"We would need to form a partnership," said Don. "What should we name our company and how much will that cost us?"

"Why not name it S & S Farms," Bob answered. "You can tell your friends that S & S stands for Sanderson and Schneider. I'll tell mine that it stands for Schneider and Sanderson!"

"Sounds good to me," Don laughed. "How much will it cost, and what else do we need to do it?"

"We can get Jim Woodsen to draft the partnership papers," Bob replied. "He does all of Dad's legal work and probably won't charge over $50 to set up the partnership. In addition, we'll need an Internal Revenue Service employer number and a checking account. The IRS number doesn't cost anything. We just pick up the forms at the local office and mail them to Kansas City. To set up the bank account, all we need to do is sign the cards so that either one of us can write checks on the account."

About that time, Mr. Schneider joined the two men on the porch.

"Sounds to me like you two boys are about to go into the farming business," he said. "Alice and I would like to see you run the farm. We've spent our entire married life here, and here's where we raised our family. It's been a good life, but now that I'm nearing retirement age we would like to be free of the responsibilities. With you two running the farm, we know it will be kept in good shape.

"Furthermore, once I start drawing Social Security, any income that I make beyond a certain amount will be deducted from my monthly check. I've paid into Social Security for more than forty years. Now they can start paying me. By leasing the farm, this income is considered rental income which does not affect my checks.

"I would like to see you run the farm. Tell you what I'll do. You can pay me $10 per acre lease and I will pay for the materials used in repairing the fences. All you need to do is provide the labor."

"Dad," said Bob, "now that you are about to retire, share with us some of your thoughts about being a farmer. Did you ever think you would have been happier as a businessman?"

"I am a businessman," replied Mr. Schneider. "The farmer is America's most frequently overlooked entrepreneur. He sells a high-demand product under high-risk circumstances and must be profit oriented. Farmers work extremely hard, run their own show, and have to develop an expertise in numerous technical areas.

"Today's farmer couldn't possibly survive without management skills. You have to be able to forecast the weather and commodity markets, make extremely complicated tax decisions, be a good bookkeeper and even somewhat of an engineer and mechanic.

"I guess the one business activity I engage in most is planning. I keep records on practically everything to facilitate my planning efforts. I keep track of prices during various times of the year, when I planted and harvested, the cattle yield, and what the weather was doing and when.

"I try to plan ahead more than one calendar year, but it's real tough to do with all of the uncertainties in agriculture. The one big certainty, though, is the need for financing. Farmers have to keep track of the cash flow just like any other businessman and watch how they time major capital investments. These have to be depreciated according to IRS regulations, so planning is mandatory.

"Dealing with the banker is one other major planning aspect of farming. He forces it on you whether you like it or not. He wants to know what you're planting this year, how many acres, expected yields, and on and on. The bank has a stake in your farm too, so the pressure to plan is understandable.

"I guess the one thing no farmer is ever really prepared for concerns contingencies—what ifs. What if the weather turns hostile; what if supply shoots up and prices fall; what if the President institutes a grain embargo against Russia. Farming is loaded with ifs."

"What type of problems could we anticipate in running the farm?" asked Don.

"As I said before," replied Mr. Schneider," just about all of my problems are caused by uncertainty: when to plant and harvest, when to sell, whether or not to sign futures contracts, and so on. Getting help during the busy times of the year is also tough. I generally end up doing most things myself.

"It's always a problem setting priorities and using time wisely. Time is our only certainty. Even when the weather is bad, you can repair equipment, fix fences, and work with the herd. Wasted time is wasted money.

"The government is another problem, that's for sure. Just like the weather, it's so unpredictable. The government has tried, through the years, to help out farmers, and I suppose it has succeeded pretty well in areas like the soil bank and disaster payment programs. But the government's pricing policies have failed. The parity system, where prices are pegged to a cost-of-living index, just doesn't enable most farmers to cover costs. Inflation is eating us up because our costs keep going up, just as for everyone else, but selling prices haven't kept pace, even though supermarket prices have skyrocketed.

"Profits are important to everyone, and I'm glad to see you boys are looking at the numbers. But don't forget the psychological rewards of being independent and self-sufficient. You are looking at this now solely for the additional income. But how long will it be before you begin to consider it as a career opportunity? I suspect there are a lot of entrepreneurial characteristics in each of you."

Analysis: What are some of the primary differences between running a farm and other types of nonagricultural businesses?

"We'll let you know in a couple of weeks Dad," replied Bob. "Don is going to look at the numbers to determine if we can make any money on the deal and what would be the best mix of corn and beef to produce to maximize our profits. Then we'll be in a position to talk more seriously."

Bill then said, "If you boys want to build the herd fast, I'll lend you whatever funds you need for your breeding stock. You can borrow the money from me at 8 percent and pay it back out of your profits. You should be able to pay it back in five years."

As the two men departed Bob cautioned Don, "When you do the numbers, don't forget to consider the risks of putting all our eggs in the same basket. Some cattle will offset the drought that could wipe out a corn crop, and some corn might be a hedge against some disease killing all our cattle."

Analysis: Are Bob and Don true entrepreneurs, since the farming venture is not their primary source of income? What is your definition of entrepreneurship?

Have Bob and Don omitted any cost factors in their informal assessment of the S & S Farms venture idea?

Bob and Don mentioned the possibility of hedging their losses by utilizing a mixture of beef and corn production. In your opinion, would this be a wise course of action? If so, what percent of the farm should be employed for beef and what percent for corn? Assume the lease will be terminated in three years.

Should Bob and Don form a fifty-fifty partnership? If not, what arrangement would you recommend? What are the potential dangers of a fifty-fifty partnership?

EXPERIENCE PHASE II
venture management

cumberland crafts

10

Ann Stanfield, president of Cumberland Crafts, Inc., comments, "I have believed in this business from the very beginning, and I think the basis for any successful venture is believing in what you are doing."

Cumberland Crafts, Inc., is a wholesaler of craft supplies and accessories located in Santa Fe, New Mexico, a town of approximately 40,000 persons in the northern part of the state. Cumberland Crafts, as well as its retail counterpart, Craft Village, is owned and operated by Ann and Dick Stanfield. The Stanfields have been in the craft business since 1975 when Ann opened Craft Village as a sole proprietorship.

Cumberland Crafts is one of only four craft wholesalers in the state of New Mexico, the others being located in Albuquerque, Tucumcari, and Hobbs. The Stanfields provide a wide variety of craft items (materials for decoupage, macrame, woodworking, plastic castings, etc.) to 350-400 retailers in a four-state area.

Background and History of Cumberland Crafts and Craft Village

Craft Village was begun in Ann Stanfield's garage as a part-time outlet for her interest in crafts as a hobby. In 1973 Ann decided to work toward the opening of a retail craft store by becoming as familiar as possible with crafts and craft accessories. She spent some two-and-a-half years in this informal learning process.

"I didn't really know how I was going to use all I was learning, but I knew

I wanted to become professionally involved with crafts because they were so interesting to me."

In 1975, Ann borrowed $5,000 (the maximum allowable) from a Santa Fe bank, withdrew the cash values from the family's life insurance policies and retirement pension plan, and opened Craft Village in a small building that rented for $175 per month. The total investment in inventory and fixtures was approximately $8,000 to $9,000. "We started out selling about $50 per day, and it gradually grew until it has now reached about $600 per day." Inventory was stored at home, in the garage, during the early months of operations.

The Stanfields initially promoted Craft Village by having Ann put on demonstrations for homemaker clubs, local high schools, and junior high schools. In 1974, due to increasing business, Craft Village moved across the street to a larger building, where it is now housed. "This was definitely a good move, because it helped us to increase our sales and our classroom space." Also, in 1974, husband Dick quit his teaching job to join the growing business.

It was at this time that the Stanfields decided to expand into wholesaling in order to capitalize on what they perceived as a regional boom in craft retailing. "Nobody in the area was providing adequate wholesaling service in general. We saw the need for a generalist wholesaler and decided to step in."

The wholesaling operation was originally located in a series of adjacent offices in one building which rented for $500 per month. While in this temporary location, the Stanfields were able to open a line of credit at the local bank, where they eventually borrowed a total of $36,000. "At this time we were heavily in debt but not to an excessive level for the kind of business we were doing," commented Ann.

In August of 1978, the Stanfields moved the wholesaling operation, which had been named Cumberland Crafts, into a central warehouse renting for $500 per month. For no additional cost, this new warehouse provided 7,500 square feet vs. 2,500 square feet in the previous location. By mid-1978, Cumberland Crafts had grown to the point where it employed four additional workers and was doing $20,000 per month in sales.

Also, during the summer of 1978, both Craft Village and Cumberland Crafts were incorporated, leading to financing problems with the local bank due to the changeover from personal liability to limited liability. As a result, a second mortgage was placed on the Stanfield's home, and their banker further recommended that they apply for an SBA loan. To the Stanfield's surprise, the SBA loan was not approved despite the backing of their local Congressman. Ann explained, "I was pregnant when we applied for the loan, and I guess the loan officer involved didn't take me very seriously. At this time we were really needing some financial backing, because we were in a tremendous growth period."

In January 1976, the Stanfields refinanced their patchwork loan arrangement with the local bank by agreeing to pay back the $36,000 on a monthly schedule over a five-year period. In addition, the bank approved a $75,000 line of credit. "So finally, after all those years of operation, we had adequate financial banking. We were able to begin really growing without our hands being tied."

Management of the Company

"I have been the main leader in the business simply because I was the one that started both of them and I had the most craft retailing experience," commented Ann in discussing the management of Cumberland Crafts and Craft Village. Ann is president of both companies, with Dick Stanfield being secretary-treasurer for both firms. While Ann has responsibility for the overall administration of the company, Dick concentrates on sales to retail customers and on finance. The remaining management team consists of three department heads and an assistant manager at Craft Village.

Kay Ridgeway heads up the accounting function, including invoicing. Kay is the product of a vocational school and several years of bookkeeping experience. Ann Stanfield feels, "She's really been a fantastic employee for us. She was a lucky find."

Shipping and receiving is staffed by four shipping clerks, three warehouse people, and a supervisor. The shipping clerks pull orders from inventory, write and price invoices, weigh, pack, and ship orders. The receiving crew checks arriving merchandise against purchase orders, prices merchandise, and places it in inventory. Bill Cannon is warehouse supervisor, responsible for the performance of the other seven employees. Bill has had some previous plant-related experience. Dick comments: "Bill's a fairly good organizer. He'll take what we tell him and execute in logical manner."

Jerolyn Poe is the customer-relations coordinator for Cumberland Crafts, responsible for meeting and greeting customers at the warehouse and for explaining sales and purchasing policies. She is additionally responsible for coordinating customer seminars, workshops and other special customer services, such as the Cumberland Crafts catalog and newspaper. Jerolyn has a degree in agriculture, previous experience with the federal government, and with Craft Village. According to Ann, "We created this position especially for Jerolyn because she's very bright and knows crafts inside and out. She's really done an outstanding job in laying out our fast-changing catalog."

The Stanfields estimate that they spend 95 percent of their time on the wholesaling operation and very little time on retailing. Craft Village is managed very much on a decentralized basis, with the assistant manager carrying most of the work load. Ann comments, "My main job at Craft Village is handling the promotions, which entails primarily running newspaper ads. Occasionally I go over there to help iron out other types of managerial problems."

The assistant manager for Craft Village, Barbara Carnes, is also viewed in a very positive light by Ann. "Barbara is a fantastic type of person in that she has a great deal of loyalty, which is very important to me. She has faith in us as leaders. The fact that she believes in us and in the business makes her very conscious of doing what she thinks is right for Craft Village. She may not always know what's right, but she'll always try to find out."

While the present employees are generally described in positive terms by Dick and Ann, this has not always been the case. Between February and May of 1979, just about all of the warehouse employees turned over as the company grew and changed performance expectations. Ann describes the morale of the present staff and warehouse employees as healthy. "For the most part, we have a beautiful working relationship among ourselves."

Ann feels employees in both organizations are satisfied with their compensation and benefits. "Just because an employee comes in for a pay raise doesn't mean he or she automatically gets one. We try to evaluate our people on the basis of their performance. We started our evaluation program recently and have already given several raises. From here on out, we intend to let the warehouse coordinator evaluate his employees twice a year, and then we will sit down with each employee and discuss raises."

Ann also feels that she and Dick are going to have to spend more time in personnel matters as the company continues to grow. "We really need to have more meetings with employees to better cement communications and instructions. Our personnel situation is tolerable but not as good as we would like it to be."

In discussing the couple's management style Ann states, "Our management style has always been very informal and loose. Lately we've grown to the point where we definitely need more formal structure and management. We're going to have to be more definite with our employees and less easygoing."

As for future goals and plans, the Stanfields plan to stay in both retailing and wholesaling and even plan to move into manufacturing on a limited basis. "We don't anticipate as much growth for the future as we've had for the past couple of years. We hope to reach a plateau at some point so we will get things under better control."

Ann comments further on the future outlook: "The longest period I've been able to plan ahead for is about a year-and-a-half to two years. I feel that the craft business is so fickle that we can't plan ahead any more than this. The popularity of different crafts changes from year to year, making it very difficult to forecast ahead. Because the craft industry is so young, it becomes difficult to base future predictions on past trends.

"For the short range, over the next year or two, I've pretty well figured what I think the business will do dollar-wise. When we get into our small-scale manufacturing, things will probably go wild for awhile. For the next five years I have a general idea that we'll still have Craft Village, although we'll probably switch locations, say to a shopping mall. I don't anticipate having a second retail store. We won't rule this out, but it's not a part of the plan simply because of the enormous effort required. Further retail growth would also depend on the availability of personnel. We'd have to come up with a strong assistant-manager type. For instance, Craft Village has not done nearly as well as it could if I gave it my full attention. Running both a retailing and wholesaling business at the same time has presented some difficulties. In the future, however, our main emphasis will be in wholesaling."

In her assessment of future business problems and challenges, Ann states, "Our major problems at this point are those of employee productivity, employee evaluation and satisfaction, and inventory control, while our biggest challenge is keeping up with our growth. Another challenge we will face over the next year is getting together a complete staff and a good group of employees. I want our people to be compatible, to do as good a job as possible, and to be happy with what they're doing.

"We get behind on some problems because other larger problems arise. For instance, we've been intending to write-up job descriptions for some time, but inventory problems have taken precedence. We probably know where most of our present problems are and among us should know how to solve them."

Analysis: What special problems might arise from the sharing of managerial responsibilities by a husband and wife team? Might unique advantages also accrue from such a family arrangement?

Do you agree with Ann Stanfield that the craft business is too fickle to permit planning beyond two years?

Marketing

The Stanfields consider that their primary market consists of the 350 to 400 retail outlets in New Mexico, Arizona, Utah, and Colorado which purchase products from Cumberland Crafts on a continuing basis. Ann feels that they do a good job with these customers: "Cumberland Crafts is fairly close to being a full-line craft wholesaler. We distribute in most of the product lines wanted by our retail customers."

Elaborating on their product line Ann states, "I can't even tell you how many different crafts you can do by going out in our warehouse." Also Ann could not give an accurate estimate of the number of different items stocked in the warehouse or displayed in the wholesaling catalog. "I can tell you in dollars, but I can't tell you by number of items."

In discussing market share Ann states that, "Cumberland's current market share of the wholesaling business in the four-state area is not a big concern of mine. This is because I'm content with the amount of growth we've had here in New Mexico. For years the state never had much in the way of crafts retailing, much less wholesaling. I think Craft Village and Cumberland Crafts have done much in this regard. A lot of small craft stores are opening up all over this area, with most of them on a shoestring. No one really knows just how much demand is actually out there. I don't suffer from a great deal of greed and I think there's enough business out there for Cumberland Crafts and its competitors."

While the Stanfields do not worry much about market share, they have made an effort to learn something about their competitors. Ann comments, "Our competitors are not really very strong. The distributor in Tucumcari handles bicycles and parts and thus doesn't really specialize in crafts; the Albuquerque company greatly overprices its items; and the Hobbs wholesaler does little more than supply his own retail shop. Cumberland Crafts is definitely the largest crafts wholesaler in the state of New Mexico. We get at least 35 percent of the New Mexico retail business. The one thing I really strive to know is the strengths and weaknesses of my competitors.

"There are two or three things which separate us from our competitors and perhaps give us an advantage over them. One is the fact that we've had a designer—someone who creates new uses for a particular craft item. We try to find unique sources and then build the demand through our designers. Another competitive edge is our fast service. We try to give one-to-two day service on most orders. We added an extra shipping clerk just to provide for this capability.

"I would say that having unique sources is another competitive advantage; that is, having good selling items which most other major wholesalers have not been able to find a source of supply for. In the craft wholesaling business, sources of supply are a real competitive weapon. You have to know where to find the unusual craft items that are being produced. We've had pretty fair success with uncovering sources—so much so that I sometimes think I should be selling sources!"

Dick is Cumberland Crafts' only salesman. He comments, "We've wanted someone else to travel for us but so far have not been able to make the right arrangements. It's hard to be real aggressive when you don't have a full-time salesman. However, I think we are the type of company that customers naturally come to because of our many competitive advantages."

The Stanfields do not plan to spend a great deal of effort developing new retail outlets. Ann states, "We would like to see most of our future growth come from existing customers because we feel that our existing retailers already know how to do business with us. New customers have to be taught how to buy and sell. I would much rather keep an old customer who already knows these things and who is likely to purchase more because of the business already built up. However, I do anticipate adding four or five new customers per month.

"We are not really very aggressive in the area of seeking out new customers because they will seek us out. We feel we get a good number of new customers from yellow-page ads and from the newsletters we send out. If Dick hears about a potential new account in an area, he certainly will call on them. Or if somebody gives me the name of a new store, I certainly will call on them.

"We have never carried out a formal market research program where we went out and tried to determine customer needs. Of course, we pay attention to market demand. When we go to a craft show, we always make a point to notice the best things at the show. Two years ago, the hottest item was macrame and you could see it bloom all of a sudden. Five years ago, you couldn't give macrame away.

"Another way we do marketing research is by talking to salesmen and asking them about how business is in different regions. For example, what's going on in California will, for sure, be big here two years from now. Our area seems to be the very last to get all the new crafts. New Mexico has just lacked leadership in the craft industry. This is the leadership we're trying to provide. Fortunately, after the start-up of a craft business you soon reach the point where you can make educated guesses about the market."

Cumberland's pricing policy follows the manufacturer's suggested retail price on most items, which normally involves a 40 percent mark-up. For other items not having the manufacturer's suggested price, the Stanfields establish price on the basis of what the market will bear. The largest profit margins are on those items which are manufactured by Cumberland Crafts, such as silk flowers. Volume discounts are offered to retailers on the basis of a smaller volume discount received by Cumberland Crafts from its suppliers. "We don't offer volume discounts on many items because we don't purchase many things on this basis ourselves, and because it makes things pretty confusing for our shipping clerks."

The Stanfields feel they could generally benefit by spending more time in the areas of advertising and promotion. "We're already reaching a point where we're large enough to help mold demand. We can creatively push a certain item and, in effect, manufacture demand for it among our retailers. In this business, it is so easy to create demand. If you know the right approach, you can create a demand for anything relating to crafts. It all starts with showing the customer how to be creative with something and then letting his or her interest catch hold."

Craft Village has generated considerable customer interest by promoting crafts classes. Ann explains that a $3 fee per class is charged "because we found that people won't come to class unless they pay for it." The store's normal procedure is to contract with free-lance instructors to conduct the classes. According to Ann the wholesale operation also promotes through classes for retailers as well as instructions and demonstrations on new craft ideas. "Usually we bring in outsiders to conduct these seminars because we don't yet have the trained people in Santa Fe to do it."

Cumberland Crafts advertises in the national trade publication, *Profitable Crafts Merchandising*, and carries yellow-page ads in Denver, Salt Lake City, and Phoenix, as well as in the several resort areas in Colorado and Utah. The Stanfields state that their purpose in advertising in *PCM* magazine is to give Cumberland Crafts the image of a national supplier. "This really helps our image and brings customers to our back door."

While the ads in *PCM* and the yellow pages are considered important by the Stanfields, the firm's chief means of promotion are its monthly newsletter (sent to over five hundred retailers) and its merchandise catalogs. Currently the company has two catalogs with a third in the works. Customers can obtain catalogs for a small deposit refundable upon first order.

The Stanfields are in the process of becoming small-scale manufacturers of selected craft items such as silk flowers. Ann estimates that the new manufacturing venture has the potential of generating $40,000 to $50,000 in additional sales per month. "Silk flowers have just gone like wildfire. We really based our initial wholesaling business around flowers and are becoming more interested everyday in flowers and related sources of supply. Getting our program for manufacturing and distributing silk flowers is going to be one of our major challenges over the next year. We are not really even sure who our distributors will be. This will open a whole new area for us to tackle."

The Stanfields have already applied for a trademark on the silk flowers and plan to market the product under a name other than Cumberland Crafts to keep their competitors (who are also potential customers) from knowing that Cumberland is the manufacturer. Ann feels that other wholesalers might also feel compelled to engage in manufacturing if they learned of Cumberland's involvement.

Ann is not sure how much it will cost to manufacture silk flowers but feels that it will be considerably less than the 91 cents it currently costs to buy them. The silk flowers are wholesaled at a 30 percent markup and retailed for $2.25.

On the subject of long-range plans for the new manufacturing side of the business, Ann states, "I would very much like always to be manufacturing at least one hot craft item, because some of the most successful wholesalers I know operate in this way. I think some manufacturing is a very healthy process."

Analysis: Does Cumberland Crafts have a distinct competitive edge? Should the Stanfields pursue silk-flower manufacturing as a top priority?

Finance

The Stanfields employ a CPA firm to provide them with a monthly balance sheet and income statement. Ann feels that this information is a vital part of the company's daily operations. "I can't run this business by the seat of my pants. I've got to have figures to work with. In addition to reports prepared by our accountant, I take figures home with me and analyze them at night. Some of the figures on our financial statement may look a little out of line, but I would say that our company is in pretty good financial shape because our future potential is so strong."

Ann states that although both companies made money from the very beginning, no salaries were withdrawn until 1976, when Dick resigned his teaching position. Ann feels certain that Cumberland is profitable but concedes that the bottom line is not her primary concern. "It's probably a mistake, but I don't spend as much time thinking about profit as I do sales. I do project sales figures and have been pretty accurate thus far. I know our sales are growing at a very rapid rate and our before-tax profit seems to be running at around 10 percent."

Business during the first four months of 1980 was very good. In fact, Ann comments, "I've been very pleasantly surprised at how brisk our sales have been this year." Normally, the company's sales exhibit a seasonal trend, peaking in the period from September to December as retailers build up their inventories for the Christmas rush. Sales fall off from December 15 to January 1 and then basically stabilize during the remaining months.

In mid-1976, the firm installed a **WATS** telephone line for most states west of the Mississippi to assist Ann with her customer contacts during the period of her pregnancy. The couple anticipates using the telephone as a sales tool, but Ann comments, "We've never really used the WATS line to sell as we could. It has not yet become the selling tool that I think it eventually will."

During the early years of operation, profits have been used almost exclusively to build inventory. In fact, Ann states, "Most of our assets are tied up in inventory, which I feel is not about to go bad. I believe in having a good inventory in the warehouse whether you pay for it or not. Most of the people we work with will give us short extensions on our payables with no problems."

Cumberland Crafts extends credit terms of 2/10, net 30, and has had less than on 5 percent uncollectable accounts receivable. Credit control is not a big problem for repeat purchases. "We watch new retailers very closely, however, because they are often starting on very shaky ground."

While the Stanfields extend prompt payment discounts to their customers, they have their own philosophy concerning the taking of such discounts. "We generally don't take advantage of early payment discounts because we like Cumberland Crafts to stay liquid. When we need cash in a hurry, as is frequently the case, I like to have it. Right now we see our liquidity as more important than discounts. Anyway, most creditors really give us sixty days before complaining, so this is an additional reason not to take discounts. We've established a good reputation with creditors so that they believe us when we say we can and will pay them back. We've had only one company ever cut off our credit." The cost of capital for both of the operations is approximately 9 percent, which the Stanfields view as quite reasonable for their region.

Neither Craft Village nor Cumberland Crafts operates on any type of budget system. The lack of budgetary controls is explained by Ann: "We have tried doing budgeting but haven't had much success. Dick and I complement one another, because he's very conservative with financing and I'm very liberal. It'll be hard for us to budget much for at least another year until we can get a better grip on our sales and be able to better predict our overall operational picture. We do have a very close budget on our advertising, however. I don't think budgeting has been a bad problem for us, because we haven't had a cancerous kind of overgrowth. We've been able to control things."

Analysis: Evaluate Cumberland's financial health and performance track record.

Operations

Cumberland Crafts now occupies 10,000 square feet in office and warehouse space with another 5,000 becoming available in the near future. However, Dick Stanfield estimates that, "This additional room will provide us with adequate space for probably no more than another year—then we'll have to move again." He comments further that, "Our present physical layout could be a lot better than it is. The facilities we have are adequate or just barely so. For instance, we need more office space and we could really use some additional classroom space. We're currently in the process of rearranging shelves and trying to make more efficient use of our warehouse. We may soon reach the point where we'll have to quit buying some items due to inadequate space. We now have a lot of clutter in the aisles which we're slowly doing away with. Over the next five to eight years, Cumberland Crafts will need in the neighborhood of 25,000 square feet of space, and I don't really know how much manufacturing capability. Demand is so dynamic."

The new manufacturing project is also putting demand on the already critical floor space. Equipment for manufacturing silk flowers has been ordered, including one press and tools for six varieties of flowers. Dick explains, "The manufacturing process is relatively simple, involving a clicker and dye. We were very fortunate recently to find someone here in town who has a clicker for cutting silk and is willing to subcontract this phase of making silk flowers. To have purchased our own clicker would have cost us $6,000. We'll buy the dies." He estimates the initial set-up cost for manufacturing to be in the neighborhood of $10,000. "We are essentially ready to set the equipment in today."

By the Stanfield's own admission, inventory control is one of the biggest problems that Cumberland faces. According to Dick, "Someone knows where certain items are kept, but not everyone knows where every item is. We sometimes waste time searching for inventory hidden in the warehouse. We've got to control this better to prevent cancerous growth.

"One of our inventory difficulties stems from the fact that today a great number of craft retailers are specialists who purchase large amounts of just one or two big-demand items. For example, there currently are numerous macrame shops that carry many macrame products but nothing else. This means that we have to greatly overstock certain items."

Another problem pointed out by Dick is that, "Many people in the craft industry are inclined to go in too many directions at the same time, ourselves included. Consequently, we currently are trying to get grips on what we have already started and to control our inventory growth better. We want to reach the point where we have a place to put every item in inventory and exert closer control over each item. Only in this way can we give our customers the kind of service they need with as few errors as possible.

"In the area of inventory control and sales, we have one big advantage over a clothing company or some other kind of business that caters to customers with changing tastes. We can have our designer come up with a new use for the item.

"Weeding out items from our wholesaling inventory is no easy matter. We don't have a cut-and-dried method for this. The only way we've had to do it so far is to go out into the warehouse to see if something has obviously been sitting there too long. We're in the process of working up some data cards on inventoried items to help with control. However, 35-45 percent of our inventory items are staples always in strong demand, such as glues, spray paint, instruction books, felt, chenille, etc.

"My answer to our ever-growing inventory control problem is to go to a small computer. We're slowly getting our inventory system on a special by-card setup designed to help us keep track of the inventory. We would like to take our control system to the point where someone could be hired to fulfull this function on a full-time basis."

Analysis: Should inventory control be a top priority project for the Stanfields?

How would a small computer be beneficial? Do you feel the purchase of a computer would be cost justified?

EXHIBIT 10-1

Cumberland Crafts, Inc.

MONTHLY INCOME STATEMENTS

for period ending Oct. 1980

	Nov.	Dec.	Jan.	Feb.	Mar.	April	May	June	July	Aug.	Sept.	Oct.
Total Sales	$ 75915	$ 39606	$ 33542	$ 51787	$ 82730	$ 61402	$ 77577	$ 70259	$ 54002	$ 73375	$ 97186	$ 99872
Less: Cost of Sales												
Beginning Inventory	176473	184556	195781	196510	192415	189472	194604	172729	179118	185863	169789	153571
Purchases	50115	41717	25079	36295	59122	51338	78384	62346	47659	38548	54568	69043
Ending Inventory	184556	195781	196510	192415	189472	194604	172729	179118	185863	169789	153571	146420
Total Cost of Sales	42032	30492	24350	40390	62065	46206	100259	55957	40914	54622	70786	76194
Gross Profit	$ 33883	$ 9114	$ 9192	$ 11397	$ 20665	$ 15196	$(22682)	$ 14302	$ 13088	$ 18753	$ 26400	$ 23678
Less: Operating Expense												
Salaries	$ 7272	$ 5087	$ 4659	$ 5854	$ 6502	$ 6838	$ 9827	$ 7159	$ 7635	$ 7180	$ 8283	$ 8122
Advertising	127	424	68	161	983	99	541	810	46	861	172	90
Rent	600	600	600	600	600	600	600	600	600	600	600	600
Telephone Expense	212	351	151	391	480	821	908	889	974	802	1006	934
Licenses and Taxes	10	17	—	5	—	—	—	30	—	242	—	2336
Insurance Expense	274	274	274	274	274	274	19	925	—	634	1289	519
Depreciation Expense	23	23	23	23	18	23	452	130	119	119	119	119
Office Expenses	315	393	839	471	547	209	534	553	387	664	407	227
Other Operating Expense	1352	1659	1259	1432	3792	2768	5310	1046	3980	2486	1689	2722
Total (Operating Expense)	$ 10185	$ 8828	$ 7873	$ 9206	$ 13201	$ 11632	$ 18191	$ 12142	$ 13741	$ 13588	$ 13565	$ 15669
Other Income or Expense	635	83	94	102	211	26	67	136	223	296	586	576
Net Profit Before Taxes	$ 24333	$ 369	$ 1413	$ 2293	$ 7675	$ 3590	$(40806)	$ 2296	$ (430)	$ 5461	$ 13421	$ 8585

EXHIBIT 10-2

Cumberland Crafts, Inc.

MONTHLY BALANCE SHEETS

for Nov. 1979 to Oct. 1980

	Nov.	Dec.	Jan.	Feb.	Mar.	April	May	June	July	Aug.	Sept.	Oct.
ASSETS												
Current Assets:												
Cash	$ 2991	$ 378	$ 1401	$ 1243	$ 1525	$ 1334	$ 5175	$ 864	$ 1721	$ 3220	$ (118)	$ 285
Accounts Receivable	44323	19526	23526	39233	51000	52774	69226	61302	46949	54748	62059	72053
Inventory	184556	195781	196510	192415	189472	194604	172729	179118	185863	169789	153571	146420
Total Current Assets	$231870	$215685	$221447	$232891	$241997	$248712	$247130	$241284	$234533	$227757	$215512	$218758
Fixed Assets:												
Furniture, Fixtures & Equipment	$ 9463	$ 9463	$ 9463	$ 9463	$ 9390	$ 11136	$ 16319	$ 15438	$ 16340	$ 16808	$ 16869	$ 16869
Accumulated Depreciation	(370)	(393)	(416)	(440)	(463)	(486)	(927)	(976)	(1095)	(1214)	(1334)	(1453)
Net Fixed Assets	$ 9093	$ 9070	$ 9047	$ 9023	$ 8927	$ 10650	$ 15392	$ 14462	$ 15245	$ 15594	$ 15535	$ 15416
OTHER ASSETS	100	100	100	100	100	7600	10100	10100	4096	4096	4016	4016
TOTAL ASSETS	$241063	$224855	$230594	$242014	$251024	$266962	$272622	$265846	$253874	$247447	$235063	$238190
LIABILITIES AND STOCKHOLDERS EQUITY												
Current Liabilities												
Accounts Payable	$ 69600	$ 52384	$ 41847	$ 26903	$ 52539	$ 59352	$103972	$ 87933	$ 83973	$ 85554	$ 66709	$ 64707
Other Current Liabilities	12978	13934	12668	14206	10889	16424	17960	17717	19357	4506	2054	3943
Total Current Liabilities	$ 82578	$ 66318	$ 54515	$ 41109	$ 63428	$ 75776	$121932	$105650	$103330	$ 90060	$ 68763	$ 68650
Long-term Liabilities												
Loans From Stockholders	$ 37428	$ 37409	$ 37409	$ 37409	$ 53050	$ 53050	$ 52710	$ 67375	$ 67375	$ 66698	$ 66355	$ 66010
Stockholders' Equity												
Common Stock	$ 5000	$ 5000	$ 5000	$ 5000	$ 5000	$ 5000	$ 5000	$ 5000	$ 5000	$ 5000	$ 5000	$ 5000
Premium on Common Stock	14600	14600	14600	14600	14600	14600	14600	14600	14600	14600	14600	14600
Retained Earnings	101457	101528	119070	143896	114946	118536	78380	73221	63569	71089	80345	83930
Total Stockholders' Equity	$121057	$121128	$138670	$163496	$134546	$138136	$ 97980	$ 92821	$ 83169	$ 90689	$ 99945	$103530
TOTAL LIABILITIES AND STOCKHOLDERS' EQUITY	$241063	$224855	$230594	$242014	$251024	$266962	$272622	$265846	$253874	$247447	$253063	$238190

the millionaire

11

Suppose you were given one million dollars to invest anyway you wanted. It could come as an unexpected inheritance from a distant relative, or from holding a lucky lottery ticket in Atlantic City, or from Howard Hughes' will. The source is really of no consequence.

Just assume you have $1,000,000 in liquid funds. It's all yours, no strings attached. What will you do with it? Be as specific as you can.

Analysis: What does your million-dollar spending spree say about your (1) personality; (2) entrepreneurial inclinations; (3) personal needs; (4) lifestyle?

Suppose you received the million dollars but were expected by a board of trustees to maximize your return on it over a 36-month period. What would you do to maximize ROI? Again, be specific.

polymar manufacturing

12

Polymar Manufacturing, headquartered in Syracuse, New York, manufactures and distributes specialty chemicals for industrial machinists and engineers. Although a healthy company with a creditable performance track-record, Polymar has experienced forecasting and planning difficulties in recent years stemming from market instability and burgeoning foreign competition.

Polymar's president, Dwight Elkins, elaborates: "We at Polymar have always prided ourselves on our ability to forecast market demand accurately and to filter this down to our manufacturing process. Even though we're not a big company with a specialized planning staff, we do our best to stay in close touch with our specialty chemicals market. Lately, the entire chemical industry has been so unstable that our planning has suffered.

"Our main problem lies with knowing what information should go into the planning process—what to leave in and what to leave out. Polymar's planning system consists of nine interlocking steps which complement one other. By that I mean that each stage in planning grows out of the previous one and merges into the next stage. This means that each planning stage has certain inputs and outputs.

"For example, when we hit the third stage of forecasting, we consider such inputs as the state of the economy, cost of capital, foreign imports, the inflation rate, and so on. Forecasting outputs include such things as identifying business opportunities and threats, and contingency plans.

"I am currently engaged in a dialogue with my production and sales VPs concerning planning inputs and outputs. With an unstable, competitive environment, we need to sharpen and clarify our understanding of what goes into and comes out of each planning stage. Only in this way can we go about improving our overall planning capability. How can any company hope to plan well if it doesn't fully understand exactly what inputs and outputs are involved?"

Analysis: Using Exhibit 12-1, list the inputs needed to execute each stage of Polymar's planning cycle and the resulting outputs. Inputs to each stage consist of information and managerial action required for successful implementation. Outputs consist of information and action which will logically result from successful implementation. In many instances, the outputs of one stage serve as inputs to the next. Pay particular attention to realism. That is, consider inputs and outputs in light of smaller company limitations and constraints.

Can you suggest any improvements in Polymar's planning framework?

EXHIBIT 12-1

POLYMAR'S PLANNING SYSTEM

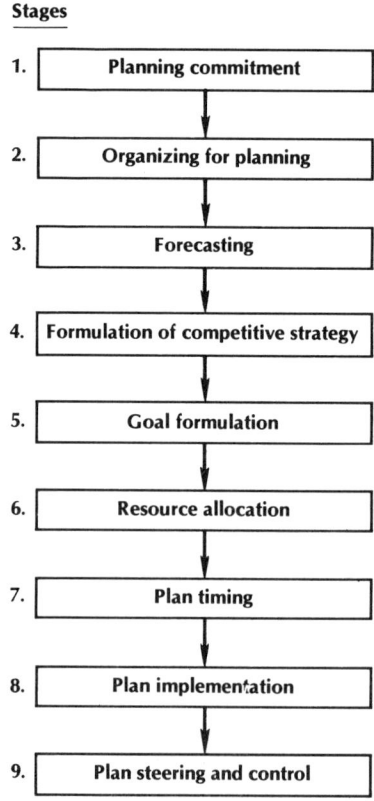

sun city delivery

13

Marie Tarvin Garland, president of Sun City Delivery, Inc., an El Paso, Texas multifaceted commercial delivery service, was named Runner-up National Small Business Person for 1977 by the U.S. Small Business Administration. Earlier she had been honored as Texas Small Business Person of the Year.

Prior to starting her business, Ms. Tarvin was a student at the University of Texas at El Paso where she pursued a Bachelor of Science degree in Electrical Engineering. Previously she had worked in the restaurant business and had been a scholarship student at New Mexico State University in Las Cruces.

Marie, tell us how you became an entrepreneur.

I was going to college in El Paso, majoring in electrical engineering, but found it difficult to make ends meet. I took a job at a local bar serving beer and wine as a way of making extra money. One day the owner of the bar approached me and asked if I would like to become a bookkeeper for his operations. I reacted with surprise saying, "A bookkeeper? You've got to be out of your mind. I may be a mathematician but I'm no bookkeeper. I don't know anything about accounting."

But my boss persisted and brought in a CPA to show me the basic procedures of bookkeeping. I found it really wasn't all that complicated. So during the day I went to class, and then from four in the afternoon until midnight I worked for the bar doing a variety of assignments including the bookkeeping.

It occurred to me one day that perhaps I had chosen the wrong major. I enjoyed engineering because of the technical demands involved, but I realized that

I was cut-out for working with people. I just couldn't visualize wearing a white coat all my life or being locked up in some laboratory with eighteen electronic machines with no one around to talk to or to interact with. I had already had some exposure to this kind of work in a co-op program with Schellenger Laboratories at the university. I did computer programming for them and other technical jobs. Although I enjoyed it, it was clear to me that I wanted to be out in the so-called real world mixing it up with people every day.

Analysis: Can only extroverted personalities become successful entrepreneurs? What entrepreneurial opportunities are available to individuals having a technical orientation, such as engineering, chemistry, or computer sciences?

It just so happened that I recently had started taking flying lessons to get my pilot's license. A group of us prospective pilots would meet at one of the local clubs near the El Paso airport occasionally, and we'd shoot the breeze. One day I happened to be talking to a man who heard that the airfreight contractor who was working for Continental Airlines in El Paso was putting his business up for sale. This seemed to be an interesting kind of business to me, I guess because of it's connection with flying. I happened to know a person, named Gary, who had some spare money and was in the process of looking for an investment.

I looked Gary up and told him what I had heard about the airfreight contractor going out of business. He seemed pretty interested and said that he would put up the money if I would handle the management end of the thing. So Gary and I put together what we thought was a fairly attractive package and I went down to the contractor and made him a presentation. I think we offered him about $50,000 for his business. He asked for twice that amount and also wanted to retain 20 percent ownership. I told him in so many words that his counter offer was absurd. After all, his company did not have a good reputation in town, they had no filing system, no record keeping—it was really wild. He got defensive about the whole thing and said that he was not going to sell out at my offer. I told him for $100,000 I could start up an operation that would put him in the shade. Well, I must have gotten to his ego because he dared me to even try opening up a business like his. He told me that he'd run me out of town.

His challenge was the best thing that had happened to me in a number of years. I went back to Gary and said that I had decided to open up a freight business to give him some competition instead of buying him out. I negotiated a deal with Gary where I would work out of a corner of his office, paying him $50 a month rent. I had a phone hooked up, borrowed some money to buy a used van, and I was in business.

Tell us about your initial experience in business.

My very first challenge was to get one client that I could start with. I went to a clothing shop where I had bought my clothes for years and asked them if I could make some of their deliveries. I got the job, and for the first two weeks I remember the business grossed something like $54.75. Nevertheless, I incorporated the business calling it Sun City Delivery. Another clothing retailer and a jewelry store signed on at the end of that two week period.

Finding additional customers proved to be a very elusive challenge, so about a month after I started up I got the idea of talking to the phone company about making some of their deliveries. The phone company had been delivering their new installations via taxicab, which obviously was a very inefficient and expensive means. I contacted a phone installer that I happened to know and did a little research on how long it took the taxi to deliver a phone. It quickly became apparent to me that I could save the phone company quite a bit of money by handling their delivery service.

I got gutsy and decided to call up Mountain Bell and discuss the possibilities of providing deliveries for them. I contacted a Mr. Chrysler and asked for an appointment to go over my proposition. To my surprise, he said, "Can you be in my office tomorrow at 2:00?"

I quickly said "Yes sir; you bet I'll be there." I figured that I was going to get some kind of a courtesy meeting and a firm "thanks but no thanks" from them.

The next day I walked into Mr. Chrysler's office and there were about six people in the room. They had the warehouse on a conference call and everyone was looking at a big map of the city. I suddenly realized that Mountain Bell was very serious about my proposal, so I made my pitch. Every now and then, they would interrupt and check out my facts with the warehouse to verify the research I had done. As it turned out, they were impressed with my planning and made me a conditional offer. I was given a ninety-day trial period to show Mountain Bell what I could do with half the city. I was ready.

I started out making the deliveries in a Cadillac, which was the only car I had besides the used van. Before long I found the need to enlist the help of my father's old Plymouth, and I even got my sister to help us out occasionally with a little Pontiac she bought to go to school in. This was my corporate fleet, if you can believe it! Before long though things got going better, so I purchased another van and had two-way radios put in.

Analysis: Do you think being a woman helped or hindered Marie in her early business experiences?

Did you make any money from the Mountain Bell deal, or were you just trying to establish your name in the El Paso area?

The Mountain Bell contract was the best thing that could have happened to Sun City Delivery—it put us on the map. It created cash flow and sales volume that allowed us to purchase additional vehicles and begin to consider other kinds of deliveries besides phones. It also gave us the prestige of being able to say that we had a contract with Mountain Bell.

Our local reputation really began to develop in the four to five years that we did business with Bell. They finally got smart enough to equip some of their own vehicles and handle their own delivery service. I was very proud that our company paved the way for them.

What happened to that guy who threatened to run you out of business?

He went bankrupt eighteen months later. He definitely should have sold his business, but I guess I'm glad now that he didn't accept my offer. I'm not sure I had enough experience or financial capability to have pulled the business through. At that time I really didn't know much about trucking or the airfreight business. All I really knew was bookkeeping and some engineering concepts. But the experience I got working with Mountain Bell, and other small jobs, prepared me to expand Sun City Delivery and to branch out in new directions.

Analysis: How can a small-business owner know when he or she is really ready and capable of taking on the new challenges and responsibilities which come from expansion?

Tell us about some of this expansion after the phone company experience.

Things got to be a little slow even with the phone company. We still didn't have enough business to support the company and me. As a matter of fact, I was forced to lease operate a bar which I promoted on nights and weekends while running Sun City during the day. One evening, my answering service said that a man's secretary had called and that he was on a flight to El Paso to talk with me about a new freight delivery contract.

Later that evening this man walked into the bar wearing a suit. The cocktail waitresses and the bartenders froze, because this was a neighborhood-type bar and, whenever someone came in wearing a suit, he was immediately suspected of being on the Alcoholic Beverage Commission. When I saw the guy, I thought it was a raid. I almost passed out! But then he showed his card and I saw that he was from the Air Borne Freight Corporation. I was flabbergasted!

At that time Emery Airfreight was number one in the business and Air Borne was no less than number two. I spent the evening talking with the man and was thrilled to find out that he was interested in contracting with Sun City to do Air Borne's delivery in the El Paso area.

The next morning we met at my office and worked over the prices and details of the relationship. As I recall, I drove a pretty good bargain with him, so that he added 25 cents to each shipment beyond his original offer. We were in business.

Did this new contract with Air Borne Freight have a large impact on your volume?

You better believe it; it was one heck of a deal. I really felt complimented for a major airfreight forwarder to seek me out to take on the airfreight business when I really didn't have much experience in this area. I guess it was Sun City's excellent reputation that made the difference.

Then imagine my surprise a month or so later when I got another telephone call. This one was from a representative of the number one company, Emery. He told me over the phone, "We're bigger than Air Borne and we can give you more volume work. I'll be out in El Paso next week and will come by to see you and discuss our mutual interests." He did, spending two days with us checking with our clients, suppliers, and bankers.

About six months passed and I didn't hear from him further, so I pretty much forgot about the whole deal. Then one day out of the blue, he called me on the phone and said, "Are you ready to sign a contract?"

They made arrangements to fly me out to Dallas to negotiate with them. When I got there, they showed me their whole operation, even allowing me to watch a freighter load and unload. We signed a contract, and to my utter disbelief Sun City had the two biggest carriers for customers. This was in February of 1971.

With this incredible success, suddenly there came another big opportunity that just fell into our lap.

Analysis: What are the advantages and disadvantages of tying a small business to large company clients?

What was that, Marie?

It started when I received a call from a friend at Emery. He mentioned to me that I shouldn't become overly dependent on one or two accounts. I asked him what he had in mind. He told me that I should give some serious consideration to dealing with some of the airlines in El Paso and making deliveries for them as well. This would be a major new source of revenue and spread our risk.

It sounded highly attractive and promising, of course, but Sun City was nowhere near big enough to handle the volume of business that the airlines offered. Besides, there was already another local company, Airfreight Services, that had been doing an awful lot of contract work for the major airlines.

I got to thinking about Jeff Niemon, who owned Airfreight. Jeff was having a lot of management problems, and I felt I could add a whole lot to his operation. So naturally the thought of a merger quickly came to mind. The airline opportunity was certainly worth initiating merger discussions.

I contacted Jeff and told him, "Look, the one thing that my company has figured out how to do is make money in the freight business. You and I pretty well have the town split in half. I think I can add a whole lot to the management of your company and that it would be very much in your best interest to discuss merger with me."

Jeff thought about it awhile and about three weeks later contacted me at home on a Sunday. He said, "Marie, I don't really know that much about running the freight end of the airline business, so maybe we should talk about a merger."

Sensing an opportunity to become more aggressive, I told him, "You know, I have decided that I really don't need your money. I'm confident I can get into the airline business without even merging with you. Would you like to talk about selling out instead of merging?"

Jeff hesitated but finally said, "Yes, I think we may have something to talk about."

So we began the negotiations that would put Sun City into another big, new area of business.

The negotiations turned into a protracted legal battle that went on for about four-and-a-half months. The problem had to do with the terms he demanded.

Tell us about the details of your negotiations.

The problem all centered around an SBA loan. Jeff had a loan with them and explained that he had an offer to sell out. The SBA said, "Fine. If the bank goes along with it, we'll go along with it." Jeff's bank was agreeable to the deal, but after a few more weeks the SBA for some reason began to get cold feet. They told Jeff that if he sold out, they were not going to allow him to pass on the note to Sun City.

Well, that fouled up his personal P & L, because the loan gave him a contingent liability of $19,000. Jeff tried to blame it on us by saying: "If Sun City were financially stronger, the SBA would let you take over the loan."

He finally wound up wanting some small amount of money—$75 or $150 a month—until the SBA loan was paid off. This was to compensate him for the contingent liability he had to carry on his personal P & L. I was tired of all the legal hassling and was seriously considering his terms.

But the troubles weren't really over because my CPA said, "Marie, I don't think you're really comfortable about buying this company." I told him that he had it figured right, because I still had doubts about buying Jeff's balance sheet. I really wanted nothing to do with his balance sheet because I suspected that it contained a lot of undisclosed liabilities that would be haunting us for years to come.

Jeff heard about my cold feet and called me up and said, "Come on, let's have one more meeting. We can work this out."

Analysis: Should Sun City buy out Airfreight Services? What is Airfreight worth? If Marie commits to a buy out, what terms should she offer?

EXHIBIT 13-1
Sun City Delivery, Inc.
BALANCE SHEET
January 31, 1974

Assets

Current Assets		
Petty cash	$ 50.00	
Accounts receivable	10,250.39	
Employee advance	42.00	
Prepaid expenses	1,224.99	
Total current assets		$11,567.38
Fixed Assets		
Autos and trucks	20,365.05	
Furniture and equipment	10,204.67	
	30,569.72	
Less accumulated depreciation	13,220.41	
		17,349.31
Other Assets		
Covenant not to compete	325.00	
Goodwill	900.00	
		1,225.00
TOTAL ASSETS		$30,141.69

Liabilities

Current Liabilities		
Bank overdraft	$ 156.00	
Accounts payable	2,780.07	
Notes payable—due within one year (Scheduled)	11,398.80	
Loans payable—stockholder	1,998.00	
Accrued taxes and expenses	1,295.68	
Total Current Liabilities		$17,628.55
Stockholders' Equity		
Capital—1,000 shares, $100 par value authorized		
21 shares issued and outstanding	$ 2,100.00	
Paid-in surplus	16,455.00	
Retained earnings	(6,041.86)	12,513.14
TOTAL		$30,141.69

EXHIBIT 13-2

Sun City Delivery, Inc.

INCOME STATEMENT

six months ended January 31, 1974

Gross Income	$95,849.06	
Less freight forwardings	29,514.14	
Gross Profit		$66,334.82
Operating Expenses	$ 459.60	
Advertising and promotion	300.00	
Bad debt expense	28.57	
Bank service charges	472.35	
Claims and losses	4,351.73	
Depreciation	4,415.18	
Gas and oil	2,776.81	
Insurance	683.27	
Interest	1,239.42	
Lease equipment	945.05	
Legal and accounting	461.45	
Miscellaneous	854.16	
Office expense	2,427.86	
Rent and utilities	13,957.62	
Salaries—officers	19,653.74	
Subcontracts	166.77	
Taxes and licenses	520.48	
Taxes—payroll	1,939.42	
Telephone	2,303.27	
Travel and entertainment	677.20	
Truck and auto—repair and maintenance	5,753.34	64,387.29
Operating Profit (loss)		$ 1,947.53
Other Income		
(Loss) on sale of assets	(467.41)	(467.41)
Net Income		$ 1,480.12
Earnings per Share (21 shares issued and outstanding)		$ 70.48

EXHIBIT 13-3

Air Freight Services, Inc.

INCOME STATEMENT

for the year ended December 31, 1974

Gross Income		$101,600.00
Less freight forwarding		32,400.00
Gross Profit		$ 69,200.00
Operating Expenses		
Advertising and promotion	$ 236.00	
Claims and losses	210.00	
Salaries	42,349.00	
Depreciation	200.00	
Gas and oil	4,700.00	
Insurance	2,750.00	
Interest	800.00	
Lease equipment	200.00	
Legal and accounting	1,600.00	
Licenses and taxes	1,100.00	
Taxes—payroll	4,200.00	
Telephone	2,200.00	
Repair and maintenance	8,300.00	68,845.00
NET INCOME		$ 355.00

EXHIBIT 13-4

Air Freight Services, Inc.

BALANCE SHEET

January 31, 1974

Assets

Current Assets:		
Cash	$ 1,500.00	
Accounts receivable	14,069.00	
Prepaid expenses	1,031.00	
Notes receivable from employees	1,000.00	
Total Current Assets		$17,600.00
Fixed Assets		
Autos and trucks	4,200.00	
Furniture and equipment	1,800.00	
	6,000.00	
Less accumulated depreciation	2,030.00	3,970.00
Other Assets		
Goodwill		1,500.00
TOTAL ASSETS		$23,070.00

Liabilities and Stockholder's Equity

Current Liabilities:		
Accounts payable	$ 60.00	
Taxes payable	210.00	
Notes payable to SBA (current portion)	1,500.00	
Accounts payable to stockholders	3,000.00	$ 4,770.00
Long-term Debt		
Notes payable to SBA (non-current portion)		17,500.00
Total Liabilities		$22,270.00
Stockholder's Equity		
Capital stock	6,000.00	
Retained earning	(5,200.00)	
Total Stockholder's Equity		800.00
TOTAL LIABILITIES AND STOCKHOLDER'S EQUITY		$23,070.00

big sky western store

14

In July 1980, H. J. Ridley, Sr., owner of the Big Sky Western Store in Rawlins, Wyoming, was wondering how he could use data processing techniques and other modern methods of operation to achieve better control and greater profit in his business. He was especially interested in two areas: (1) controlling inventory which had grown from $94,000 to $207,000 in one year; and (2) having available for his customers the most demanded sizes of hand-made boots in quantity.

Competitive Environment

In the Northwest many people own horses and usually wear western clothes, especially boots and western dress-pants or jeans. The Big Sky Western Store is located in a part of Wyoming where a great deal of the social activity calls for dressing in western styles. Horse shows are held from early May to late October at all of the small, surrounding communities and even in many of the more metropolitan ones.

Law-enforcement agencies are also outlets for western wear. Most of the law officers from the local deputy through the Wyoming Highway Patrol wear boots and western dress-pants similar to those sold by Big Sky. In close proximity is a large university oriented toward agriculture where students still wear western clothes as their standard dress. In addition, surrounding communities hold various rodeos and fairs all through the spring, summer, and fall. These and the statewide rodeos and fairs combine to encourage everyone to wear western clothes. Even for people who do not have horses and do not plan to attend rodeos, the informal comfortableness of western clothes makes them attractive.

At present Big Sky has no appreciable local competition, although several merchants in the region have begun similar stores. One vendor opened a store in a town six miles away and stocked western merchandise thinking he would get the overflow. Because his store did not attract business, he soon closed and sold much of his merchandise to Big Sky at reduced prices. Twelve miles away another merchant opened a similar store and immediately stocked it with much out-of-style western wear. Currently he has an attractive, orderly store with quantities of merchandise—but few customers.

One deterrent to competition is the difficulty of buying merchandise from wholesalers. At present in the western-wear line, especially in the jeans group, wholesalers are very reluctant to open a new retail account. Their standard reply is that they may be able to talk to a prospective new customer "next year."

Still another roadblock to truly direct competition is the very large inventory carried by Big Sky. Most merchants who want to compete can hardly afford such a substantial initial investment, as least until they know whether or not their store will have customers.

Analysis: What strategy would you use to compete against the Big Sky Western Store?

Overview of Retail Operations

Originally Big Sky was the usual general store in a small town, selling merchandise typical of a rural community. The father of the present owner started Big Sky in the 1920s. During the last ten years, under the guidance of the current owner, the merchandise has become more and more "western flavored." In both 1978 and 1979, the store grossed over a million dollars in revenues.

As the present owner recognized the increasing popularity of discount houses, the store began to offer quality merchandise at very reasonable prices. Realizing that people generally appreciate a bargain, Mr. Ridley offers only top quality merchandise. No "seconds" are permitted in the store, although a favorite ploy of competitors is to imply that the reason for Big Sky's lower prices is that the merchandise is not first-class.

Current discounts on merchandise are appreciable, with many items being sold nearly at cost. For example, a Tony Lama hand-made boot sold elsewhere for $70 to $85, is retailed by Big Sky for $59.75. At the upper end of the boot price-range, the genuine alligator boot sells at $237.50, compared with the $285 to $350 price typically asked by competitors.

Word-of-mouth has been partly responsible for people realizing that Big Sky is not the typical discount store where only the most popular sizes are stocked. Instead, the store offers much more variety in both styles and sizes than the usual discount operation. One of the things of which Mr. Ridley is especially proud is that he stocks boots to fit men in sizes from 6-D to 14-AAA and ladies in sizes from 4-B to 9½-B. Children sizes are carried for all age categories, beginning with one year.

Divided into two parts, Big Sky consists of a larger store housed in three connected buildings and a smaller economy store two doors down the street. In the larger store, only hand-made boots and Red Wing work boots are sold. Down the street, children's boots and the less expensive boots for adults are sold.

Until the store started selling Tony Lama boots—hand-made boots manufactured in El Paso, Texas—that brand was not widely known in the Northwest. Now, primarily due to the number of people who purchase boots from Big Sky, Tony Lama is one of the two most popular brands of hand-made boots in Wyoming. Justin boots are also very big sellers at Big Sky. As a matter of fact, in 1979 the Justin boot salesman who called on the store was the top salesman of the Justin line, principally as a result of the volume sold to Big Sky.

The appeal of true quality merchandise at a moderate price is strong enough that people travel for many miles to purchase this western wear. On numerous occasions, customers have flown in from Montana, Idaho, and the Dakotas. On one recent Saturday, customers came from such distant and diverse places as Laramie, Pocatello, Boise, Fargo, and even Denver.

Boots have been mailed to Australia, England, and North Africa. Brown and Root construction men working on an off-shore rig off the coast of Africa regularly use their intercontinental phone line to call for Red Wing working boots to be mailed to them.

During the Christmas shopping season, crowds of customers can get so large that the store doors actually have to be locked. At certain times of the day, new customers are admitted to the store only as others leave. People have sometimes waited in line for several hours, even during the cold or rain. Recently the owner added a steel building, across the back of the three main buildings, as a comfortable waiting area for eager shoppers.

In large measure, the success of Big Sky stems from the purchasing ability of Mr. Ridley. He has the knack of acquiring merchandise at bargain prices, especially since he orders in such large quantities. High merchandise volume and turnover permit the unusually low prices. Traffic through the store is of such intensity that one salesman remarked, "Even your mistakes sell when so many different people come through."

Overall volume is substantially increased by outfitting numerous sheriff's posses, riding clubs, and western bands. Many high school western-drill teams also buy their boots from Big Sky.

Unlike discount stores, where most of the service consists of the clerks "pointing" customers to the merchandise, Big Sky offers true service in fitting boots. Originally boots were openly displayed on shelves to enable customers to browse through the boxes. As the business grew and the inventory increased, the open-shelf method had to be abandoned for several reasons.

Customers would often put boots back in the wrong box or put a boot of one kind and a boot of a different kind in the same box. The open display system also lent itself to pilferage, especially on busy Saturdays when the crowds are so large. The open-shelf arrangement also made it difficult for clerks to find the size or type boot needed for a particular sale, since customers often moved boots from one location to another.

Analysis: Why is a price-intensive strategy particularly appropriate to the Big Sky Western Store?

Identify at least three other different retailing situations where an aggressive pricing strategy would probably not succeed. Explain your reasoning.

The Merchandise

In western wear, just as in other types of merchandise, styles prevail. Styles do not change as quickly in the western field, but they are definite. Quite a variety of merchandise is sold at the Big Sky Western Store. All brands and types of jeans, in all fabrics from the favored blue denim to the recently added knits, are available. Western pants in the fabrics worn by the real cattlemen and ranchers are also stocked in many colors, materials, and sizes. Big Sky is unique in that it handles shirts with extremely large neck sizes such as 18, 19, or 20; western dress-pants up to size 50; and western suits up to size 52. The average merchant is reluctant to stock such seldom-requested sizes.

Western hats (which are custom-steamed to the customer's favorite crease) follow the seasonal demand, with straws for spring and summer and felts for fall and winter. Again, low pricing prevails. For example, Bailey and Resistol Hats, which retail for $25 to $110 at other stores, sell for $20 to $65 at Big Sky.

Various-priced western shirts of name-brand manufacturers, western jackets, western-style suits, and western vests are carried. For men, Nunn-Bush shoes are also available in several styles and colors. One part of the store handles staple items, such as underwear, socks, towels, sheets, material for making women's dresses, and hose.

Although numerous brands of boots in wide price ranges are sold, Big Sky's two principal suppliers of boots are Tony Lama and Justin. For both of these brands, Big Sky sells more boots than any other single store in Wyoming. The wide variety of styles and sizes accounts for much of the volume. Very few retailers stock a variety of either styles or sizes for immediate delivery. Oftentimes, competitors require customers to order boots from the catalogue with a six-to-nine-month waiting period, especially for the hard-to-fit sizes.

The Justin Company makes some styles and fabrics of boots especially for Big Sky, such as an ostrich boot, which is a top seller. Several patterns or styles that were originally created as special orders for Big Sky have now become part of the regular lines of both Tony Lama and Justin.

Mr. Ridley categorizes the store's merchandise by approximate sales volume as follows:

- Hats   8%
- Jeans, pants, suits, shirts   20%
- Children's boots   2%
- Cheaper adult boots   15%
- Tony Lama, Justin, Red Wing boots   48%
- Miscellaneous   7%

Inventory Control Challenge

A recent study revealed $111,000 in inventory with about 50 percent consisting of boots. Mr. Ridley feels that considerable investment in inventory can be reduced by keeping only eight styles of Tony Lama and Justin boots in the most requested sizes. While Mr. Ridley and the sales staff think they have an idea of which are the more popular sizes, no true consensus exists about the eight best-selling styles.

Mr. Ridley anticipates several problems in implementing any inventory control system. Aside from the mundane problem of coding items for punched-card use, the paramount problem centers around clerk resistance.

Should an unfamiliar punched-card method be implemented, resistance is sure to appear if for no other reason than unfamiliarity of application. Most of the clerks have very little understanding of a punched-card's purpose. In Mr. Ridley's opinion, they will be likely to resent anything that appears to make the sale more time-consuming, especially since their commissions derive from gross sales.

Boot Inventory-Coding Proposals

Several ideas are under examination for identifying and coding the biggest-selling styles and sizes. For example, the Tony Lama Company now puts a reorder card in the bottom of each boot box. These are not punched cards, but they do contain all pertinent information about the particular pair of boots. These cards are often lost as a pair of boots may be shown many times before sold. Clerks are aware of the cards but typically attach little importance to them. The owner believes that Justin will place a similar card in each box upon request.

Various ways of utilizing a punched card are being considered. If the card is placed inside the box it can easily be lost. If it is attached to the boot, it may possibly interfere with the fitting. Even stapled on the boot box, the card might get lost.

An inexpensive, plastic holder for punched cards is also under consideration. The holder can be attached to the front of the box much as price tags are attached to items. The identifying card would fit in the holder and could be easily removed at the time of sale. The proposed card would contain the style number, the company name both coded and in full, and the size of the boot in code and in full. Codes would be designed for quick computer utilization, while the printed name and size would benefit the sales clerk. On the surface, this information seems sufficient for present inventory-control needs.

Summarized below is additional, miscellaneous information about the boot-inventory system and accompanying coding proposals.

1. Both Tony Lama and Justin boots come in the following colors: chocolate brown, brown, tan, suntan, benedictine tan, bone, sorrel, bay, black, olive, and tree bark. Since eleven colors are included, two card-columns would be needed for the color code.

2. Two general classes of western boots exist: those for men and those for women. With only two classifications, one card-column could handle this information.

3. Sizes for men range from 6-D to 14-AAA, and for women from 4-B to 9½-B. Three card-columns would thus be necessary for the size, with a "5" being used to indicate the "½". Numerical coding probably should be used for the widths, with one card-column being adequate.

4. The three boot brands (Tony Lama, Justin, and Red Wing) could be coded with one column on the punch card. Even if lower-price boots are added later, one column would still be adequate, because there are only four other boot suppliers.

5. Red Wing's classification scheme would be easier to code, since there are only nine styles, in sizes 6-16. These styles and their descriptions are:
   a. 1177—oil-treated work boot, slip on
   b. 1155—oil-treated slip on
   c. 1122—crepe-sole work boot
   d. 1199—rough-out leather work boot
   e. 967—climbing boot with 12" top
   f. 617—climbing boot with 16" top
   g. 214—unlined, shell-hide, lace-up hunting boot
   h. 812—lace-up, mock toe, insulated hunting boot
   i. 976—safety steel, wing-toe boot

The actual style number could be punched on the card, taking only four columns.

6. Presently Tony Lama puts an identification card in each box, with the size and the pertinent information about that boot style. Mr. Ridley thinks the Justin Company will include a card if requested to do so.

7. Justin has a stock number for each boot style, with the number being unique for a particular pattern, color, toe, top, and heel. If the same style boot is sold in another color, Justin gives that boot a different number. When a boot is modified in any way, such as a different type sole, a letter is placed in front of the original

stock number to designate the style change. An example of Justin's method is as follows:
- a. 1536—mule-hide boot, with spur ridge on back, saddle-stitched top, round heel, leather toe, flat heel
- b. 4601—the same boot described above but with a hypelon sole
- c. 2345—chocolate-brown boot with a 12-inch top, narrow, round toe, calf vamp with caribou algonquin plug on top of the foot
- d. S2345—the same boot as above except 11-inch top
- e. S369—the same boot above in black

8. Both Tony Lama and Justin boots come in the following leathers: kangaroo, calf, lizard, alligator, sea-turtle, camel, elephant, and water buffalo. Two card-columns would be necessary, because other exotic leathers may conceivably be used in the future.

9. Tony Lama calf boots could be identified by these names, although each represents a grade of calf leather: Kip, Kitty Tan, Flambeau, or Calf.

10. A big problem is encountered with the Tony Lama boots, as their stock numbers do not identify a unique boot. Since the Tony Lama stock number can mean many things, the coding process is complicated somewhat. The problem can best be assessed by analyzing a schematic on the front of a Tony Lama boot box:

STYLE 8030					
TOP	TOE	HEEL	HEIGHT	SIZE	LEATHER & COLOR
500	R	3	12"	490	Alligator Lizard Peanut Brittle

Note that there is a place for the description of the top, heel, height, size, width, type of leather, and color.

Style 8030 could have variations of all seven of these items, or possible combinations of these. In order to list correct information for the current inventory, all seven of these items would have to be coded along with the style.

The Tony Lama Company eventually hopes to have an identification number, similar to Justin's, for each unique style and to incorporate all seven of these features in that style. That possibility, though, is in the future. It appears that there is no alternative solution for the present other than to actually include all seven of these items on the punched card.

Analysis: Design a computer punch-card format that could serve as a prototype for Big Sky's boot-inventory system. Concentrate on making your card format complete, logical, and simple to utilize.

Provide pragmatic guidelines for overcoming the resistance of sales personnel in implementing the new inventory-control system.

telguard services

15

Lyle Wanamacher is majority shareholder and board chairman of Telguard Services, a national leader in the electronics security industry. In the following wide-ranging interview, he discusses Telguard's competitive strategy, growth evolution, and future designs. Throughout the interview, Mr. Wanamacher highlights the entrepreneurial spirit within Telguard and his own entrepreneurial management philosophy.

Would you please give us an overview description of Telguard Services?

Telguard is a diversified electronics company offering a range of security services for both the residential and commercial markets. I started the company in 1972 to market smoke-detector alarms and gradually expanded into a systems-based, electronics security company. We offer a full array of security products and services, including burglary alarms, visual-monitoring stations, and property watch.

Telguard stresses complete security systems in marketing, however. By this I mean that we strive to provide our customers with security protection in all areas simultaneously: fire, burglary, vandalism, and so on. By no means are we a single-product or single-service firm.

In 1979, Telguard grossed over $23 million in sales with 700 employees and 145,000 square feet of manufacturing facilities. We have two plant locations, one in Oakland and another in upper New York state. I personally control 86 percent of company stock, with the remainder spread among twenty-one other stockholders.

I have no intention of going public, because I cherish my freedom too much. I've relied mostly on retained earnings to finance Telguard's growth so far. I see no reason to depart drastically from this in the future.

Lyle, please tell us how you started Telguard Services.

It all happened because I retired prematurely! After finishing school in 1957 at UCLA, I went to work for Wescos Oil Company in their investments department. I left in 1965 to form my own independent investment brokerage company. We specialized in private placements, mutual funds, and over-the-counter securities.

Within seven years I built the largest independent brokerage house in America. At thirty-five years of age I sold out to a large conglomerate and retired. One day, not long after that, I came home and found my wife crying. "I'm sick and tired of telling people you're retired at thirty-five," she said. I quickly decided I had better get back to work! So I did.

I became a distributor for another firm's security products. It didn't take me long to recognize the enormous growth of security services and products—smoke alarms in particular. I stayed with the distribution business long enough to learn the industry and then incorporated Telguard in Oakland, California, in 1972. We grossed $123,000 that year, compared with over $23 million in 1979.

We sold smoke detectors under the Telguard label and rode out that industry's truly amazing growth curve. It took just slightly over seven years for smoke detectors to run their course. For more typical consumer products, the growth curve may last twenty to thirty years.

Analysis: Name other products marketed over the past decade which had rapid growth curves.

What can companies do to avoid product obsolescence?

By 1976 we began to diversify our product and service mix, recognizing the rapidly diminishing potential of smoke alarms. We began manufacturing additional alarm systems, such as for automobiles, and initiated aggressive expansion into both commercial and residential security markets. We concentrated on developing a technical edge over competition through using telemetry, which incorporates the use of integrated circuitry and microprocessors in security devices.

Today Telguard is the market leader in electronic security systems. We protect our customers against theft, arson, fires, vandalism, burglary, inventory loss, and industrial espionage. Our surveillance systems monitor everything from oil wells and petrochemical plants to air-conditioning systems, automated-production lines, and refrigerators. Our strongest national competitors include Honeywell, 3M, A-T-O, and Rollins.

You know, in retrospect I never envisioned myself becoming the head of a large manufacturing company. I had always felt that my calling was in the financial community. Neither did I ever previously see myself getting into a hot growth-industry like security services. But I have been an entrepreneur all of my life. Even at age nine I was making spending money selling seeds. I feel entrepreneurial management has had a lot to do with the rapid growth and success of Telguard.

Why do you say that, Lyle?

I feel the company has been more than a little innovative in some of its marketing and manufacturing practices. For example, Telguard pioneered a unique sales approach with smoke detectors, and we have carved out a distinctive niche in the security industry.

Please explain your sales approach to us.

Up until 1975, all smoke detectors were sold through traditional retail channels of distribution. At that point in Telguard's growth history, we simply didn't have the financial clout to build a big brand-name for our smoke detector. So I searched for some sort of a marketing edge to penetrate the market with. Ironically enough, we found it via the Occupational and Safety Health Act. OSHA was cursed by most corporations but not by us.

OSHA stipulates that all companies with at least a hundred employees must periodically hold safety meetings. I saw my opportunity right there. I designed a safety orientation program which corporations could hold in-house. Telguard would become safety consultants to these companies.

We developed a ten-minute audio-visual slide presentation that focused on fire safety. We put this on for a company free in exchange for allowing us to present our smoke detector to employees immediately afterwards. For employees interested in obtaining a smoke detector for residential use we offered a discount plan as a further incentive.

Before long corporations all across the country were clamoring for our program. We would run safety meetings back-to-back in a given company from 8:30 in the morning until 5:00 in the afternoon. In some plants we even held meetings all night long for the graveyard shifts. Some of the office towers had thirty or more floors, like the Pennzoil building in Houston. We would spend weeks within the same building going from floor to floor.

Fifty-two percent of employees ended up purchasing a smoke detector from us. To show you what an extraordinary batting average that really is, consider that the sales closing-ratio for the insurance industry is only 10 percent.

Over the five-year span from 1972 to 1976, we secured more than five hundred corporate clients, almost all of which were in the *Fortune 1000*. We didn't have to solicit them; they sought us out. We took some of the sting out of OSHA for them. They cooperated with us because we reduced their workman's compensation and gave them a channel for providing good employee PR.

Analysis: Can you think of additional examples of how small companies have benefited from federal government legislation or policy?

Lyle, tell us some more about Telguard's sales organization and approach.

Currently we have around four hundred sales reps working the U.S. and Mexico. They're one of the finest trained sales forces in the country. They work on a referral basis only, rather than soliciting cold from door-to-door. The three basic categories of professionals we rely on for the bulk of our referrals constitute the key to our sales success. These three groups are insurance agents, glass installation companies, and locksmiths.

Stop and reflect a moment. Who's the first person you call, after the police, when you've been burglarized? Your insurance rep. Then you call a glass company to repair the window where the burglar gained entry. Finally you call a locksmith to install new locks or to change the old ones. Our sales people have all three bases covered. We pay our contacts a generous finders fee for their efforts and thereby cement a nice long-term business relationship with them.

You know, simplicity is truth's most becoming garb. In marketing Telguard's products and services, we have never lost track of simplicity. We market peace of mind.

How did Telguard respond when the smoke-detector market matured so quickly and prices began to drop?

Boy did they ever begin to drop! The same smoke alarm selling for $66.50 in 1975 under our corporate discount plan currently goes for $9.95 at any Sear's store. This left no doubt in our minds that we were going to have to broaden our product line, and quickly. In 1977, 137 companies sold smoke alarms. Today six are left. That's what you call a shake-out!

We recognized the enormous potential of the security business in general and again went niche-picking. Here was a $400 million market up for grabs. Our new strategy was to expand into nonvolatile markets buffered against the cyclical ups-and-downs of the economy.

We also wanted to pick a growth area technologically related to security equipment which offered marketing carryover. Once again the answer was simple: energy conservation and protection. Not only did we want to expand our traditional security services but we also wanted to offer companies and homeowners protection against energy waste. With dramatic increases in energy costs, the need for protection was obvious. This is where we want to stake our claim for the remainder of the century.

With our sophisticated monitoring equipment and telemetry, we can see to it that commercial and residential customers don't over air-condition or under-do it. We can control air temperature, humidity levels, insulation levels, and so forth.

Here's a growth market that is certainly a mandated national priority and which will hardly run its course in just seven years!

Besides your own entrepreneurial drive and innovativeness, what is Telguard's most important resource?

Unquestionably, our people. We have a truly outstanding and unique personnel force. For instance, Telguard has an R&D staff of fifteen highly productive people. If one of our researchers has patented a product marketed by the company, he realizes full royalties. Most corporations would make him sign a waiver, but we don't. One of our people made $300,000 last year from royalties received.

I also like to surround myself with Ph.D.s as my vice presidents. Of course this goes contrary to the common stereotype that academics are useless eggheads who don't know how to make a buck. My staff is not only profit-minded but also highly articulate, creative, and intellectually stimulating to work with.

Telguard also places great stock in the plant employees. They are highly motivated and productive, largely because we employ teamwork and encourage healthy competition between the various work crews. Even though we don't practice paternalistic management, the company tries diligently to recognize performers.

For example, at the end of each week the work team with the best weekly performance record is presented with a large ten-foot-long banner that is hung over their work station for the following week. We recognize employee birthdays and anniversaries by sending a red rose to their home or by bankrolling supervisors to take them out to lunch. Most of the production people eat out only at inexpensive fast-food places. When their supervisor takes them out to a decent restaurant, it makes a lasting impression.

My motto is simple: forget your people and forget your productivity. Telguard Services definitely recognizes that people are the building blocks of the company. We want everyone to behave as entrepreneurs.

Analysis: What do you think Lyle Wanamacher means when he says he wants all Telguard employees to behave as entrepreneurs?

What can larger companies do to promote an internal entrepreneurial spirit among employees?

What are your future plans for Telguard Services?

We want to pursue acquisitions in our identified growth niche relating to security and energy conservation. There's an awful lot of poorly run companies limping along out there that I'd like to go after. As Telguard's sales continue to grow from $13 million to $50 million and more, we're not going to be able to invest all of our excess cash internally. Acquisitions will become vitally important.

I also would like to step up my efforts in providing guidance to fledgling entrepreneurs who need both capital and solid business guidance. I have no desire to become a venture capitalist and suck the blood out of new ventures. Rather, I get real satisfaction out of being able to lend a helping hand to struggling businesses.

I take a certain percent of the action and then function sort of as chairman of the board, questioning decisions, lending advice, and encouraging innovative performance. Any time the entrepreneur is fed up with me, he can fire me and buy back my ownership interest. I'm in it for the personal satisfaction, not the money. I'm rich enough already.

Anlaysis: What general guidelines do you think Telguard should follow in making future acquisitions? Do you feel playing the acquisitions "game" is an entrepreneurial activity?

In what ways could an inexperienced entrepreneur benefit from the advice and guidance of Lyle Wanamacher? Be specific in your answer.

In closing, Lyle, would you please describe your lifestyle for us?

I am basically a loner. I cherish my personal independence and freedom and have a strong need to do things my own way. I like to express my personality and individuality through my work.

I am driven by work. I have very little family life, even less social life. I have tunnel vision because I am so strongly goal-directed. I guess I'm not a very interesting person to be around because I'm so company-oriented. I have no hobbies to speak of and few outside interests other than politics. My family suffers a great deal because I am an entrepreneur. I guess, in a way, I'm a nut!

My day begins at 4:30 in the morning and I'm at the office by 5:45. For the first fifteen minutes of each day, I plan my daily schedule by setting action priorities. At 6:00 I go over the financial reports for the previous day.

From 6:30 to 7:00 I breakfast with my executive team. We discuss current problems and priorities. Between 7:00 and 9:45 I meet personally with department heads. I spend the remainder of the morning troubleshooting operations problems or getting involved with projects of one sort or another.

From 12:00 to 12:30 I generally eat lunch with a business executive in another firm, or with a politician. I try to expose myself to the outside world in this way and gain exposure for Telguard. From 1:00 to 1:30 every day I nap in my office. After that I return phone calls for an hour or so. The remainder of the afternoon is typically spent meeting with employees and managers from all through the company to discuss both work-related and personal problems. I try to take my open-door policy very seriously.

From 3:30 to 5:00 I study production reports and cost figures. I am home by

5:30 to eat supper and visit with my family. I'm back at the office by 7:00 to work on competitive analysis until 10:00 or 11:00. I also catch up on my reading during this time. I'm in bed about 11:00 to midnight. My days are all busy but satisfying. To be successful, you have to be willing to pay the price.

Analysis: Is effective time management a prerequisite to business success?

Would you personally be willing to work as hard as Mr. Wanamacher to achieve great business success?

Do you feel entrepreneurs can succeed on an 8:00 to 5:00 schedule?

EXHIBIT 15-1

Telguard Services

BALANCE SHEET

December 31, 1979

Assets

Current Assets		
Cash	$ 178,310	
Accounts receivable—trade	1,870,925	
Inventory—at estimated cost	817,323	$2,866,558
Property and Equipment		
Sales and manufacturing equipment	$1,319,287	
Office furniture	63,817	
Automobiles	10,300	
	$1,393,404	
Less accumulated depreciation	317,277	$1,076,127
Other Assets		
Lease deposits	$ 1,350	
Licenses	5,082	$ 6,432
TOTAL ASSETS		$3,949,117

Liabilities and Stockholders' Equity

Current Liabilities		
Current maturities of notes payable	$ 88,500	
Accounts payable—trade	751,650	
Federal income taxes payable	203,133	
Total Current Liabilities		$1,043,283

EXHIBIT 15-1 Continued

Long-term Debt

Noncurrent portion of notes payable	$ 70,856	
Notes payable—stockholder	42,651	
		$ 113,507

Stockholders' Equity

Capital stock	$ 6,000	
Contributed capital	100,000	
Retained earnings	2,686,327	
Total Stockholders' Equity		$2,792,327
TOTAL LIABILITIES AND STOCKHOLDERS' EQUITY		$3,949,117

EXHIBIT 15-2

Telguard Services

1979 INCOME STATEMENT

Sales		$23,337,000
Cost of Sales		20,903,000
Gross Profit		$ 2,434,000
General and Administrative Expenses		
Officers' salaries	$279,560	
Salesmens' salaries	153,900	
Office salaries	148,300	
Legal & professional services	47,920	
Rent—office & manufacturing	57,000	
Office expense	31,800	
Telephone	23,550	
Insurance	36,121	
Payroll taxes	193,817	
Advertising & promotion	51,010	
Postage expense	37,418	
Freight expense	40,717	
Travel & entertainment	51,820	
Bad debts	25,000	
Interest expense	11,800	
Depreciation expense	25,333	
Equipment expense	31,787	
Total Expense		$ 1,246,853
Income before Federal Taxes		$ 1,187,147
Federal Income Taxes		$ 593,761
NET INCOME		$ 593,386

emergency mobile garage

16

Nolan Wolfe established Emergency Mobile Garage seventeen months ago in Davenport, Iowa. From his modified Chevy van, Nolan operates a fairly complete mechanic's shop equipped to troubleshoot auto and truck repairs, as well as other miscellaneous repair problems.

Explains Nolan, "I go where the customer needs me—at home, at work, in a parking lot, at the airport, or wherever. If someone has a car problem, they don't have to tow it to a garage. They can give me a call, and most times I'll be there within thirty minutes. I am literally a mobile garage."

Approximately half of his calls come from people with stalled cars. This is particularly true during Davenport's cold winter months, when radiators freeze up and batteries run down. Wolfe is also regularly called upon at various times of the year to fix lawn mowers, repair small appliances, and to overhaul air conditioners.

Wolfe would prefer to confine his services to motor vehicles, since this is where his real expertise lies, and where he can make the most money. However, in the relatively brief time he has operated Emergency Mobile, he has not received enough auto calls to permit specialization in this one area. Nolan explains, "I have needed the other kinds of repair jobs to make a decent living."

Wolfe clearly recognizes the need to begin advertising his service in order to expand his auto repair clientele. Thus far, he has relied solely on word-of-mouth for promotion. At the insistence of his wife Adele, Nolan borrowed $5,000 from a Davenport bank to use in promoting Emergency Mobile Garage.

"I was reluctant to make the loan," Wolfe admits, "but it's obvious that the business needs more exposure. There is definitely a strong demand for mobile repairs, because my customers have been more than willing to pay my $20 service charge plus regular labor. When they call me, there often is an emergency, so money is a secondary consideration.

"There's no doubt in my mind that Davenport will support my service well. It's just a matter of spreading the word. That's my problem. I don't really know how to put the $5,000 to the best use. Running a business is all new to me. I realize that $5,000 is not a lot of money, but it's all I can afford right now. Besides, I'm not that big a business, so maybe I don't really need a larger sum.

"The only thing I do know is that I want Davenport to be aware of Emergency Mobile. Once the word gets out, I'm confident that the business will prosper."

Analysis: Design a promotional strategy for Emergency Mobile Garage that would make optimum use of Wolfe's $5,000. Be specific in your recommendations.

the vessel apparel shop

17

The Vessel Apparel Shop is a sole-proprietorship owned and operated by Edwin and Susan Stockley. Located in the small rural farming community of Adairville, Kentucky, the Apparel Shop carries a line of sports clothes and accessories for men and women. Since taking over Vessel nine months ago, the Stockleys have more than doubled average weekly sales on their product line. The store currently stocks approximately $15,000 in inventory of thirty well-known brands and labels. The Stockleys, who are both in their mid-thirties and still attending college, employ one part-time sales clerk to help with customer service.

The Stockleys paid $16,000 for the store, which included $6,000 of merchandise inventory, and agreed to pay off the principal over ten years in annual lump sum payments of $1,600. They presently rent the building from the previous owner for $100 per month.

Ed Stockley has no prior experience in retailing but has worked as a realtor and manufacturer's sales representative. Ed currently holds several part-time positions in Adairville, including emergency medical technician and police-court justice of the peace. Both he and his wife are finishing up their undergraduate degrees in business administration at Western Kentucky University (located fifty-five miles to the northeast in Bowling Green). Sue Stockley has had prior retailing experience as a buyer for the Top Dollar General Store chain. She also worked for a county attorney's office. The Stockleys have no children.

Ed Stockley feels that the overall track record of the store over its thirteen years of previous ownership was inconsistent. "I think the store had some good years and some bad years. Still, when I looked into the business before purchasing it, I felt strongly that it could be doing better than it was. From talking with the previous owner, I know that there were some unprofitable years, but I have no idea when they were. One of the problems with the previous owners was that they would get into and out of different lines, such as children's clothes, and lose money."

Operational responsibilities at Vessel are divided up fairly equally between Ed and his wife. Sue takes care of the merchandising activities, including buying, inventory control, and displays. Ed concentrates more on the financial end of the business, such as credit and bill-paying. Both the Stockleys wait on customers and carry out maintenance duties on the physical facilities. Ed states, "The day-to-day management of the store is played by ear. We certainly don't fight over who's boss."

In discussing his goals for Vessel Apparel Shop, Ed Stockley comments, "As far as the major goals my wife and I have discussed for the store, two broad alternatives are seen: expanding by setting up a chain of clothing stores in the Western Kentucky area or selling out, whenever the time is right. The real problem with either goal is finding someone either to help us expand or to buy us out. Finding motivated, capable people isn't easy."

Ed plans to continue with running Vessel Apparel upon his graduation from college, but he doesn't know what he wants to be doing over the long-run. "I know I want to continue as the town's medical technician and that I want to buy a new house here in Adairville. However, I haven't really decided on a long-run goal, except that we know we won't stay with just one store for any length of time. We will either sell out or start a chain. We haven't been in business long enough to finalize our long-range plans. I do know that once I get clear of school and my term as judge runs out in four months, I'll have a lot more time for planning."

The Stockleys have not tried to formulate an overall competitive strategy. Sue explains, "We don't have any competition—we're the only clothing store in town." Beyond their long-range plan to expand or sell out, they have not worked up any operations goals or policies. "Right now we pretty much try to make it from day to day. We really don't know where we stand after just eight months of operation. We are definitely open to suggestions from knowledgeable outsiders on where to go with the business."

Sue Stockley goes to trade shows in Louisville and Lexington, Kentucky, as well as Nashville, Tennessee, where she purchases the Vessel Shop's line of sportswear for men and women. She shops for age thirteen and up, maintaining a slightly larger inventory for women than for men. Even with its limited inventory, Vessel Apparel carries a fairly full line of sizes and age-group styles. According to Sue, "We try to cater to mainstream fashions but definitely not youth-oriented fads. Adairville is a rural farming community and people are fairly conservative. We do carry quite a wide selection of inventory, even though carrying enough sizes is difficult. We take care of most customers with no problems though."

Besides sportswear, Vessel handles a few jewelry and gift items, as well as belts, purses, wallets, and a few linens. "We don't carry watches because they are too expensive to handle, and besides, the mark-up on watches isn't very good."

Under its previous management, Vessel catered largely to the fashion needs of older women. The Stockleys decided to reverse this trend and to emphasize instead more youthful fashions. According to Ed, "We want to keep our older trade but at the same time pick up more younger people."

Ed Stockley feels his store has difficulties marketing to older men. "One of the problems we have with older men is that they often don't realize that we carry what they're looking for. The younger trade know us better and they're profitable. They'll come in and pay as much money for a pair of fancy jeans as they will for dress slacks."

In the area of generating a marketing information system, the Stockleys have found lack of time to be a real problem. "Sue and I have talked about doing some sort of a marketing survey, but we really haven't had the time." The Stockleys try to talk informally with customers in order to get a better idea of their needs, and a list of customers purchasing gift items in the past has been kept. "We try to make sure that we know the names of our better customers, but there are plenty of $5 and $10 customers whose names we never have learned."

The Stockleys are uncertain which group of customers constitutes their most profitable market, but they have observed quite an increase lately in the patronage of teenagers. Ed estimates that "50 to 60 percent of the people who come in usually buy something, but I'm not sure what our average sale per customer really is. We probably get from fifteen to twenty people in a day."

In promoting Vessel Apparel, the Stockleys have relied primarily on word-of-mouth local advertising. The store has experimented with advertising in a Russelville, Kentucky newspaper and over that town's youth-oriented radio station, but the Stockleys felt the results were lackluster. "Word-of-mouth is our best approach to advertising. The other, more costly, means just don't appear to be that effective in a small town like this."

Since taking over the store eight months ago, the Stockleys have seen sales increase at a fairly steady rate. The Apparel Shop's sales began at a level of $500 per week and since that time have reached as high as $1,200 weekly. The unfortunate lack of financial records for previous years of operation has made it all but impossible for the Stockleys to identify the store's sales trends and seasonal fluctuations. Despite sketchy information about Vessel's financial performance, however, Ed Stockley perceives the store to be in satisfactory financial shape. Humorously he explains, "I pretty well leave it to my accountant to tell me if we're about to have any financial troubles. I've done business with that lady for about thirteen years and have come to trust her advice and thinking. As long as she accepts my check for her services, I figure the business must be okay. When she refuses to take my check, then I'll know the business is in trouble!"

Commenting further on sales performance, Stockley notes that sales peaked in December, dropped sharply in January, and then resumed growth in February. "We haven't had any week less than $500, however. This appears to be our breakeven point as nearly as I can figure." Stockley feels confident that sales can continue to grow. "I think the growth is there if we can just find a way to tap into it." He projects that the store's weekly sales potential is at least $2,000 to $3,000.

Financial statements for Vessel Apparel have been drawn up only once since the Stockleys assumed management. Ed Stockley explains that he has been too busy with running the business thus far to study his accountant's reports. "Once things settle down, I expect to review financial statements about every six weeks."

Vessel Apparel has no outstanding receivables and has been granted a credit line of $3,000 by the local bank. "Credit is no problem for us. We really can get all we want from our banker. The problem is knowing if we can pay it back. Right now, we're not sure enough of our cash-flow situation to feel very confident about borrowing. This is the biggest financial matter worrying me now." Stockley feels occasional sixty-day notes from the bank are sufficient for handling financial needs in the foreseeable future.

Stockley refers to inventory financing as his number one operational problem and managerial headache. He points to cash flow dilemmas caused by having to purchase large inventories of merchandise often far in advance of sales. Inventory ordered at trade shows is shipped by the twenty-fifth of the month specified by the Stockleys, with payment due by the twenty-fifth of the following month. If payment is made by the tenth of the following month, a discount of 8 percent accrues on all ladies' fashions. No such discounts are available on merchandise for men.

Stockley elaborates on his inventory purchasing problem: "Our inventory payment schedule and resulting cash balance are pretty much hit and miss. We try to keep track of when ordered merchandise is about to arrive and hope that there will be enough cash on hand to handle it."

Stockley is also troubled by the absence of a purchasing and inventory budget. "It worries me that we don't have a purchasing or inventory budget, but in just eight months we haven't been able to figure out things well enough to lay out a budget. As a result, cash is a real problem, particularly in financing the inventory. I would like to be able to know how much we're going to pay for and sell each month."

Ed estimates that inventory is purchased approximately four times a year for women, and three times annually for men. Fashions for each group are selected two seasons ahead, something Stockley describes as "a very difficult thing to do because of the long lead-time involved."

"Getting back to the cash-flow thing, I'd have to say that our number one problem is having to pay for merchandise before we have a chance to see it. Occasionally, a lot of ordered merchandise comes in but sales are slow. Coordinating the two has eluded us at times. You think that everything has come in but then find a large shipment arriving that you had forgotten about. We haven't been able to plan our purchases well. It's sort of like using a credit card; you don't realize all you spent until you get the bill at the end of the month."

The Stockleys have not yet prepared any financial plans or cash-flow statements in their management of Vessel Apparel. They are in the process of gathering sales information for the past eight months, however, which they hope to use in plotting sales trends.

Ed Stockley offers these comments on his future financial plans for Vessel: "We have talked about opening up a second clothing store in Adairville by transferring our men's apparel to a separate retail establishment. The banker seems to be cooperative about this. We might even want to sell out, although I don't know that we could find someone to pay what we'd want for the store."

Analysis: To what extent have the Stockleys actively planned for Vessel's operations over the past nine months? What planning deficiencies are evident?

In what specific areas is more planning warranted by the Stockleys? What aspects of their personal lives require additional planning?

What are the most important planning issues for Vessel in the short-run? The long-run?

What does the case illustrate about the realities of entrepreneurial planning?

sonics systems— audio arts

18

Sonics Systems is a stereo components retail outlet located in Allentown, Pennsylvania. Co-owned by Monty Cayman and Vernon Elder, Sonics Systems specializes in top grade stereo components and sound reproduction equipment. The two owners also operate a commercial servicing business, Audio Arts, specializing in commercial sound systems, paging devices, and intercoms.

Monty Cayman, the majority shareholder, is forty-two years old and chief executive. Sonics Systems is his first business venture, having been opened in 1980. Previously Mr. Cayman was a commercial photographer for Polaroid.

Vernon Elder, thirty-nine, has 35 percent ownership and serves as Sonics Systems' electronics expert. For the previous eight years, Mr. Elder worked as head engineer for an Allentown radio station.

Sonics Systems is located in a "strip" shopping center in the heart of Allentown's retailing district. Approximately $10,000 worth of inventory is carried in the retail business, with another $5,000 in the Audio Arts commercial venture. Combined, the two businesses generated approximately $193,000 in revenues during 1981.

Sonics Systems employs two permanent, full-time individuals: a bookkeeper and salesman. Audio Arts is staffed solely by temporary personnel, employed on a subcontracting basis.

Two other merchants in Allentown compete directly against Sonics in selling top quality stereo components. Both firms are well established and carry larger inventories than Sonics. A number of discount houses, led by K-Mart, offer competition with lower quality, single-unit sound systems.

Marketing

Monty Cayman is frank in his critical appraisal of Sonics' marketing performance: "Our sales effort really leaves much to be desired. I guess our retailing problems stem from the store's inconvenient location. Although we're in a prime business location, our walk-in business is limited. Our store occupies the corner slot in the shopping center and is adjacent to three fast-flowing traffic arteries. Our small sign and window displays are almost obscured by traffic lights and street signs. It's not very easy to turn directly into our parking lot either, because of the intersection bottleneck. In short, Sonics suffers from lousy visibility."

On the other hand, the store is located close to a popular record and tape store and a Radio Shack, situated at opposite ends of the shopping center. "These establishments are what originally attracted us to the site. Being close to record and radio stores is a plus for us as far as I'm concerned," explains Mr. Cayman, "because people who purchase records are naturally interested in top quality reproduction equipment. The record store and Radio Shack serve as free advertising for Sonics."

Mr. Cayman and Mr. Elder agree that gaining greater customer visibility is Sonics' most pressing current marketing problem. "Vern and I are both confident that sales will gel when people discover our whereabouts," comments Mr. Cayman. "It's simply a matter of time and advertising before the store takes off. We've been in existence for just a couple of years. Miracles don't happen overnight in this competitive business."

Vernon Elder adds that, in his opinion, Sonics will also benefit in the future from Marvin Norwood, the store's new floor salesman. "Marvin is a born salesman, and he really knows electronics. We hired him three months ago from a competitor in town, and our customers seem to be very pleased with his attentiveness and know-how."

Mr. Elder admits that Sonics suffered in the past from poor floor sales. "Monty and I did the best we could to work with customers, but we really were too busy with administrative matters. Besides, I don't think either of us has a real flair for sales. Monty's an entrepreneur, and I'm an engineer."

Cayman and Elder feel there is definitely a viable market for "top-drawer" stereo components in Allentown. With a local population of 120,000 and only two direct competitors, the two men are confident of Sonics' future potential. According to Mr. Cayman, "Lack of capital is really the only thing holding us back right now. With more cash, we could crank up our advertising and really stimulate the store's market visibility. We have the product, expertise, and drive to propel us ahead."

"We also have Audio Arts," adds Vernon Elder, "which has virtually unlimited potential in this town. It's our ace in the hole."

Audio Arts

Audio Arts is the commercial arm of Sonics Systems, run out of the back room of the retail store. "We work on bid contracts," explains Cayman, "for anyone in town who needs commercial sound work done. This includes installation of in-plant communication systems, office intercoms, wiring for Musak-type setups in buildings, and so on. I run the business end of it, while Vernon handles most of the technical stuff."

Thus far Audio Arts had completed fourteen jobs, the majority being small in nature. "We've had mostly $500 to $1,000 contracts, which obviously hasn't made us rich," explains Cayman. "However, we've gotten some very valuable experience and begun to establish a reputation locally. The real beauty of Audio Arts is that it offers us an alternate source of income for when the retail business is lagging."

Cayman characterizes the business of Audio Arts as sporadic. "We've had fat months and lean months. Sometimes Audio Arts has generated as much as 80 percent of our monthly revenue; other times, it has contributed nothing. But the slow periods certainly aren't disastrous for us, because Audio has virtually no fixed costs—only current costs. Sonics Systems carries the fixed costs. Thus, Audio Arts pays its own way. When business is poor on the retail floor at Sonics, Vern and I can make ends meet by seeking out commercial contracts."

Vernon Elder elaborates further on the necessity of operating Audio Arts: "The stereo components business is a strange one from the standpoint of supply. Top-of-the-line manufacturers, like Jensen, Marantz, Fisher, and Sony, work through exclusive distributorships only. They won't sell merchandise to just any old retailer. A long-term continuous supply relationship is essential. We couldn't operate Audio Arts, therefore, without Sonics Systems, which assures us of our distributorship status. If we didn't operate Sonics Systems, we couldn't operate Audio Arts. Our supply would vanish. We need too much sophisticated electronics equipment in our commercial work to free lance it without a legitimate retail distributorship."

"So Audio Arts needs Sonics Systems," sums up Mr. Cayman, "and Sonics needs Audio from the standpoint of cash flow and revenue generation. The two businesses actually complement one another quite well, even though the marketing dynamics of each are dissimilar. I feel both are close to exploding with success—especially Audio Arts. Vern and I have got a bold new strategy in mind for it."

Cayman feels that Audio Arts is on the verge of landing several highly lucrative commercial contracts. Over the next eighteen to twenty-four months, a large apparel manufacturer is scheduled to begin construction on a new plant in Allentown; a local aerobics health center and spa plans to undergo considerable expansion; and a new indoor mall will be near completion. Mr. Cayman views all three projects as golden opportunities for Audio Arts.

"We're talking about big bucks in contracts for any of the three construction projects—$50,000 and up. We've already got the inside track on the apparel plant. They are ready to accept our bid of $58,000 to install a plant-wide sound system contingent on our fronting the equipment costs of approximately $30,000. In other words, we've got the job if we can finance the $30,000 worth of equipment on our own.

"If we decide to sign with them, the contract will call for us to receive the $58,000 in four equal installments synchronized with a three-month completion timetable for the plant-wiring job. However, I have a hunch that they are flexible about the specific terms of the payout. As soon as I can find enough time to put pencil to paper, I'm going to work up an alternate proposal that hopefully will take some of the financial burden off our shoulders. Ideally, they would finance the $30,000 themselves and help us out that way. But even if they're not willing to go that far, I hope that their enthusiastic endorsement of our bid will put them in a compliant mood."

Vernon Elder is currently engaged in studying the other two construction opportunities from a technical point of view. "I'm especially excited about the mall," he comments. "Their sound needs are not ultra-sophisticated. We can handle them easily from our backlog of experience. The size of the project is much larger than anything we've previously tackled, but Audio Arts isn't going to get off the ground until we land a big fish or two. We could use the business badly."

Elder views the aerobic center as a more sophisticated electronics project, but is undaunted. "I love a challenge, and from what I've seen of the spa, we'd have something to really sink our teeth into. If we could pull that one off, our local reputation would be established. I personally would like for Audio Arts to be known for its ability with both large projects and sophisticated ones. Talk about a competitive edge!"

Financing

"There's just no question about it, financing is the key to our future." Monty Cayman elaborates further: "Vern and I have put about $26,000 in equity into our two businesses, but it hasn't been enough to keep operations fluid. We have always had a funds-flow problem; our near-term financial situation has therefore always been pinched. Now that we have fashioned a new growth plan for Audio Arts, we are on the verge of developing a long-term capital crunch as well. The age-old adage that 'it takes money to make money' applies perfectly to our present bind. I'm determined to get the money we so desperately require."

Cayman's number one current financial priority is thus to attract new investors into the twin companies. He has a commitment from his bank to match him with one dollar of debt for every dollar of new equity he is able to secure.

Cayman estimates his monthly breakeven point for both operations to be in the vicinity of $12,000 to $13,000. Approximately 33 percent of his financing needs are tied up in financing Sonics Systems' inventory.

According to Constance Hataski, bookkeeper for the two businesses, "Sonics' balance sheet needs cleaning up in the worst possible way. We've got payables over a-year-and-a-half old. Needless to say, our chronic cash shortage prevents us from taking advantage of most purchasing discounts, which in our business can sometimes run as much as 20 percent." Constance estimates that Sonics' monthly breakeven point could be lowered 15 to 20 percent by retiring existing short-term debt.

Monty Cayman attributes his persistent cash shortage to several factors, including the newness of his business, extensive inventory financing, shortage of equity, and the onset of the 1980 recession. "We're going to turn the corner with the apparel account, or one of the other two big projects within our reach. If we can swing one or more of those deals, the mass infusion of cash will revive us. Then investors will come courting us for a change."

Analysis: Formulate a short-term and long-run competitive strategy for Sonics Systems and Audio Arts.

EXHIBIT 18-1

Sonics Systems—Audio Arts

1981 CONSOLIDATED INCOME STATEMENT

Sales	
Retail merchandise	$ 95,010
Commercial contracts and misc.	98,500
Total Sales	$193,510
Cost of Sales	
Retail	$ 48,491
Commercial	78,000
Gross Profit	$ 67,019
Operating Expenses	
Advertising	$ 1,550
Accounting	1,231
Automobile	1,250
Factoring	425
Bad debts	675
Freight	1,480
Insurance	2,713
Interest	3,219
Miscellaneous	1,324
Office supplies and postage	741
Contract labor	10,946
Payroll taxes	4,119
Rent	4,296
Repairs and maintenance	945
Salaries	18,444
Store supplies	1,394
Telephone	2,694
Utilities	1,455
Total Operating Expenses	$ 58,901
Operating Profit	$ 8,118
Other Expenses	
Depreciation	2,204
Amortization of organizational expenses	519
Total Other Expense	$ 2,723
NET PROFIT	$ 5,395

EXHIBIT 18-2

Sonics Systems — Audio Arts

1981 CONSOLIDATED BALANCE SHEET

Assets	
Current Assets	
Cash and savings accounts	$ 2,081
Accounts receivable	32,119
Inventory	16,894
Total Current Assets	$ 51,094
Property and Equipment	
Furniture and equipment	$ 3,456
Auto	3,891
Accumulated depreciation	(1,904)
Total Property and Equipment	$ 5,443
Prepaid Expenses	
Prepaid rent	$ 425
Prepaid interest	444
Organizational expense	3,423
Prepaid taxes	98
Total Deferred Assets	$ 4,390
TOTAL ASSETS	$ 60,927

Liabilities and Stockholders Equity	
Current Liabilities	
Note—auto	$ 1,294
Accounts payable	50,665
Payroll taxes payable	265
State and city taxes payable	894
Total Current Liabilities	$ 53,118
Long-term Liabilities	
Note—G. Livingston	$ 2,450
Note—H. Jennings	2,900
Total Long-term Liabilities	$ 5,350
Stockholder Equity	
Common stock	$ 26,000
Retained earnings	(23,541)
Total Equity	$ 2,459
TOTAL LIABILITIES AND EQUITY	$ 60,927

atkins machining

19

Odell Atkins recently opened a small machine shop in Cleveland. After working for fifteen years as head machinist for Hydraulic Systems in Cleveland, Odell put together $93,000 of savings and borrowed capital to open a small machining shop with two close associates. During 1980, the company's first full year of operations, the shop grossed $345,000 and employed five full-time machinists.

Atkins clearly relishes his newfound entrepreneurial role. He comments that, although he works long, hard hours, he enjoys his job and no longer has any motivational problems on Monday mornings.

"It's amazing how many new responsibilities I have in managing the shop. We're mighty small, especially in comparison with Hydrolic Systems, but nontheless I always have more than enough to do. Sometimes too much."

Atkins describes his daily schedule as "fragmented," because he must engage in a wide variety of activities without much continuity. "I deal with a customer over the phone for a few minutes, then troubleshoot a production problem, maybe write a letter, and so on. I wear an awful lot of hats around here!"

According to well-known management writer Henry Mintzberg, managers must perform nine functions in addition to being entrepreneurs. Each role carries a certain set of performance responsibilities and expectations. The nine roles are:

1. Coordinator: tying together and synchronizing the work of others.
2. Disturbance handler: resolving conflicts and promoting beneficial compromise.

3. Resource allocator: establishing resource priorities and promoting efficient resource utilization.
4. Leader: setting a professional example and motivating and directing employees.
5. Monitor: checking and evaluating the work of others.
6. Spokesperson: representing subordinates and the organization to others.
7. Figurehead: performing ceremonial functions.
8. Negotiator: representing different viewpoints in making decisions.
9. Communicator: sending and receiving a broad array of messages.

Analysis: For each of the nine roles above, cite at least one managerial activity that is an example of the role. You may use Atkins Machining, or any other entrepreneurial situation you are familiar with, as the basis of your examples.

As the manager of a small machine shop, which two or three roles do you feel Mr. Atkins spends most of his time performing?

Which of the nine roles do you feel are most crucial to the success of a new venture?

Interview an entrepreneur in your community. Have him or her comment on each of the nine managerial roles—which they find most challenging, most time-consuming, and so forth.

magic carpet travel agency

20

Brook Stevens, owner and manager of the Magic Carpet Travel Agency in Trenton, New Jersey, is worried. According to the New Jersey Travel Agency Association (NJTAA), the state legislature is giving serious consideration to a new bill which would grant airline passengers the right to receive ticket purchase discounts.

The legislation, currently under committee review, would enable airline passengers to receive a fare discount when they arrange their own reservations. Such discounts currently accrue only to travel agencies, which traditionally have relied upon reservation services as their commercial mainstay.

Consumer advocates in New Jersey are pushing the new bill, dubbed the "discount equality" law, on the grounds that individuals wishing to make reservations directly have a right to receive the same fare rebates as travel agencies do.

Mr. Stevens, along with the NJTAA, vociferously opposes the bill. "The so-called discount equality law would ruin travel agencies. Take away our airline rebates, and most agencies would have little business remaining. Magic Carpet here in Trenton would be completely wiped out, because I derive 85 percent of my revenue from reservations."

Stevens elaborates further: "Travel agencies provide an invaluable service to passengers and airlines alike. Travel agents are carefully trained individuals who perform an array of technical services. We understand how the complicated air reservation systems operate, and we are very conversant with the myriad of scheduling procedures employed by the various airlines. We know how to place reservations properly in airline computers and how to issue and validate tickets.

"My gosh, if the airlines had to deal directly with all passengers, they'd have to triple their already overworked reservation staffs. Quality of reservation service would be bound to suffer. More mistakes would occur, passengers would get tied up on the phones, and airport ticket counters would be inundated with people. All of this would inevitably mean higher fares."

The New Jersey Travel Agency Association is meeting in three weeks to consider options for opposing the legislation. Brook Stevens plans to be in attendance to contribute what he can.

Analysis: What actions should the NJTAA and Brook Stevens take in seeking to thwart the "discount equality" bill?

Do you feel the bill is ultimately in the best interest of consumers?

Assuming that the NJTAA is successful in stalling the bill for the short-run but that passage is virtually assured within five years, what strategic actions should Stevens take in managing Magic Carpet?

omni ski productions

21

OMNI Ski Productions, of Aspen, Colorado, manufacturers a line of ski equipment for advanced skiers. Started in 1957 by Darren Pledger, a former member of the U.S. Winter Olympics team, OMNI manufactures skis, poles, boots, and bindings.

OMNI's financial controller, Lee Sklair, met with Mr. Pledger in December, 1980, to derive the company's monthly sales forecast for 1981. Pledger voiced considerable displeasure at Sklair's lackluster forecasting records for 1979 and 1980, which were considerably off the mark from actual sales.

Determined to improve his 1981 forecast accuracy, Sklair prepared a seasonal index for OMNI's sales from 1976-1980. (See Exhibit 21-1.) He also derived the following trend equation for that five-year period: $Y' = 2574 + 45.5(X)$, where Y' = projected monthly forecast for 1981 and X = number of months beyond January, 1976 (the X=0 base period). Thus, the X value for January, 1981 = 60 (being the sixtieth consecutive month after the starting base period in January of 1976).

Sklair assured Pledger that this new forecasting approach had the advantage of considering seasonal variation in OMNI's sales. Forecasts in previous years had failed to make a seasonal adjustment, thus producing inaccuracy. Mr. Pledger expressed his sincere hope that the company could straighten out its forecasting problems in order to expedite production scheduling and sales deliveries during 1981.

Analysis: Derive the 1981 sales forecast for OMNI Ski Productions using Lee Sklair's equation and the seasonal data in Exhibit 21-1.

EXHIBIT 21-1

SEASONAL INDEX FOR OMNI SKI PRODUCTIONS

Month	Index
January	63
February	80
March	85
April	93
May	100
June	97
July	95
August	98
September	104
October	120
November	130
December	135

colonial american kitchens

22

On a beautiful New England autumn day in 1979, sixty-eight year old Bill Bradley, the president of Colonial American Kitchens (CAK) and inventor of a new-shaped hot dog bun and hamburger bun, sat in his small one-room office reviewing the events of the past two years. His company was experiencing unexpected financial and technical difficulties.

Mr. Bradley remarked, "If we could just solve the automation problem, our troubles would be over. At this time we are only able to produce our Good Buns in a semi-automated manner using a scrapless moline table-cutter running at a rate of 100-dozen buns per hour. We must find a way to get that rate up to 1000-dozen buns per hour before they will become acceptable to the big wholesale producers."

He concluded that he had only two alternatives. First, he could market the buns more slowly on a local basis, using bread route-men who would sell them to a few key bakeries on a commission basis. At the same time he and his associate, Bob Towers, would continue to search for an automated production machine which would produce the buns at the required 1000-dozen rate. The second alternative was to sell his bread-pan and baking-process patents to a large baking company for approximately one million dollars and pay off his debts. That might be the end of his dream to revolutionize the traditional hot-dog and hamburger buns.

Bill Bradley was born in Wellesley, Massachusetts, in 1911, He entered the baking trade early in his career, working in a number of small-size and large-size bakeries. Over time, Bill began to develop an idea for a new hot dog bun shaped like an ice cream cone. The goal of his efforts was to design a bun shaped in a way that would prevent condiment spillage. He began to experiment with different mixtures of dough and cone-shaped buns in his home kitchen. None proved successful because they were hard to form and would not cook uniformly in the usual flat horizontal baking pans.

One day he experimented with a dinner tin by forming a hump in the center of the tin and placing dough around it. He baked it and, much to his surprise, it worked. The discovery of the up-side-down raised-indentation baking form was not experimentally proven. From 1972 to 1974 he began to experiment with handmade wooden molds and tin foil materials in his basement workshop. He was successful.

He showed his invention to his baker friends at work. They encouraged him to form a company, since he had acquired a patent on the process. One of the bakers went so far as to circulate a list of persons who would like to buy stock in Bill's new invention. Twenty-five thousand dollars in savings were subsequently pledged.

Bradley began to get publicity in local newspaper articles. The pressures continued to build for the company to seek additional process patents. In 1975, Bill retired from his bakery job and began to pursue his life's dream: to be known as the man who revolutionized the traditional hot dog and hamburger buns.

Demand for Hamburger and Hot Dog Buns

The consumption of soft buns—the "hots and hams"—reached $1.5 billion in wholesale business in 1978. This boom was rooted in the growing preference for eating more meals away from home. Fast-food firms, such as McDonald's and Wendy's, bought 270-million-dozen hamburger buns per year at an estimated $100-million wholesale value. Soft buns, in addition to variety buns, were the fastest growing segments of the wholesale bakery industry.

The food-service industry had been growing at a 10 percent annual rate and was a $40 billion industry. Fast-foods operations accounted for at least $12 to $15 billion of this amount.

Market Research Corporation of America used a consumer panel to keep diaries of family food consumption. Their revenue census showed the following results for consumption of bread-type products per 1,000 individuals in 1972 through 1978:

EXHIBIT 22-1
CONSUMPTION OF HAMBURGER AND HOT DOG BUNS, 1972-1978

	In Home	Net Change	Away From Home	Net Change*	Total	Net Change
Hamburger Buns	13,259	+21%	22,066	+20	35,325	+47
Hot Dog Buns	8,777	+35%	4,885	+31	13,662	+32

*Adjusted for population increases.

Supermarkets were aggressively going after bakery food business. The number of in-store bakeries had increased from four thousand in 1974 to ten thousand in 1979. Correspondingly, sales increased from $500 million to approximately $3 billion over this same period. From 75 percent to 85 percent of new supermarkets planned to include in-store bakery facilities. Gross profits for such facilities ordinarily ran from 65 to 70 percent.

Many supermarkets were experimenting with combining their bakery shop with either a coffee shop or deli. These combined operations typically accounted for 7 or 9 percent of total grocery sales. ITT's Continental Baking Corporation advised its customers that the bakery department provided an opportunity for one of the biggest dollar producers per square foot in the supermarket. One supermarket in Effingham, Illinois, averaged $8.75 in sales per square foot of bakery department space.

Initial Market Test of Good Buns

Colonial American Kitchens' management believed that the market gains Good Buns might make during 1978, the first full year of test marketing, would be at the expense of conventional bun sales. They were confident that consumers would be eager to try the new hamburger or hot dog bun even at the cost of a slight price premium of five cents over conventional buns.

An agreement was made with a regional bakery, United States Bakery, to test market approximately 50,000 packages in Wellesley supermarket chains in a six-week period, May through June. Various radio and television advertising spots were used to tempt consumers to buy Good Buns. It was hoped that homemakers and teenagers would be eager to purchase the product for its uniqueness and convenience.

Both the boat-shaped hot dog bun and the round hamburger bun were tested. It was believed that six weeks would be long enough to see if consumers would switch from conventional buns. The test buns would be baked by the semi-automated molding table technique requiring manual intervention. This was the first time a large number of buns were baked.

The initial market introduction was not successful from two points of view. United States Bakery, using the molding table method, said that it cost too much to produce the 50,000 buns. They had trouble producing the buns using the semi-automated method. They felt it cost too much to place the proofed dough on the special crown-type molds by hand. Even more discouraging, consumers seemed unwilling to purchase the eight-pack buns for a 5-cent premium over conventional buns priced at seventy-nine cents per package. Only two-thirds of the buns were sold in supermarkets. Most unsold buns were returned or found their way into day-old-bread stores.

Mr. Bradley concluded that consumer buying habits were too difficult to change in four months. A more sustained advertising program was necessary, but the firm didn't have money for that in the summer of 1978. Bradley began to rethink the pricing policy adopted for the new buns. Apparently, Good Buns were priced too high to get consumers to try them for the first time. Even with the coupons offered in daily newspapers, the 5-cent premium was still too high. The bun market proved to be much tougher to penetrate than anyone had suspected, even the United States Bakery executives. Mr. Bradley was convinced more than ever that the key to success lay in getting the automated production perfected. During 1978 and 1979, he devoted his entire energies to achieving this goal.

Production Problems

Exhibit 22-2 illustrates the production process designed to produce 100-dozen Good Buns per hour. Ingredients were mixed using the special Colonial American flour selected for Good Buns. The flour was rolled into sheets of dough, cut into exact dough shapes by a special cookie-cutter roller assembly, placed on crown-type molds in baking pans, and put in the proofing boxes to cure. A bottom pan was used to form the dough on the indentation molds. The product was then baked, cooled, wrapped, and packed into cartons.

During the latter part of 1978, the Baking Division of Johnson Food Service Group, a large supermarket chain, began to work with CAK to perfect a cookie-cutter roller assembly and ingredient mixture which would allow molding-table production of the new buns. Initial tests demonstrated the feasibility of this manual production technique. Correctly cut dough, ready to be baked in CAK baking pans, was produced. However, Johnson soon discontinued experimentation to perfect the ingredient mixture and ceased conducting test production runs.

Various problems developed in finding a proper ingredient mixture that would reduce dough sticking on the roller assembly. Johnson felt that CAK should bear the expenses for these experiments. A favorable test report was necessary before Johnson would allow CAK to approach their chain-store owners selling Good Buns distributorship rights.

After headquarters approval, CAK expected to approach the Johnson chain-store owners for the purpose of selling contracts for frozen Good Buns dough to be baked in their stores. As soon as the technology could be perfected, Johnson representatives stated that they would send a product approval letter to their chain stores in exchange for exclusive production rights and other considerations. In 1979, CAK had yet to negotiate this total package of rights, responsibilities, and duties.

Since 1977, Mr. Bradley had worked to perfect a roller cutter assembly attachment and the associated production process that would be used to cut the round and long dough shapes, roll them, and finally drop them precisely in the center of a special mold producing the exact indentations necessary for the hollow buns. Various production problems had been encountered and solved in the development of this process. The roller cutter assembly was not satisfactorily per-

EXHIBIT 22-2

**COLONIAL AMERICAN KITCHENS
SEMI-AUTOMATED PRODUCTION PROCESS**

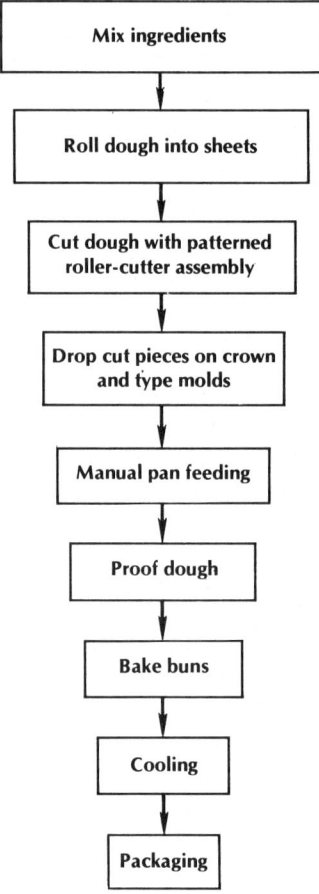

fected by the first engineering consultant hired. A new design tested by Johnson Food Services seemed to work well, even though it continued to cause sticking dough. A Teflon coating was expected to solve this problem.

There were continuing problems in establishing a suitable ingredient mixture which would produce a non-sticking dough necessary to yield a precise dough-drop on to the indentation mold. However, the most important technological problem facing the firm was to develop a high speed production system that would automatically drop the dough precisely on the center of the molds. This critical production problem had to be solved before CAK could go into the fully-automated mass production necessary to serve large numbers of consumers.

Mr. Bradley had faith that this problem could be solved. He arranged to have the Donut Corporation of America advise him on the feasibility of using the fully-automated baking technique employing one of their modified donut baking units. Their initial report was due to be sent to Mr. Bradley in early 1980.

Colonial's Chief Market Assumption

Mr. Bradley believed that homemakers of middle-income families, and above, would purchase Good Buns on a regular once-a-week basis after full acceptance had been obtained. He further felt that market research data could assist the firm in establishing a profile of the typical consumer who would tend to purchase both hot dog and round bun styles. It remained to be seen if the shape of the bun itself could win new buyers away from the conventional buns.

Mr. Bradley believed that some middle-income consumers might be taste-conscious as well as convenience-oriented. He restated the firm's chief market assumption: Good Buns will be accepted by consumers primarily because of the convenience of having an enclosed and fillable bun structure. However, taste was thought to be of utmost importance. The firm may later engage in product-development activities in order to observe the effects of a variety of grains on consumer product-acceptance.

These developmental activities were to be postponed until well into the next phase of product development, the regional test market period. Mr. Bradley admitted that the firm had not engaged in extensive market research to test this critical assumption. The most important problem he saw was perfecting the mass-production process to produce 1000-dozen buns per hour.

Potential Distribution Channels

Ultimately, Mr. Bradley believed that there were two major multiregional channels of distribution feasible for Good Buns. The first was the regional mass-market units, the supermarkets, in which Mr. Bradley expected to get 80 percent of the firm's total sales after full consumer acceptance of the product concept. After the introductory phase, full product-acceptance would include the use of supermarkets which had their own baking facilities. Bradley believed it would be easier for him to monitor supermarket bakeries and control any baking production problems which might have arisen during this period.

At a later stage of acceptance, the products would be produced for all types of supermarkets and quick-shop stores. The other 20 percent of fillable buns sales would come from fast-food restaurants as either an addition to the usual product line, or as a product base around which a potential franchise could be oriented. When asked if these plans had been formalized in writing, Mr. Bradley pointed out that the plans were still in the talking stage since he did not have the staff to conduct formalized planning.

Colonial's Management Team

At the height of CAK's growth, the firm consisted of personnel shown in Exhibit 22-3. Joyce and Jim Stork were silent partners who played no active part in the firm's daily management. Very early in the venture Bill Bradley admitted the limitations of his marketing knowledge. In 1976, he decided he needed someone to help him put his product on the market. A few of his friends suggested he should be attempting to franchise the buns.

One day he went to the library and found the name of a local business person in a franchising periodical. That person, Joseph Gene, agreed to become Bill's executive director. Mr. Gene was an impulsive, fast-moving, self-educated salesman who had little formal education and a habit of keeping his cryptic sales-expense records on his checkbook stub. He had no formal or practical knowledge of marketing, management, or finance.

He immediately began to aid Mr. Bradley in setting up and operating the Colonial American Kitchens Corporation. He formulated a plan for licensing bun production with the right of establishing regional distributorships by states. Gene then initiated an aggressive national sales campaign. Within the next two years, more than four licensing contracts had been signed. Cash began to flow into the company.

In October, 1977, a shareholder-investor's meeting was held. The officers of the firm distributed the financial information contained in Exhibits 22-4 and 22-5 to the more than fifty people who attended the informal meeting. Mr. Gene's efforts were perceived positively at the meeting. His salesmanship seemed to have made up for any lack of formal knowledge or experience concerning marketing research, finance, planning, or record keeping.

Technical problems persisted, however. One avenue after another was pursued. Consultants were hired to help find a way to produce dough on a fully-automated production scale using a Pan-O-Matic attachment. Other technical problems were under consideration. Roller assemblies for both long and round buns had to be designed so that the dough would not stick to the rollers. The designs for two different styles of baking pans had not been firmly established for high-speed production processes. The ingredient mixture required coordinated development as well.

The firm operated on the assumption that these problems would eventually be solved. During this period no budgets of any type were formulated or used to control expenditures. In November 1977, Richard Thomas, one of the firm's investors, began advising Mr. Bradley on financial matters.

The Current Situation

With the test-market failure in the summer of 1978, events began to run against the firm. The sale of licensing agreements was halted for legal reasons. Cash-flow problems arose immediately. The staff was advised that the firm had no available funds. Mr. Bradley sought legal assistance but continued to work on the technical problems of meeting the 1000-dozen per hour production requirement. In October 1979, the letter illustrated in Exhibit 22-6 was prepared for mailing to stockholders.

EXHIBIT 22-3
COLONIAL AMERICAN KITCHENS
ORGANIZATIONAL RELATIONSHIPS, 1977

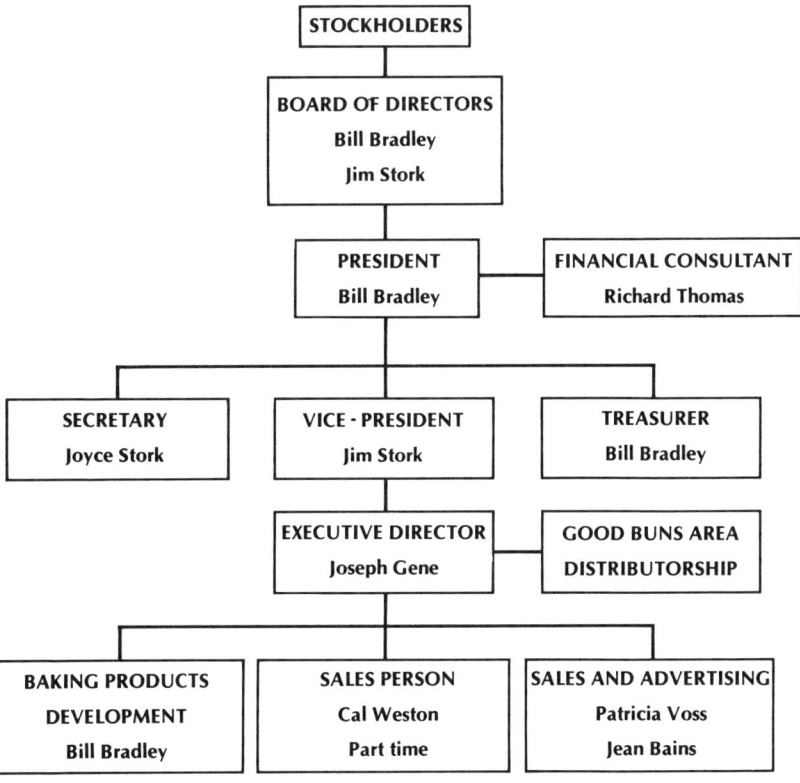

EXHIBIT 22-4

Colonial American Kitchens

BALANCE SHEET

October 31, 1977

Assets		
Cash*		$ 4,046
Deposit—royalty		1,000
Prepaid expenses		
Insurance	$ 601	
Advertising and sales promotion	25,909	26,510
Research and development (Unamortized portion)		
Consulting fees	103,782	
Travel	6,215	
Product development	21,810	131,807
TOTAL ASSETS		$163,363

Shareholders' Equity		
Capital stock		
Common stock		
"A" $1 par—40,000 authorized	$156,500	
issued and outstanding—156,500		
"B" 5¢ par—60,000 authorized	26,375	
issued and outstanding—590,000		
	182,875	
Paid-in surplus	37,500	$220,375
Deficit		
Balance—January 1, 1977	(8,874)	
From current operations**	(48,138)	(57,012)
TOTAL SHAREHOLDERS' EQUITY		$163,363

*$27,500 additional cash due to distributorship contributions and an $18,000 increase in paid-in surplus for a total cash balance of $49,546.

**November expenses $6,750.

EXHIBIT 22-5

Colonial American Kitchens

STATEMENT OF OPERATIONS

January 1, 1977 to October 31, 1977

Income		$ —
Operating Expenses		
Selling costs	$ 1,663	
Rent/Storage	2,320	
Telephone	3,662	
Office supplies	734	
Donation	314	
Equipment depreciation	825	
Sales promotion/advertising	1,888	
Travel	2,870	
Insurance	500	
Amortization—Reserve and development	33,362	48,138
NET INCOME (LOSS)		($48,138)

EXHIBIT 22-6

Colonial American Kitchens

LETTER TO STOCKHOLDERS

October 31, 1979

Dear Stockholders:

I would like to provide you with an evaluation of our recent operations. Enclosed is a financial summary for the year 1978. As you can see, we are currently in a loss position. Let me advise you of the steps the company has been taking to turn our venture around.

The biggest technological problem is to achieve automated bun production in quantities of 1,000 dozen per hour. At the present time, our semi-automatic technology will produce 100 dozen per hour and it requires manual intervention. We are investigating two pieces of equipment which we believe can be satisfactorily modified to produce the desired production rate while maintaining the desired product quality. One is produced by the Donut Corporation of America, a division of DCA Food Industries, with headquarters in New York City. We have visited one of their production facilities located here in Wellesley. Their production processes have certain apparent advantages which we are now evaluating. A second system which, with modification, may be suitable to produce our buns, is manufactured by Autoprod of Hyde Park, New York. Feasibility studies are now under way. We will keep you advised of our progress as we continue to evaluate these and other systems.

United States Bakery has tested our existing semi-automated processes and has not achieved desirable results. Basically, we concluded that consumers wanted the product, as evidenced by the June 1978 market introductory program. During a three-month period we sold 46,000 packages of Good Buns. However, American Bakeries could not foresee the possibility of producing the buns at the 1,000-dozen bun rate with their existing technology.

Our company has loaned pans to twelve companies or individuals for further baking tests. For example, Inglish Rolls Bakers is now producing our Good Buns for soft drink vendor carts.

Our creditors are trying to help us by being patient in collecting what we owe. We are making every effort to meet our obligations to them. I have worked with no salary since October, 1978. I will continue to work without salary because I believe that consumers want our buns and, most importantly, I want to strive to protect your interests.

EXHIBIT 22-6   Continued

What is your company doing to try to find a solution to these problems? We are moving very vigorously to solve our major technological problem. We expect to have some results on this soon. Second, we have moved to establish independent sales and delivery merchandisers using our semi-automated production techniques in local bakeries. We feel we can ultimately be successful using this slower marketing approach. However, our major priority continues to be to seek an automated process.

May I make a personal request? I need your continued patience while I implement the plans sketched above. Time is needed to work out these problems. I feel we are close to discovering how to achieve the desired production rate. Once that is accomplished, we will have the means to make our future secure.

My pledge to you is to work as hard as I can to solve the problems I have outlined. I will keep you advised on the moves that are being made. If you have any questions, please call me.

Sincerely,

Bill Bradley, President

Analysis: What apparent mistakes did Mr. Bradley and his associates make in developing Good Buns?

How might the product-development phase have been better handled from a marketing point of view?

What should Colonial American Kitchens do now?

What responsibilities does Mr. Bradley have to his stockholders?

infomatics corporation

23

Infomatics Corporation manufactures computer terminals for public transportation companies. Harper Knowles was named chief operating officer nine months ago when his predecessor, Douglas Sladek, resigned abruptly upon conviction of bribery and perjury charges.

Mr. Sladek and two Infomatics executives were convicted in 1979 of paying bribes in excess of $100,000 in exchange for long-term leasing contracts on Infomatics terminals. Harper Knowles was selected as COO by the Infomatics board on the basis of his highly successful fifteen-year track record with Infomatics and his reputation for honesty and integrity.

Knowles pledged to the Board of Directors that the highest possible ethical standards would be maintained during his administration. To ensure ethical behavior on the part of the company's 128 employees, Knowles requested that all operating managers post official policy statements regarding ethical business conduct.

Much to his chagrin, Knowles quickly learned that Infomatics had never developed policy statements on ethics, nor had any of its competitors done so. The board requested that Knowles initiate immediate action to draft ethical guidelines for Infomatics employees to follow.

Knowles appointed a special committee to identify ethical issues germane to company operations for which policy statements should be developed. The committee reported back three weeks later on the results of an extensive in-house study. The report, entitled "Survey of Ethical Concerns for Infomatics Corporation," recommended that formal policy statements be drafted, reviewed, and approved pertaining to the following operating issues:

1. Financial disclosure
2. Expense accounts
3. Executive stock options and perquisites
4. Advertising and public relations
5. Giving and receiving gifts
6. Employee use of drugs and controlled substances
7. Competitive tactics and standards

Analysis: Draft policy statements for the issues above. Make the statements clear, specific, implementable, and tough.

In addition to formalizing company policy on ethics, what else should Harper Knowles do to maintain high ethical standards throughout Infomatics?

What constitutes ethical behavior?

chama steelworks

24

A television news crew pulled up to the entrance gate of Chama Steelworks, a medium-size steel fabrication plant adjacent to a Denver middle-class suburb. The two security guards at the gate shook their heads at one another. "Frank Chama ain't gonna be too pleased by this," one of the guards commented to his partner.

The guard immediately picked up the phone and dialed Mr. Chama's number inside the plant office. "Mr. Chama, Channel 7 News from Denver would like an interview with you. Should I run them off like I did the reporters yesterday?"

Frank Chama groaned and clenched his teeth. "Yeah, tell Channel 7 to hightail it back to the city where they belong. They have no business stirring up trouble out here."

Chama lit a cigarette and then suddenly picked up the phone receiver again. "On second thought, Johnny, tell the news team to come right on in the plant and park in the executive lot."

Chama tightened his loose tie, donned his suit jacket, and combed through his hair. "Might as well look decent if I'm going to be on T.V.," he thought to himself.

"Hey Dale," Chama yelled across the hall to the adjoining office, "guess who's on the way in?"

"Who?" queried Dale Stoner, the personnel Director for Chama Steelworks.

"Television reporters from the city."

"You're kidding," ventured Stoner, rising from his desk. "Who let them past the gate?"

"I did, Dale. Just got through inviting them in. They're pulling up in the lot now."

"Are you nuts, Frank? We've got enough troubles as it is with that SIN bunch. Now you're going to get us a passle of bad publicity. Just what we need!"

"Don't get all hot and bothered," responded Chama. The general public needs to hear our side of the story too. Can you think of a better forum than the biggest T.V. station in town?"

"Frank, I sure hope you know what you're doing," moaned Stoner as he retreated into his office and shut the door behind him.

The news team made its way into Chama's office, quickly set up their equipment, and the taping commenced:

Reporter—Mr. Chama, do you intend to comply with the request of the group calling themselves Stop Industrial Noise? They want you to lower the noise level of your steelworks plant.

Chama—Our company already has.

Reporter—Not according to SIN spokesperson, Charlene Telson.

Chama—Oh! What has she told you now?

Reporter—That Chama Steelworks refuses to make further noise reductions in the plant. I believe Ms. Telson quoted you as telling her group that they could all go to hell. Is that correct Mr. Chama?

Chama—Is what correct—that I refused to lower noise levels further or told them where they could go?

Reporter—Did you tell them both things?

Chama—Well, I discussed the decibel thing with the lady but I can't really recall telling her where to go.

Reporter—You do admit, then, that you have refused to lower your plant's decibel level?

Chama—Let's get a few facts straight. Eight months ago Chama Steelworks invested $85,000 in decibel moderation equipment. That's a great deal of money, but our company is conscious of being a good citizen in the community. We voluntarily carried out a significant noise control program.

Then this neighborhood group formed, calling itself SIN. Without anyone else in the neighborhood asking them to, they came up to my plant and made a series of demands about decibel reduction. That's some gratitude for our $85,000 program!

Reporter—But the group contends that your plant is still too noisy, not to mention a hazard to clean air.

Chama—Chama Steelworks has one of the finest clean air records in Colorado.

Reporter—What about noise pollution though, Mr. Chama?

Chama—I honestly don't think the neighborhood has that much to complain about. Our noise control program has really made a difference.

Reporter—That's not what Charlene Telson and SIN say. According to them . . .

Chama—SIN is made up of a bunch of malcontents. Most of them don't even live in the neighborhood. They claim to represent the neighborhood, but I don't believe it. Our plant has resided along side the neighborhood peacefully for over twenty years. Why the fuss all of a sudden?

Reporter—According to Ms. Telson, your plant has recently undertaken night operations. She claims the people in the neighborhood can't sleep at night because of it.

Chama—Let's get another thing straight. Chama Steelworks located here over twenty years ago when this part of Colorado was desolate and open. Can we help it if Denver's urban sprawl ended up in our lap? The people all moved here voluntarily. We were here first but have been mighty good neighbors through the years.

Reporter—Is operating at night being a good neighbor Mr. Chama?

Chama—I think so. You see, over thirty families in the neighborhood owe their livelihood to Chama Steelworks. In some cases, both husband and wife are employed with us. By operating a night shift, we can continue to provide work for our employees and further expand the personnel force.

Reporter—SIN intends to bring suit against you if the plant's decibel level is not substantially reduced. How will you respond to this Mr. Chama?

Chama—We've got lawyers too! But I really see no need for SIN to waste everyone's time and money with irresponsible legal action. I can only hope that the good people of this neighborhood wake up to the trouble being precipitated by SIN before anything gets out of hand. Chama Steelworks is a responsible member of the community—always has been and always will be!

Analysis: Is Chama Steelworks being irresponsible in refusing to take further noise control action?

Is SIN acting responsibly?

What political realities about business management are illustrated in this case?

Evaluate Frank Chama's public relations effectiveness.

If SIN does bring suit against Chama, what action should the company take?

Do smaller companies have any social responsibilities beyond providing a product or service and jobs for their local communities?

midwest municipal airport

25

Gilbert Martinelli, aviation director for a small municipal airport in the upper Midwest, likens the airline industry to a twentieth-century railroad. "In past generations, American communities by-passed by the railroad were in big trouble. They were all but doomed to stagnation. Today cities that lack a viable airport are experiencing an array of civic growth problems. I'm afraid our city may be in this fix."

The community's 193,000 citizens are currently serviced by only one commuter airline, Peninsula Airways. Three other carriers have initiated and withdrawn commercial and passenger air services in the region over the past six years.

Comments Martinelli: "The city's market for air services is obviously limited, but I honestly feel that we deserve better coverage than we've received. A couple of carriers opened here for less than six months each and then abruptly withdrew. You can't tell me that was long enough to generate any real success. Currently Peninsula Airways has all of the town's business, and they're making no real effort to upgrade their meager services."

Peninsula flies three times daily to Detroit, Lansing, and Ann Arbor. No other flights are currently scheduled. Martinelli would like to see several new routes opened, especially east across Lake Michigan into Milwaukee and Chicago. He comments, "If our citizens want to get to Chicago or Milwaukee they either have to drive or fly into Detroit to make connections."

Martinelli points out that when one carrier pulls out, others are naturally reluctant to open up. Compounding the problem is a severe slump currently being experienced by the airlines as part of the 1980 economic recession. An increasing number of summer travelers are staying home, and incoming air freight deliveries are 18 percent below the 1979 level. Passenger traffic at Midwest Airport is 22 percent below the 1979 average.

The escalating cost of energy has worsened the airline industry's economic woes, with fuel costs up 70 percent in twelve months. Other areas of airport operations have also been affected. Mr. Martinelli comments, "For the past year-and-a-half, I've been trying to get airport runways and parking lots resurfaced. The price of asphalt has skyrocketed, since it's made from petroleum. Resurfacing work, completed in 1977 for $60,000, now costs in the vicinity of $175,000."

Martinelli looks to the future with some optimism, however. He expects the airline slump to end by late 1981 and for the industry to bounce back as the automobile becomes increasingly uneconomical for long distance traveling.

He is also pleased with continuing industrial development in and around the community. "Although the town is predominantly blue collar, a greater number of white-collar type businesses are moving here. Since traveling businessmen are the bread-and-butter of any airline, I'm optimistic that the airport can attract a larger clientele."

Just seven years ago, the community was serviced by a large northeastern airline with three jet flights daily. However, service was canceled in 1974 as energy-conscious airlines began switching from mid-size DC3s (40 seats) to the larger DC9s (90 seats). When jet service was canceled, the community lost flights to Chicago, Milwaukee, and Lansing.

Between 1976 and 1978, two small commuter lines briefly flirted with the city's market. Both withdrew their services after a few months. Martinelli explains that one of the companies, Beacon Airflight, failed to advertise its schedules and was chronically late. Its predecessor by nine months, Airstream Aviation, sought to cater to the city's business community but never seemed to synchronize its flights with an 8:00 to 5:00 schedule.

"That left us with only Peninsula Airways," Martinelli notes, "and they're interested solely in a few bread-and-butter runs. They are unwilling to experiment with new routes."

Convincing the public of the need for a more viable airport in the community is another obstacle faced by Martinelli. Midwest Airport is 70 percent self-funded, with the city financing the remaining 30 percent, which amounted to $65,000 in 1980. "The city officials would like to see our services expanded, because they clearly recognize the linkage between civic growth and air traffic. But getting the average resident to realize this is no easy matter."

Martinelli's top priority is generating new air services for the city. "I would like to see new routes open up as well as some new competition for Peninsula," he comments. "I sincerely hope that our citizens don't wake up one day and realize that progress has passed us by."

Analysis: Provide suggestions for how Mr. Martinelli can attract new business to Midwest Airport.

Do you agree with Martinelli that civic growth is vitally linked to air traffic services?

EXHIBIT 25-1

ARTICLE IN THE LOCAL NEWSPAPER

September, 1981

A recessionary economy has reduced passenger traffic at Midwest Municipal Airport 15 to 20 percent below the 1980 level, airport manager Gilbert Martinelli said Friday.

Addressing the airport board's monthly meeting, Martinelli said passenger traffic generally swells during the summer season. This summer, however, sagging economic conditions curtailed vacation traffic. Martinelli said he anticipates less of a decline for the month of September as business traveling stabilizes.

Most other airport utilization statistics also showed a summer decline, according to Martinelli. This included amount of fuel consumed, number of cars rented, and receipts for the airport's restaurant. One area, freight loaded, did show an increase for the month of August.

In other action, the airport Board approved a plan to lease additional land near the airport for placement of billboard advertisements.

eberhardt products, inc.

26

Three years ago, in 1978, Cole Eberhardt opened a small production facility in Roanoke, Virginia, to manufacture and distribute a rust-deterrent compound for automobiles. Called RustRid, the product chemically treats metal to resist rusting and general corrosion. It is distributed through 425 retail outlets in Virginia, West Virginia, North Carolina, Delaware, and Maryland.

Sales grew steadily throughout 1979 and 1980, and Eberhardt Products doubled its plant capacity. Cole Eberhardt, sole stockholder and president, was elated with RustRid's excellent reception in the market and readied plans to manufacture a companion product to be called ReFinish. A liquid chemical like RustRid, ReFinish was designed to restore luster to corroded metal and hard compounds.

Eberhardt admitted that he was dragging his feet in marketing ReFinish, because he wanted time to develop a means for gathering marketing information to use in selling the new product. He explained that, despite excellent sales for RustRid, his knowledge of why it sold was limited. He wanted to sharpen his understanding before marketing ReFinish, so that the latter's introduction could be fully exploited.

Specifically Eberhardt wanted to develop a consumer profile of RustRid users: age, income level, family status, geographic location, etc. In addition, he wanted to determine what kind of vehicles RustRid was used on and how frequently the product had been purchased and applied.

Eberhardt professed to have more of an affinity for chemistry than marketing and was unsure of how to proceed in conducting market research. He summed up his feelings as follows: "I know what I want out of this research. I want to learn how to market RustRid better and how to optimize the introduction of ReFinish. What I'm unsure of is, what information to gather and how to go about gathering it. I really don't want to continue depending on luck in selling Eberhardt products."

Analysis: Design a marketing research campaign for Eberhardt Products. Be sure to specify what information is to be gathered and how it is to be gathered. Make your design realistic and pragmatic.

kath surgical equipment

27

Kath Surgical Equipment, a subsidiary of Jayton Corporation, is a small manufacturer of specialty hospital and surgical equipment. Following unprofitable performance for the past eighteen months, Kath's management team was replaced and a turnaround begun.

Chad Meador, Kath's new General Manager, is in the process of redesigning the firm's accounting system, beginning with the cash-flow statement. He seeks to determine how much the company will have to invest to stimulate long-run profitability and if any short-run financial problems are imminent.

Kath produces two basic products: a stainless steel autoclave for sterilizing surgical instruments, and a pressurized steamer for cleaning surgical gowns and hospital linens. The autoclave sells for $5,000 and the steamer for $7,500.

Autoclaves have been selling at a rate of five per month. Over the next four months, Mr. Meador predicts autoclave sales of ten, twelve, fourteen, and sixteen for each respective month. The steamers have been selling at a rate of four per month. Meador expects sales to increase to six in the third month. Price increases are not foreseen for either product.

Past data show that materials for the autoclave represent about 30 percent of selling price, while labor runs about 20 percent. Materials for the steamer cost 25 percent of selling price, and the labor is 25 percent. Inventory has been depleted and needs to be increased at a rate of $2,000 per month. Because of past late payments, Kath is COD with its suppliers. Payroll tax and certain employee benefits are 12 percent of gross salaries and wages. Shop supplies and maintenance represent 2 percent of sales. Rent is $24,000 per year. Depreciation on equipment is

$36,000 annually. The shop employs two supervisors at $24,000 per year each. Workman's compensation insurance in the shop is 6 percent of gross salaries and wages. All other direct overhead costs will amount to approximately $4,000 per month over the next four months.

Meador will receive a salary of $48,000. His secretary and office manager receives $1,100 per month. Workman's compensation insurance for office workers is 1 percent of salaries. Costs for advertising and promotion will run about 2 percent of sales, but no expenditure will be made in the first month. Sales commissions are 5 percent of sales. All other expenses are fixed at $3,000 with the exception of an equipment loan outstanding against the division. The equipment principal plus interest payment is $3,000 per month, due on the twelfth day of the month. The interest rate is 16.75 percent on the remaining principal balance.

The accounts receivable, as of October 31, will consist of $25,000 between thirty and sixty days old and $60,000 between zero and thirty days old. Typically, the company has collected all of its over thirty day accounts in the following month and two thirds of its current, that is, zero to thirty day accounts.

Meador confidently estimates that a statement of condition as of October 31, 1979, will appear as follows:

EXHIBIT 27-1

Kath Surgical Equipment

STATEMENT OF CONDITION

for the year ended October 31, 1979

Cash	$ 30,000	Accounts Payable	$ 98,000
Accounts Receivable	85,000	Current Portion of Long Term Debt	25,900
Inventory	15,000		
Current Assets	$130,000	Current Liabilities	$123,900
Equipment (Net)	208,000	Long Term Debt	46,100
		Equity	168,000
	$338,000		$338,000

Analysis: Develop a cash-flow statement for Kath for the four-month period beginning with November 1. State any assumptions you make.

fantasia music company

28

Fantasia Music Company has been located in the same downtown site in Winona, Minnesota, for forty-seven years. The store is owned and operated by Doyle Albrecht, who purchased it from its founder in 1974. Fantasia is a full-line music service company serving a clientele consisting primarily of band and orchestra students in Winona's public schools.

Mr. Albrecht characterizes his background as "varied," citing previous experience in television, journalism, and sales. He purchased Fantasia because of his love for symphonic band music and fond memories of band activities in high school and college.

"I do a little of everything at Fantasia," he comments, "but I guess I spend most of my time on music ordering and inventory control. These activities are the heart of our business. Here's where my three biggest operating problems come from."

The problems Mr. Albrecht refers to concern the vagaries of ordering sheet music for school bands during marching and contest seasons. "I've got to order the right music at the right time and then figure how to get rid of what doesn't sell," explains Albrecht. "All this is easier said than done, because the market is just not all that certain. I can never be sure what kind of pieces will sell best from year to year. That's my first challenge. Getting rid of dead inventory—compositions that nobody wants—is a second problem. The publishers won't buy it back and the music often becomes dated from year to year—kind of like pop tunes on the radio."

Seasonal sales is Mr. Albrecht's third and, in many ways, most perplexing problem. "We have two big sales periods on music orders during the year. During June and July the band directors come in and order marching-band music for the coming football season. Then during late November and early December, the rush is on for symphonic compositions for the concert season in the spring. In other months the demand for sheet music is virtually nonexistent. The resulting cash-flow crunch is very difficult for Fantasia to absorb."

Product Line Strategy

Fantasia carries a full line of musical instruments, accessories, and supplies in addition to sheet music. "People come to us because we have it all," Mr. Albrecht explains. "This is the only way I can compensate for the store's poor location in town and our rather spartan physical facilities." Fantasia Music is located in Winona's outmoded downtown district which, as in so many communities, has been rendered semi-moribund by the flight of retailers to suburban malls.

Fantasia carries a complete line of top-quality musical instruments to facilitate its rental program with city schools. "Although instrument rental is not a real profit maker for us, it paves the way for sale of accessories and supplies which do have a nice mark-up. I figure if the schools and parents seek us out to rent instruments, they will also purchase supplies here and get their instruments repaired here."

Fantasia has a long-standing arrangement with the Winona school system to rent instruments through the schools to beginning band and orchestra students. "The school board drives a pretty hard bargain, so the rental program is really just a breakeven proposition for us," explains Albrecht. "However, we can turn around and sell the instruments to many of the students who decide to stick with the music program. We definitely make some money here."

Albrecht estimates that approximately 40 percent of the students eventually apply accumulated rental towards the purchase of their instruments. "The amount of profit we make from converting a rental to a purchase depends on how soon the conversion is made. The longer we have to carry a renter at breakeven, the less we profit when purchase takes place. We have a real incentive to keep the rental period to a minimum."

Mr. Albrecht has encountered difficulties in predicting rental conversion patterns. The rate of conversion differs from instrument to instrument, as might be expected. The smaller, less expensive instruments, such as coronets, clarinets, and flutes have a high conversion ratio. But the larger pieces, such as Sousaphones, bass drums, and baritones, are generally left in perpetual rental. "Any profit we make here will have to come from accessories and supplies."

Profit margins on instrument support products (reeds, lubricants, mutes, polishes, and the like) average about 35 percent. "These are good items for the cash flow because of the rapid and regular turnover throughout the school year."

Fantasia has a large repair service housed in the rear of the store. Subcontracted to an independent craftsman, Travis Preevy, the repair service is another breakeven operation for Fantasia. "Trav does a darn good job for us, even if he doesn't make us much money. He charges a flat rate of $18.50 per hour to the customer and gives us a 20 percent commission. We provide him with shop room to work in and purchase any capital equipment he might require from time to time. We're content with this arrangement, even though it doesn't generate much for the bottom line, because skilled instrument repairmen are very scarce and the repair service is yet another source of customer traffic."

Competitive Edge

Mr. Albrecht assesses the competitive dynamics of his business. "Our sole competitive edge is service. There are three other music stores in Winona, but Fantasia is the only one that really caters to band directors and their needs. Our competitors are geared up more for the general public—what we call the walk-in trade. They carry only a few instruments and accessories, offer no repair, and don't really stock much in the way of sheet music outside of piano and guitar pop tunes. They make their money on pianos, organs, records, and stereo sales.

"Even though there's no way to reflect it on the balance sheet, Fantasia's greatest asset is goodwill. We have developed real rapport with band directors in Winona. They trust us and respect us for our knowledge of the school music business. I have developed a simpatico sense with the directors because I love the band-music literature right along with them. I'm well-versed in who the favorite and most playable composers are, what's involved in choreographing marching routines, and what band clinics are all about. I talk the band director's lingo and relate to his own special world. I'm willing to go the extra mile to meet their needs."

Going the extra mile includes such services as taping band concerts for schools at cost, distributing complementary copies of demonstration recordings of new music, and providing directors with a listening room. "Fantasia Music is the band director's headquarters," sums up Albrecht. "They come here because we appeal to their professional interests. We're like a second home for many of them. No other music store in town can make that claim."

Sheet Music Sales

"We rise or fall on the basis of our sheet-music sales," observes Albrecht. "Our competitive approach, based on band director rapport, highlights the role of sheet sales. We simply have to have what the band people want—the right tunes, in the right style, and within the proper difficulty level."

Albrecht prides himself on his "gut feel" for the band and orchestra market. "I know which of my directors have conservative musical tastes and which are more contemporary. Some of them like a halftime show composed almost exclusively of classic marches—say from Sousa, Goldman, and King—while others want a contemporary, upbeat sound keyed to recent Top 40 type hits. I have noticed more of an infatuation lately for the pop stuff, I guess because more and more of the directors are young. Disco arrangements have been particularly big in the last two seasons.

Albrecht orders from nine mainline music publishing houses on a continuous basis and from two or three others intermittently. Orders flow in at a heavy pace in early spring and fall in anticipation of the two distinct band seasons. "Most of the publishers will carry me for 90 days, and sometimes longer, which is vital to cash flow. If we had to pay for new music before peak sales season, we'd really have a messed up short-term financial picture. Selling music is one heck of a seasonal business. It's awfully volatile too, and becoming more so every year given the growing popularity of Top 40 arrangements. You know how unstable and fast changing that whole business is."

Albrecht laments that he has only limited control over the profitability of sheet-music operations. Some publishers offer a larger discount on purchased music than others do, with the amount ranging from 30 to 60 percent. "Obviously, we'd rather sell the heavily discounted stuff, but it doesn't always fit the directors' needs. They aren't likely to purchase a composition just because it has an attractive price. They're educators and artists, not purchasing agents. I can only hope that the most heavily discounted sheets will also be among the most popular. Forecasting in this area is hit and miss at best and certainly not very scientific. This is why it is so essential that I keep in close touch with my local group of directors and with national trends in the band market. Fortunately, national patterns are beginning to coalesce, although regional differences in what schools want to play are still somewhat prevalent.

"There's not really a whole lot I can do personally to influence what music the directors will select. I try to maintain my credibility with them, so that they will be open to consultation. Beyond that, it's just a matter of having a variety of things on hand for them to look at during the key ordering seasons."

Despite Mr. Albrecht's "insider" feel for the market, he confesses that nearly one-third of the sheet-music packages he orders fail to sell. "I'm caught between a rock-and-a-hard-place in ordering. If I get real cautious about how many new compositions I order, I run the risk of not having enough on hand to fire-up the enthusiasm of directors. On the other hand, the more I over order, the more inventory I will end up having to eat. Striking the happy medium is mostly a matter of luck."

Publishers rarely extend refunds on unsold orders, preferring not to make their business more risky than it already is. Consequently, they tend to gravitate towards a strategy of flooding the market each year with reams of new compositions to increase success probabilities. Despite the reluctance of publishers to make refunds, they do cooperate closely with retailers in such areas as providing demonstration recordings and filling last-minute rush orders.

"Anytime I find myself fretting too much over dead inventory, I remind myself that selling music to Winona bands and orchestras is what Fantasia Music Company is all about," Albrecht comments. "Our strategy revolves around sheet-music volume. Some dead inventory is inevitable." Determining what to do with this inventory has proved to be virtually an insoluble problem. "Occasionally, I can pawn it off on another store in the region, but this is rare. If it won't sell in Winona, it generally won't sell anywhere else nearby. I wish I could get rid of it merely by lowering the price, as in most areas of retailing, but things just don't work that way in this funny industry."

Physical Facilities

"I hate to say this, but it's a real testimony to our service that Fantasia has so many loyal, long-term customers. Our in-store accommodations are not luxurious, to say the least," Albrecht candidly admits. "Not only are we stuck down here in town where business is dead, but our building is nearly a half-century old. We're definitely not hurting for floor space, or anything like that, but our products and services simply aren't well showcased."

Albrecht factitiously describes Fantasia's furnishing as "early American make-do. Most of our furniture was either bought used or made for us. And I don't mean made like it was manufactured; I mean a guy sitting in his garage with a hammer and nails!

"I suppose we had better get in gear someday soon and fancy up the place. I've been reluctant to do much about redecorating, however, until I can get the bottom line straightened out. Our financial picture hasn't exactly been on an even keel since I took over in '74. I'll admit that. But I'm more concerned with serving the music education needs of Winona than I am with getting rich. My heart's in the music, not the cash register. Fantasia offers a unique kind of service to a special clientele. I think that's something to be rather proud of."

Analysis: Evaluate Fantasia's financial performance since Doyle Albrecht took over. In your opinion, how could the store become more profitable? Recommend appropriate action in this regard for both the short-run and long-run.

Evaluate Mr. Albrecht's managerial strengths and weaknesses. Do you admire his philosophy of customer service before profit?

EXHIBIT 28-1

PRODUCT LINE ANNUAL SALES VOLUME
(Thousands of Dollars)

	1974	1975	1976	1977	1978	1979
Instrument rental	$115	$124	$138	$147	$174	$203
Instrument sales	38	47	59	77	92	112
Instrument accessories and supplies	23	29	33	48	63	89
Instrument repair commissions	1.5	2.3	3.3	4.9	4.9	5.2
Sheet music sales	70	78	84	87	92	105
Miscellaneous	10	13	12	17	22	31
Total	$257.5	$293.3	$329.3	$380.9	$447.9	$545.2

EXHIBIT 28-2

MONTHLY SALES AS A PERCENT OF ANNUAL SALES

January	6.7%	July	17.7%
February	3.9	August	7.9
March	4.9	September	4.9
April	4.3	October	2.9
May	4.5	November	15.3
June	14.2	December	12.8

EXHIBIT 28-3

Fantasia Music Company

COMPARATIVE INCOME STATEMENTS, 1974-1979
(Thousands of Dollars)

	1974	1975	1976	1977	1978	1979
Sales	$258	$293	$329	$381	$448	$545
Less: returns	2	3	2	1	4	3
Net sales	$256	$290	$327	$380	$444	$542
Cost of Goods Sold						
Instrument rental	76	88	102	132	155	210
Instrument sales	15	21	30	24	32	33
Instrument accessories						
and supplies	13	17	19	25	25	33
Instrument repair commissions	8	6	2	6	11	5
Sheet music sales	82	95	100	113	124	166
Miscellaneous	16	12	16	16	14	19
Total cost of goods sold	$210	$237	$269	$315	$361	$466
Gross Profit on Sales	46	53	58	65	83	76
Operating Expenses	41	46	50	53	59	63
Income Before Taxes	5	7	8	12	22	13
Income Taxes	1	2	3	4	8	5
NET INCOME	$ 4	$ 5	$ 5	$ 8	$ 14	$ 8

EXHIBIT 28-4

Fantasia Music Company

COMPARATIVE BALANCE SHEETS, 1974-1979
(Thousands of Dollars)

	1974	1975	1976	1977	1978	1979
Assets						
Current Assets						
Cash	$ 11	$ 12	$ 15	$ 11	$ 12	$ 12
Accounts receivable	45	43	50	52	57	86
Inventories	41	45	49	59	84	130
Total current assets	97	100	114	122	183	228
Other Assets						
Equipment	5	6	9	10	15	17
TOTAL ASSETS	$102	$106	$123	$132	$168	$245
Liabilities and Capital						
Current Liabilities						
Accounts payable	$ 43	$ 27	$ 41	$ 55	$ 78	$ 52
Notes payable	15	30	28	15	14	34
Total current liabilities	$ 58	$ 57	$ 69	$ 70	$ 92	$129
Capital						
Capital stock	40	40	40	40	40	72
Retained earnings	4	9	14	22	36	44
Total capital	44	49	54	62	76	116
TOTAL LIABILITIES AND CAPITAL	$102	$106	$123	$132	$168	$245

people providers

29

People Providers of New Haven, Connecticut (PPNH) is a small employment agency managed by Felix Heinlein and Neal Albee. The New Haven office is tied to People Providers of America, a national employee recruiting chain with 178 local offices in the U.S. and Canada. PPNH specializes in recruiting technical personnel for computer services and accounting firms.

Heinlein and Albee own equal interests in PPNH, which is set up as a partnership. Felix Heinlein is thirty-five years old and holds an MBA degree from Northwestern. Before forming PPNH in 1978, he worked for the Connecticut Department of Human Resources for three years as a specialist in job placement of the handicapped. Neal Albee, thirty-seven years old, started his career with Gulf Oil doing personnel work. Then he worked two years with Manpower, Inc., leaving in 1978 to go with People Providers.

The two partners profess to be "fairly satisfied" with how the New Haven office has performed in its first two years of operation but feel it has not come close to realizing its true potential. They discuss their operations and future designs in the following dialogue.

Description of Services

Albee—Just about all of our work is done over the telephone contacting companies within a seventy mile radius of New Haven. Occasionally we may hop out a bit farther than this. We work almost solely with personnel officers in companies that have a lot of turnover among accounting and computer positions. Sometimes we do work directly with a computer center director or staff accountant.

Heinlein—In our two years of operations, we have done business with more than 300 different offices. Some of these contacts came through sister People Provider franchises and others we initiated on our own.

Albee—I should explain that all People Provider offices are independently owned and operated. We paid a $5,000 franchise fee to People Providers when we opened, and they receive 8 percent of all our commissions. In return we can plug into their information network as a valuable source of finding clients.

Heinlein—We have a fairly simple and straightforward fee system. When we place a person with a company, we receive from 10 percent to 30 percent of the first year's salary. The higher their salary, the bigger our percentage. We seldom have any problems getting the company to pay the fee, because in most instances it costs the company more to do their own placement work. Our surveys show that we generally save our clients 20 percent plus in placement expenses.

Albee—Our services become even more essential in tight job markets such as our two specialty areas, accounting and data processing.

Heinlein—Yes, there is a 30 percent shortage of qualified personnel in the DP field and accounting is almost as bad. Several of our larger client firms are so desperate for technical employees that they have what amounts to a standing order with us to supply X number of jobs per month or quarter.

Albee—Of course, the most valuable service we offer is not so much just locating employees for companies but rather attaining a good fit between the two. Both the employee and company have a preconceived set of expectations about what constitutes a good fit. The more aware we are of these criteria, the more valuable our service becomes.

Heinlein—Neal has identified the real essence of our business there—we're brokers or matchmakers. We generate synergy between employees and companies. By that I mean simply that our service adds more to the employee-company relationship than would be there without us. The employee and the company need us and we certainly need them.

Operating Strategy

Heinlein—PPNH would be nothing without marketplace contacts. Along with whatever goodwill and image our office has in the community, our only other asset consists of the network of contacts we have built up, in and around New Haven, and with other P.P. franchises.

Albee—People Provider's national motto is, "Using what you have to get what you need." In other words, use current contacts to generate future ones. For example, every time we get in a new resume or vita we add to our contacts from the references listed of former bosses and co-workers. Ten resumes could possibly multiply into a thousand or more contacts in chain letter fashion. Here again is the synergy concept referred to before.

Heinlein—We strive very hard to form steady, long-term relationships with our client companies. Contacts are worthless if they don't cultivate anything. Repeat service clients are essential as the bread-and-butter of the agency. They pay the overhead and give us some measure of stability in what otherwise is a very fluid industry.

Albee—Our records show that about 30 percent of our clients have come back to us at least twice for placements. Felix and I hope to raise that percentage steadily over the next few years.

Analysis: Suggest ways in which PPNH can increase its repeat customer percentage over the next few years.

Heinlein—Placement percentage is another performance yardstick Neal and I use. We are concerned not only with the number of repeat customers we have, but also with our success in filling job vacancies and placing those seeking employment. On the demand side, Neal and I are proud of the fact that we successfully fill 60 percent of the openings brought to us by client companies. In less than 10 percent of our placements has the company ended up being dissatisfied with the employee after six months on the job.

On the supply side, we are successful in finding jobs for better than 45 percent of our employee clients. This is really fairly high considering that many job hunters aren't really totally serious about making a new career move.

Albee—That's one of the real headaches of running an agency—determining who is really serious about wanting a new job. Some people who visit our office are what we call "tire kickers." They're not really interested in changing jobs but only in seeing what they're worth in the market—just testing the water.

Heinlein—And for the serious job hunters, there's often emotional trauma associated with making a change. This sometimes becomes a real impediment to our placement efforts. When the client is uptight, our role as counselors really comes to the fore. Neal and I have to function as "security blankets."

Analysis: Suggest ways in which PPNH can further increase its placement percentages on both the demand (company) and supply (employee) sides.

Heinlein—People Providers helps each of their franchise offices develop what they call a grid for growth. This consists of an overall strategic growth plan for the franchise in keeping with its size, client mix, geographical area, and identified market niche. Naturally, each office has a unique grid.

Albee—Felix and I are currently in the process of crystalizing our grid for the 1980 to 1985 period. We thought it would be a fairly easy exercise until we really got into it. For the past three-and-a-half months we've been struggling with our strategy grid.

Heinlein—You'd better believe it! We have some fairly definite ideas about where we want to go with the agency but the big picture isn't clear to us yet. It's not so much a case of Neal and I disagreeing about goals and priorities as it is our mutual inability to clearly define these. After just two years in the business, we both realize that we have a lot to learn.

Albee—But we heartily agree with the national headquarters that a strategy grid needs to be developed soon. They've given us another month to develop something fairly concrete. So far, we have developed a series of short statements—Felix likes to call them propositions—about PPNH. We view these as our starting point in developing the grid. It's quite possible that additional propositions will be needed before the grid can be finalized, but the seven we have developed so far will certainly get us going.

Analysis: Using the grid format in Exhibit 29-2, formulate the optimum six-year strategy plan for People Providers of New Haven. Feel free to alter any of the strategy propositions in Exhibit 29-1.

EXHIBIT 29-1

STRATEGY PROPOSITIONS FOR PEOPLE PROVIDERS OF NEW HAVEN, 1980-1985

1. Generate at least $40,000 in annual salary for each partner by 1982.
2. Minimize office overhead costs: secretarial help, furniture and decorating appointments, size of office, and so forth.
3. Specialize in accounting and data processing clientele.
4. Strive for quality of relationship with clients rather than quantity: long-term relationship, repeat patronage.
5. Branch out somewhat in client target markets and services offered.
6. Take maximum advantage of the People Providers national information network.
7. Build a higher profile in the New Haven-East Coast area.

EXHIBIT 29-2

STRATEGY GRID FORM FOR PEOPLE PROVIDER FRANCHISE OFFICES

	1980	1981	1982	1983	1984	1985
Target revenue						
Placement percentage						
Repeat patronage percentage						
New clients: demand side						
New clients: supply side						
Target markets *(client groups)						
New services offered*						

*Requires in depth analysis on separate sheet.

EXHIBIT 29-3

People Providers

INCOME STATEMENT

for the year ended December 31, 1978

Fees Earned		$108,765
Less Operating Expenses		
Franchise commissions	$ 8,701	
Wages and salaries	63,000	
Rent	3,450	
Supplies	3,100	
Postage	2,400	
Furniture and equipment depreciation	2,300	
Utilities	1,623	
Telephone	1,175	
Miscellaneous	693	
Total operating expenses		86,442
NET INCOME		$ 22,323

EXHIBIT 29-4

People Providers

INCOME STATEMENT

for the year ended December 31, 1979

Fees Earned		$122,475
Less Operating Expenses		
Franchise commissions	$ 9,798	
Wages and salaries	68,000	
Rent	3,600	
Supplies	2,400	
Postage	2,184	
Furniture and equipment depreciation	2,300	
Utilities	1,824	
Telephone	1,200	
Miscellaneous	784	
Total operating expenses		92,090
NET INCOME		$ 30,385

EXHIBIT 29-5

People Providers

BALANCE SHEET

December 31, 1979

Assets

Current Assets			
Cash		$ 3,628	
Accounts receivable		7,380	
Supplies		302	
Total current assets			$11,310
Fixed Assets			
Equipment and furniture	$23,000		
Less accumulated depreciation	4,600	18,400	
Franchise fee and deposits		5,300	
Total fixed assets			23,700
TOTAL ASSETS			$35,010

Liabilities and Capital

Current Liabilities			
Accounts payable	$ 1,230		
Wages payable	270		
Taxes payable	110		
Total current liabilities		$ 1,610	
Long-Term Liabilities			
Notes payable		20,400	
Total liabilities			$22,010
Capital			
Albee, Capital	6,500		
Heinlein, Capital	6,500		
Total capital			13,000
TOTAL LIABILITIES AND CAPITAL			$35,010

cameron mobile homes

30

"The union is after my plant people, and I'm not about to give in." Boyce Cameron, founder and chief executive of Cameron Mobile Homes, related his problem to Ramsey Curtis, a free-lance labor relations consultant in Atlanta. "Ramsey, you have an excellent reputation in the Southeast for your ability to troubleshoot union problems. Would you give me some advice on how to ward off the union?"

Cameron and Curtis sat down alone in the company's large executive meeting room, poured coffee, and proceeded to discuss the latest attempt to unionize Cameron Mobile Homes. Their dialogue follows.

Curtis—Boyce, before we start talking specifics, please fill me in on your company's background.

Cameron—My father built Cameron Mobile Homes in 1923 on the outskirts of Atlanta. Today, of course, we're right in the middle of the industrial district. My brother Lyle and I took over in 1959 when my father passed away. Currently Lyle is treasurer and I'm head of plant operations. We make a variety of home styles in the plant and sell primarily to dealers in Georgia and Alabama.

We're profitable and growing. Even with the lousy economy last year, we grossed over $15 million in sales. 1982 promises to be a much better year if the economy picks up again.

Curtis—How many people do you employ currently, Boyce?

Cameron—As of the first of the month, 125 or so—17 in the office, 4 sales reps, and the rest plant people. Nine months ago, in June of 1980, we layed off 40 of our wage people due to soft sales. We still need to pare down the work force by a dozen, but we plan to do that strictly by attrition.

Curtis—Did the union situation heat up after the layoffs?

Cameron—Obviously it did. Although very few people with much seniority were affected, the work force was not pleased with the layoffs. But what choice did I have? The 1980 recession hurt companies all across the country. Cameron was no exception. You can't employ people when there isn't enough work for them.

Curtis—What exactly did the union do?

Cameron—In July, after the layoffs, representatives of the steelworkers union out of Birmingham, Alabama, began visiting with our plant crew both in the plant and outside. The union reps were fairly low key about it all, but they were persistent. I quickly got with my legal counsel but found that everything was perfectly legit.

Curtis—Did the union get any of your employees to sign cards indicating their interest?

Cameron—I am not aware of any such activity but don't know for certain if it occurred. I do know, however, that things seemed to die down going into the fall of '80. I began to breathe easy again. Then in February of 1981, the union made another move. Again our plant people were visited and talked to. That was last month.

Curtis—Has the union been real active in the last month?

Cameron—Visible but not necessarily highly aggressive.

Curtis—Then why did you tell me a few minutes ago that the union was definitely after your people?

Cameron—It just seemed awfully apparent to me. Why else would they be talking to Cameron workers?

Curtis—It's possible that the union is still waiting for more employee interest to develop. Organizers are professionals nowadays, and they rarely seek a representation election until they're sure they've got the worker votes lined up.

Cameron—Maybe I have over-reacted to it all.

Curtis—That's understandable. No businessman wants to be hassled by unions. It's entirely possible that things are not yet ripe for the steelworkers union to step in. At this point they may be simply testing the water. If they couldn't get enough votes lined up for an election immediately following the summer layoffs, they probably are poised for another attack.

Cameron—Well, what should I do in the meantime to build employee relations and better assure staying unorganized?

Curtis—I wish there were a simple set of rules I could pass on to you that would guarantee safety from unions. Unfortunately, the situation is always too complex for that. What a company does after a union has been voted in is never as important as what the company was doing before hand.

Cameron—What do you mean Ramsey?

Curtis—Unions don't get started by accident in companies, Boyce, at least not in the South where unions haven't traditionally been a part of the landscape as they have in the Midwest and Northeast.

Unless a company has inherited a union, unionization generally signals a breakdown in labor relations. Job security is one of the classic reasons why blue-collar employees side with a union. But beyond that, employees today are very demanding and hard to please. If they feel they're not participating enough in operating decisions or not being treated like adults, they may start sympathizing with the union.

Cameron—You're definitely right that workers today are a different breed of cat! They are demanding a lot of things besides money and working conditions. So where does that leave me? What can I do to stave off the union?

Curtis—Since they apparently have not gotten Cameron workers to sign union cards, I'd say the union is only trying to build up goodwill with your people at this point. An organizing drive is sure to be in the planning stage but perhaps not in the near future. My best advice to you, besides keeping an eye out for further union activities, is to get your house in order.

Cameron—Exactly what do you mean, Ramsey?

Curtis—Strive to create a working atmosphere in the plant that keeps people reasonably satisfied. Don't give them any obvious reasons to rekindle their interest in unionizing.

Cameron—You mean quit laving them off?

Curtis—Well, certainly that is a sore point for your plant. You definitely will have to tread lightly there. But job security still won't guarantee a union-free shop. Today's blue collar worker wants not only job security but also a voice in determining the terms of employment, protection from arbitrary management decisions, and a feeling of self-respect. As I said before, Boyce, management has to create a working climate that wins the respect and loyalty of employees.

Cameron—How can I create that kind of climate here?

Curtis—It's tough to be real specific because we're dealing with the attitudes of management. But let me give you five guidelines to follow. First, allow operative employees to share in managing their own jobs. Participation breeds commitment. Second, make certain that employees share in the success of the overall company so that they will have a strong reason to want the company to prosper. Third, provide all of your people with opportunities to develop and grow in their job—to mature professionally. Fourth, treat them like adults. That means you have to be open-minded and, at least occasionally, open to compromise. Finally, and most importantly, treat them fair and square. And if you don't know what that means, you are in trouble!

Cameron—All right, that sounds sensible enough to me. But tell me specifically how to go about implementing your philosophy. What can upper-level management, working along with first-line supervisors, do here at Cameron to create the non-union environment you've described?

Analysis: Answer Mr. Cameron's question as completely as you can. Be specific, concrete, and pragmatic.

EXPERIENCE PHASE III
venture transition

janeck furniture

31

Janeck Furniture, originally the Springfield Furniture Mart, is located in a thirty-year-old building in downtown Springfield, Illinois. Hershel Janeck, the current owner and sole proprietor, purchased the store and all of its assets from the Furniture Mart in 1966.

Janeck Furniture sells used furniture, unfinished furniture, and a line of modestly-priced new furniture. The store's cramped floor space, limited inventory facility, and undesirable location have led Mr. Janeck to investigate the possibilities of expanding to a second location in Springfield. His expansion feasibility study, completed in 1978 and submitted to a local banker, follows.

Feasibility Study for Expansion of Janeck Furniture

Part I: Estimate of Sales

Springfield's 1977 population was 97,000 with 38,800 households. Annual per capita expenditure in Springfield for furniture and home furnishings was $207 in 1977. Nineteen furniture stores currently compete directly against Janeck Furniture with an aggregate sales floor space of 339,000 square feet.

EXHIBIT 31-1

ESTIMATED SALES FLOOR SPACE
(Square Feet)

Store Name		Estimated Floor Space
Barney's		12,000
Dawsons		45,000
Goldblatt's		6,000
Hendricks		14,000
J.V. Grand		25,000
Leaths		30,000
Lee's		4,000
Madisons		12,000
Myers Brothers (2 Stores)		16,000
Southtown		6,000
Stahls		12,000
Stern's (2 Stores)		27,000
Tiskos		50,000
Wolfsons		12,000
Sears Roebuck		10,000
Stix Baer & Fuller		6,000
Famous Barr		8,000
	Total	295,000
	25%*	69,940
	TOTAL	368,750

*Estimate of the floor space of Springfield retailers who sell furniture as a secondary component of their product line (e.g., Woolco, Pennys, etc.)

Shown in Exhibit 31-2 is the analysis of excess sales demand for furniture in Springfield. The figures estimate that Springfield could accommodate an additional 60,000 square feet of furniture showroom space. Assuming sales of $50 per square foot of space, currently the average for Janeck's downtown store, there currently is $3 million of untapped market demand in Springfield for furniture.

EXHIBIT 31-2

ESTIMATE OF ADDITIONAL DEMAND
FOR FURNITURE IN SPRINGFIELD

Retail sales per household	$13,675
Furniture sales per household*	$547
(.04 x $13,675)	
Individuals per household	2.5
Potential furniture sales volume per capita	$219
Total city population in 1977	97,000

EXHIBIT 31-2   Continued

Potential furniture sales volume	$21,234,000
(97,000 x $219/res)	
Approximate out-of-city purchases (10% assumed)	$2,124,300
Net furniture sales volume	$19,919,700
Square feet of furniture store sales space in city	339,000 ft²
Sales per square foot of showroom	$50/ft²
Sales generated by existing stores	$16,950,000
(339,000 ft² x $50/ft²)	
Excess sales demand	$2,969,700
Square feet of sales area needed at $50 of sale per sq. ft.	59,394
($2,969,700−$50 per sq. ft.)	

*National business statistics indicate that residents spend approximately 4 percent of annual income on furniture.

To determine what share of the $3 million could be reasonably attained by a second Janeck Furniture store, it is assumed that the new store's customers will be from low to middle income levels (effective gross income of under $15,000). In 1977, 19,070 Springfield households were in this target category, distributed as follows:

9,826	households−less than $8,000
2,641	households−$8,000−$10,000
6,603	households−$10,000−$15,000
19,070	households−average $10,700

A conservative estimate of the effective buying income of the target households is $10,700. Assuming the 4 percent annual income expenditure for furniture (Exhibit 31-2), the 19,070 target households will spend approximately $8,161,000 for furniture during the year. This represents approximately 38 percent of the total furniture purchasing power in Springfield ($21,243,000 in Exhibit 31-2). It could be expected that 38 percent of the $3 million in excess furniture demand would go to Janeck's target population group, totaling $1,140,000.

The share of the $1,140,000 which Janeck's second store could capture depends on its location, quality of furniture offered, and extent of customer services. Given the downtown store's past record of success with selling to the target customer group (a 70 percent repeat customer rate from 1966 to 1977) and the planned attractiveness of the second store, it is estimated that Janeck's new venture could realistically capture half of the $1,140,000, or $570,000. If just 15 percent more patronage could be elicited from income groups above Janeck's target, the second store's projected annual gross revenue would be $650,000.

Future population growth projections for Springfield are auspicious. The growth rate for 1970 to 1980 is currently at 19.9 percent. Another 17.9 percent increase is foreseen for 1980 to 1990. Twenty-two thousand additional housing units are also projected for the eighties.

Part II: Estimate of Expenses

Exhibit 31-3 is a pro forma profit and loss statement for Janeck's proposed second store. Gross receipts of $640,000, derived from Part I above, are assumed.

Plans are to construct a 16,000-square-foot structure in the southwest part of Springfield. The building will be constructed and owned by Janeck Furniture on land that will be purchased for that purpose.

Mr. Janeck will provide the $80,000 equity necessary to purchase the land. The construction of the building will be $270,000. This will be financed for twenty-five years at 11.5 percent interest. Monthly loan payments will be $2715.

The initial $80,000 inventory will also be financed with a ten year-11 percent note. Monthly payments on this note will be $1102. Approximately $70,000 of additional guaranteed financing will also be available during the start-up period. The guarantee would not cost anything unless called.

In summary, 100 percent financing will require payments of approximately $3817 per month, or $45,804 per year. The pro forma profit and loss statement shows a profit of $23,183 after the bank debt has been serviced.

Part III: Conclusions

It is obvious from the preceding analysis that Janeck Furniture should expand to a second store. The local demand and future growth outlook for Springfield auger well for the proposed expansion. It should be undertaken in the near term.

Analysis: Carefully evaluate Mr. Janeck's expansion study from the standpoints of thoroughness, adequacy, and persuasiveness. What improvements can you recommend? Be specific.

If you were Janeck's banker, would you be willing to finance his new venture?

EXHIBIT 31-3

FIRST YEAR PRO FORMA PROFIT AND LOSS STATEMENT

			Percent of Sales
Gross Receipts		$640,000	100.00
Cost of Goods Sold			
Opening inventory	$ 80,000		12.5
Materials	0		
Direct labor	0		
Subcontract costs	0		
Purchases	320,000		
Overhead	0		
Total		400,000	
Less Ending Inventory		80,000	
Cost of Goods Sold		320,000	50.0
Gross Profit		320,000	50.0
Expenses			
Employee wages	30,000		4.68
Accounting & legal fees	6,250		.98
Advertising	30,000		4.68
Depreciation	13,000		2.03
Supplies	1,000		.15
Utilities	21,000		3.28
Telephone	3,000		.47
Repairs	600		.09
Sales tax	10,000		1.56
Insurance	4,500		0.70
Bad debts	3,000		.47
Miscellaneous (postage, etc.)	4,200		.66
TOTAL EXPENSES		126,550	19.77
Net Profit (before taxes)		193,450	30.22
Less federal income tax (50%)		(96,725)	
Less state income tax (4%)		(7,738)	
NET PROFIT (after taxes)		$ 88,987	

EXHIBIT 31-4

PRO FORMA PROFIT AND LOSS STATEMENT
WITH INTEREST EXPENSES

			Column 1*	Column 2*
Gross Receipts		$640,000	100.00	100.00
Cost of Goods Sold				
Opening inventory	$ 80,000		12.6	
Materials	0			
Direct labor	0			
Subcontract costs	0			
Purchases	320,000			
Overhead	0			
Total		400,000		
Less Ending Inventory		80,000		
Cost of Goods Sold		320,000	50.0	59.08
Gross Profit		320,000	50.0	40.92
Expenses				
Employee wages	30,000		4.68	14.17
Accounting & legal fees	6,250		.98	
Advertising	30,000		4.68	5.73
Depreciation	13,000		2.03	
Supplies	1,000		.15	
Utilities	21,000		3.28	
Telephone	3,000		.47	
Repairs	600		.09	
Taxes	10,000		1.56	
Insurance	4,500		0.70	
Bad debts	3,000		.47	
Miscellaneous	5,200		.66	
(postage, etc.)				
OPERATING EXPENSES		$127,150	19.86	39.86
(Col. 1 excludes debt retirement)				
Net Profit (before taxes)		192,850	30.13	3.05
Less federal income tax		⟨96,425⟩	15.06	
Less state income tax		⟨7,714⟩	1.20	
Net profit (after taxes)		88,711	13.86	1.77
Less withdrawals		⟨20,000⟩	3.12	
NET PROFIT BEFORE DEBT SERVICE		$66,711	10.42	
Debt Service		45,804		
NET PROFIT AFTER DEBT SERVICE		$20,907		

Note: Column 1 expresses each expense as a percentage of net sales. Column 2 represents the 1977 average for stores of comparable sales.

prudhoe bay oilfield servicing

32

Prudhoe Bay Oilfield Servicing is on oilfield general services company located in Prudhoe Bay, Alaska. PBOS specializes in doing field maintenance work on oil-drilling rigs located in and around the Bay area. Organized as a three person partnership in 1975, the company is currently in transition due to the sudden death of Austin Beall, majority partner.

The company's other two partners, Nance Kizer and Mitchell Granger, are reshuffling their administrative responsibilities and reassessing Prudhoe Bay Oilfield Servicing's future strategy. The following interview with Nance Kizer was held nine months after the death of Austin in November 1980.

Please provide us with background information about Prudhoe Bay Oilfield Servicing.

Austin and I formed the partnership in 1975 with equal contributions. Austin kicked in some additional funds in 1977 and became majority partner. Shortly thereafter, Mitch was invited in. At the time of Austin's death, I had 34 percent ownership and Mitch had 10 percent. Austin had the rest.

Prudhoe Bay Oilfield Servicing was originally founded to perform general welding work on oil rigs in the Bay region. As time went on, we gradually branched out into additional maintenance services, such as mud pumping and acidizing. Currently we are the largest free-lance general maintenance contractor operating in the Bay.

We work largely on a subcontracting basis. PBOS makes contact with the rig, troubleshoots maintenance needs, and then contracts with independent operators in the region to do the work. In many instances we can do the work ourselves when it's modest in scope.

Austin and I complemented each other well in running the company. He handled most of the administrative matters in the office, while I spearheaded the technical work in the field. Austin coordinated personnel, dealt with customers over the phone, and pretty much determined what services we would offer. I'm troubleshooter for problems out on the work site. Although we both had engineering degrees, our talents lay in opposite directions.

Mitch Granger was more-or-less a silent partner while Austin was alive. Mitch runs a flying service here in the Bay and spends most of his time managing it. For the past several months he has stepped into the vacuum here to assist me.

PBOS established a good track record under Austin and me. In our five years together, we tripled our assets and topped a million in sales. We expanded our mix of services greatly and laid the foundation for a professionally managed firm.

Nance, describe for us the transition period after Austin died.

Our biggest problem by far has been filling the administrative vacuum left by Austin. Even though we had $250,000 in key-man insurance on him, money is hardly any substitute for the loss of our chief decision-maker. Or for the loss of a close friend.

One day Austin was there in the office and the next he wasn't. That's how suddenly and unexpectedly he died. Mitchell and I were in shock right along with Austin's family. The whole world suddenly changed for all of us. We weren't ready for it; but who ever is?

Mitch and I met together six days after the funeral to somehow come to grips with the situation. Life had to go on for Austin's wife and two daughters, and Prudhoe Bay Servicing faced its first severe crisis.

I was the only person among all of our twenty-three employees who could even attempt to take over the office's administrative burden. Fortunately, we had just recently hired a second engineer to assist me in the field. He is now going to have to go it alone. Mitch helped with some miscellaneous paperwork chores but didn't really know enough about the business to do much more.

Austin's wife, Maureen, was able to fill me in on a lot of the office routine since she had worked closely with our accountant to computerize our books. Between the two of us, we've managed to keep the wheels moving for these past nine months. Maureen has been a big, big help.

I hate to admit this, but I really didn't know all that much about the inner workings of the company until my crash learning program began. I knew quite a bit about welding and related maintenance services but comparatively little about such areas as our bookkeeping, personnel records, job scheduling, and cash flow. I've sure been learning though!

Prudhoe Bay Oilfield Servicing has lost its continuity and momentum since Austin died. It's been strictly crisis management. New brushfires break out everyday. I'm frankly worried about our ability to make more forward progress, to use a football analogy.

I'm working sixteen to twenty hours daily just to barely keep up with all of the problems. But I have almost no time for looking ahead or for doing any innovative thinking. I get together with Mitch and Maureen a couple of times a week for lunch. That's just about the only time I have for charting our new course.

What is Maureen's role in the business at this point?

That's a very good question. I guess she has both an informal and formal role. Let me explain. When Austin died last November, Maureen inherited all of his ownership interest. She's now the majority partner in PBOS.

You see, Austin, Mitchell, and I never drew up any sort of buy-sell agreement to allow us to redefine our ownership roles. We were all tight with money and short of time, so we just never got around to seeing a lawyer. I guess that sounds awfully myopic, but we never dreamed any of us would die unexpectedly. We were all so wrapped up in making the company go that we didn't make time to legally plan for the future.

Without a buy-sell agreement, Maureen automatically assumed Austin's ownership position. Unfortunately, she also inherited Austin's liability for the company's debt. This amounts to $185,000 for her alone. If PBOS should go belly-up in the near term, she would be ruined financially. I hate that reality but can't alter it.

Maureen is an excellent businesswoman. She works thirty to forty hours a week in an informal role. She handles a great deal of paperwork, coordinates some jobs, and does great PR work with customers. She also has a very good strategic instinct and contributes to our planning discussions. The office employees respect her, and she enjoys their company.

Describe a typical work day for you Nance.

It's not very glamorous. I generally arrive at the office by 6:00 A.M. and don't leave until 9:00 or 10:00 in the evening. I've had only three days off in the last six months. I spend about a third of my time on the phone coordinating jobs and talking to clients. The rest of the day is spent going over reports and figures and doing paperwork. I doubt if I ever stay with one job for more than thirty minutes due to endless interruptions.

I zealously look forward to the time when I can get back to a more normal schedule that affords me some leisure time. I'm not cut out to be a "workaholic" like Austin was. Work was his whole life. I have always had hobbies, such as remodeling old cars.

I'm also looking forward to the day when somebody else can step into the office management role. I miss field work, even in our cold Alaska weather. I have profited greatly since assuming Austin's former role, but I don't want to stay in administration forever.

My management style is the exact opposite of Austin's. He was autocratic, impatient, and a nondelegator. I delegate well and don't push people nearly so hard. Maybe that's because I'm less committed to office administration than Austin was.

What is your future, long-run plan for Prudhoe Bay Oilfield Servicing?

Let me candidly say that a long-range plan has not yet crystalized. In a way, PBOS is a new business once again, now that I'm at the helm. Nine months hasn't provided enough time for us to plan a definite future. It's too early to say yet. We're still very much in a state of flux.

I can say, though, that I plan to reduce our scope of activities and services. Austin was much more ambitious than I in this regard. He wanted to expand our package of oilfield maintenance services as fast as possible. I'm not so strongly growth oriented—especially now that I have so many new responsibilities.

Austin got us into several deals that just barely broke even. I don't want to repeat those mistakes, if I can help it. I think we need to pick a niche and stake our claim there. Maybe in welding or mud pumping. Time will tell.

In the meantime, Mitch and I plan to continue to work closely with Maureen until we can get through the crisis phase completely. I think the three of us approach the future optimistically. It won't be easy, but we'll make it.

Analysis: What major needs does Prudhoe Bay Oilfield Servicing have in the short-run? How can these be met? What changes would you recommend?

Do you feel Prudhoe Bay Oilfield Servicing will continue to thrive under Nance Kizer?

What actions can smaller companies take to avoid the transition problems experienced by PBOS when Mr. Beall died?

philmark productions

33

"How can I know for sure when it's time to turn this operation over to a professional manager?" Sheldon Doctorow, productions director and majority stockholder of Philmark Productions, was conferring with his friend Charles Dante over lunch.

"Are you thinking of retiring when you're just fifty-two years old, Shelly?" Charles Dante registered considerable surprise at Doctorow's question.

"No, I wouldn't retire Charlie," Doctorow responded, "but I would turn over daily operations to someone else. Maybe to Tony Davis. He knows our operation backwards and forwards."

"Tony's a good man. As lead film editor I should know," Dante asserted. "I have worked closely with Tony over the past year-and-a-half helping him with the MCA deal. Tony's the best project manager at Philmark. But you're the mentor, Shelly. You started Philmark eleven years ago and have guided us with a sure rudder all the way. Why are you considering turning it over to Davis?"

Sheldon Doctorow leaned back in his chair for a moment and let his mind fondly reminisce. He had started Philmark Productions in Los Angeles in 1970. Everyone laughed at the effort, saying the movie industry was already oversupplied with film-editing companies.

But Doctorow had something new—a laser technology editing process—which the more innovative film production companies soon clamored for. Philmark Productions was suddenly very much in demand and quite profitable. Subsequent diversification lead Philmark into cable television, home-movie film processing, and most recently into distribution of video cassettes for VTR's (video television recorders).

Philmark was no longer a struggling venture seeking to break out of the red. Sales hit $38 million in 1980. That's what was troubling Doctorow: had the company outgrown him?

"Why am I considering giving it to Davis?" Doctorow finally answered, breaking his reverie. "I guess it goes back to my self-concept. I'm an entrepreneur. I love to dream up new ideas and gadgets and find a market for them. Lately, I've been having to spend more and more time on administrative matters—performance evaluations, forecasting, budgeting. I don't have a lot of flair for that stuff and not a lot of interest either.

"Maybe it's time for me to get out of daily operations and into some other phase of the company. Mayby I should even sell out." Doctorow then stood up from the table and looked out the window. "What do you think I should do Charlie?"

"Just don't rush into a decision Shelly. Maybe you're over-reacting to all those committee meetings lately. They could make anyone hate administrative work!"

"No," answered Doctorow, "It's not anything that superficial. The company has been changing a lot in recent years, but I haven't been. I guess I'm like the paternalistic father who never really wanted his kids at home to grow up.

"One thing's for sure: I'm an entrepreneur, not a professional manager. Whether or not it's time to turn Philmark Productions over to a professional is the tough question I still have to answer."

Analysis: How can a company determine when the time is right for a professional manager to succeed the entrepreneurial founder?

What is the difference between an entrepreneurial manager and a professional manager? Do you feel many people have the capacity to be both types of managers?

If Sheldon Doctorow were to turn over the daily operations of Philmark Productions to Tony Davis, how could Doctorow continue to make vital contributions to the company? Assess his options in this regard.

Is it really feasible for Doctorow to relinquish the chief executive position given that he is majority stockholder?

iron kettle restaurant

34

Louis J. Guinn is a successful real estate appraiser in Salina, Kansas, who is currently giving serious consideration to the purchase of a defunct local restaurant. Thanks to his prospering realty firm, Guinn has put together $135,000 which he wants to use as seed money for a new venture. Although Guinn has no intentions of personally managing the new business, he would like to serve as a supportive consultant-stockholder. He is especially attracted to the prospect of purchasing a restaurant, since he made his start in business twenty-two years ago as the manager of a successful steak house in Kansas City.

In the following interview, Guinn details the restaurant's past trackrecord and assesses its future potential.

"The Iron Kettle here in Salina is up for sale by Hugh Dyer. Hugh owns a food-franchise operation called the Chisholm Trail Chuckwagon. He has four of these in Kansas, including one unit here in town. The Chuckwagon serves barbeque and cold trimmings on styrofoam plates in a stand-up cafeteria line. The restaurants are heavily decorated in a cattle-drive western motif—you know, lots of knotty wood-paneling, seats shaped like saddles, and six guns on the walls.

"Based on over twelve years of success with the Chuckwagons, Dyer decided he would like to use the same food formula in a slightly higher class setting. So in the summer of 1978, he opened up a place called the Barbeque Barn in a subdivision on the outskirts of Salina. It sat on 3.29 acres of land with a split-level stone house built during the fifties.

"He paid in the neighborhood of $60,000 for the property and then sunk another $10,000 to $15,000 into redecorating the house. He put in new plumbing and heating and air and recreated the western, cattle-drive type motif inside. The setting was more elegant than the Chuckwagon—more tasteful and less garish.

"He set up a cafeteria-style serving line again using disposable plates and utensils. However, customers could take their food to any of three large rooms and eat in quite comfortable surroundings. They could even go out back and dine on shaded picnic tables. The Barbeque Barn's menu was more varied than at the Chuckwagon and somewhat more expensive—in the $5-$7 range.

"The Barn lasted just about a year before it folded. I attribute its failure to lack of promotion and customer confusion. Dyer did almost no advertising whatsoever, despite the fact that the Barn was almost hidden from public view on its large, shaded lot.

"To make matters worse, the way he set up his menu was very confusing. He featured too many dinners that were almost alike. For example, the Barn served chopped barbeque beef, pinto beans and potato salad on the Trailblazer dinner. The Trailboss dinner had chopped beef, potato salad, and corn muffins. Then the Maverick dinner was simply a combination of the previous two: beef, potato salad, beans, and muffin. Very confusing. In all, thirteen dinners were served with little differentiation. And, incredibly, the Barn listed peanut butter sandwiches on the menu for $1.20 and large dill pickles for a buck each. Now who's going to go to a supposedly nice restaurant and order that?

"In a last ditch attempt to keep the doors open, Dyer unsuccessfully experimented with a few marketing gimmicks. He gave away free homemade ice cream with every meal; he had an 'all-you-can-eat' sirloin steak night; he even gave away cheapie cowboy hats to children under eight years of age. All to no avail. The Barbeque Barn finally closed in July of 1979.

"Then in November, Dyer reopened the restaurant under the name 'TJ's.' He put his son-in-law in charge and undertook extensive interior remodeling. Two new stone fireplaces were installed. The cafeteria line was abolished. Snazzy carpeting and drapes were put up and a small dance floor was installed over in one corner.

"Dyer's son-in-law introduced a new decor to the place. He wanted it to be more cosmopolitan and sophisticated. A liquor license to serve mixed drinks was obtained. The menu was completely reformulated, this time emphasizing chicken, shrimp, seafoods, and a massive salad-bar table molded into two large letters, T and J. Customers were waited on at their tables.

"TJ's made an attempt at advertising initially by putting a mobile sign in the long driveway entrance way promoting the revised menu and availability of liquor. They also took out a small ad in the television-log section of the local newspaper. The ad read: 'Come to TJ's for a memorable evening of dining elegance.'

"Business never caught on at TJ's. I think Dyer had not learned his lesson from the Barbeque Barn experience. The image of TJ's was never really clearly defined for potential customers. TJ's diverged sharply in menu and decor from the Barbeque Barn, but you couldn't tell it from the rustic exterior of the building—which wasn't renovated at all—or from the meager advertising. People didn't seem to know whether or not it was a family restaurant because of the liquor. Also much of the western motif left over from the Barbeque Barn lingered at TJ's—like the paneled walls and wrought iron fixtures.

"Dyer's son-in-law wasn't experienced in the restaurant business and certainly didn't excel as a manager. After five months of operation, he and Dyer mutually agreed to close TJ's. The son-in-law went back to college full-time.

"In April of 1980, Dyer put the property up for sale. That was six weeks ago. He wanted $175,000 and offered to carry the mortgage himself for 10 percent, which was two-and-a-half points under the prevailing prime. The purchasing price included the land, building, and all restaurant equipment. Estimating somewhat conservatively, I figure Dyer has $90,000 to $110,000 tied up in the place. How desperate he is to unload it I don't really know.

"Several parties have looked at the property for possible use as something other than a restaurant. A group of doctors looked at it as a potential clinic site but lost interest when the need for extensive remodeling work became apparent. A local real estate firm toyed with the idea of moving their headquarters there but eventually backed off.

"I still have great faith that a restaurant can be successful there. With some aggressive marketing and dedicated management, there's no real reason why a restaurant wouldn't succeed. It would certainly make for an interesting challenge.

"I could see calling the place the Iron Kettle Restaurant and pitching it as a family-style eatery with home-cooking and moderate prices. The decor is already set up for this kind of operation.

"The facility is located on a major highway next to an upper middle-class subdivision in Salina. It's not far from a new strip-type shopping center presently under development. That should help traffic flow to this end of town and enhance surrounding property values.

"I'm really intrigued with the idea of the Iron Kettle, although I haven't completely convinced myself to take the plunge. But the situation does look attractive; there's no doubt about that."

EXHIBIT 34-1

DESCRIPTION OF PHYSICAL FACILITIES

Lot: 3.29 acres, including numerous shade trees; 200-yard long winding driveway entrance; complete landscaping adjacent to the restaurant; underground sprinkler system; asphalt parking lot for 150 cars: 7 redwood picnic tables and benches.
Building: 4200 square feet; split-level rustic stone exterior; screened in back porch dining area; 44 table and chair units seating 150 people; nearly new furnishings and interior decorating; wood paneling throughout; 2 serviceable fireplaces; dance area and bandstand covering 30 feet by 25 feet; fairly new central heating and airconditioning system.
Equipment and Utensils: Well-appointed kitchen with commercial microwave oven and dishwasher; complete dining utensils for 200 people; small cold-storage room.

Analysis: Should Mr. Guinn purchase the property and open the Iron Kettle? What would be a fair purchase price?

Assuming Mr. Guinn decides to "take the plunge," what advice would you offer him to promote the venture's short-run and long-run success?

casner filtration systems

35

Casner Filtration Systems manufactures air-conditioning filters, heating filters, and specialty filters for heavy-duty construction equipment. Started in 1954 by Mendal Casner, the firm prospered through the years and currently employs 158 workers in its downtown Minneapolis plant.

Mendal Casner visited his physician recently and received a grim surprise; he was diagnosed as being terminally ill with cancer and given only six months to live. Casner accepted the news with remarkable courage, insisting that he had enjoyed fifty-six contented years and had amassed a rather sizable estate to pass on to his family.

He had just one concern revolving around his lifelong desire to pass on his business to his only son, Keith. Keith Casner was finishing up his B. B. A. degree and working part-time in the evenings as a production supervisor in the filter plant. Keith has always felt that he would, one day, succeed his father in the business but had hoped to pursue a career in public accounting for a few years before taking over Casner Filtration. His plans had changed abruptly.

By mutual agreement with his son, Mendal Casner was determined to spend his final months preparing Keith to assume the leadership role at Casner Filtration Systems. Both father and son were committed to making a successful transition.

Analysis: Formulate a detailed plan of action for the Casners to follow in preparing Keith to take over the reins of Casner Filtration Systems. Bear in mind the limited amount of time they have available.

What are the primary problems Keith Casner is likely to encounter when he initially takes over the company?

animator toys

36

Animator Toys, Inc., is co-owned and managed by Boyd Dameron who founded the company in 1964 in Van Nuys, California, its present headquarters. Animator operates seven retail stores of varying size in a five-city region of southern California: Van Nuys, 1 store; Glendale, 2 stores; Altadena, 1 store; Monrovia, 1 store; and Arcadia, 2 stores. Dameron holds 51 percent of the company's common stock. All other stock is held by three individuals: Burrell Dulany, Animator's treasurer, 31 percent; Chester Wolske, operations superintendent, 15 percent; and Alton Ballard, a Van Nuys physician, 3 percent.

In 1980, Animator's seven stores generated just over $5 million in gross revenues, leaving an operating profit in excess of $550,000. Forty-eight full-time employees in addition to the four owners work for the chain, including a warehouse crew of five. Besides the seven retail outlets, Animator owns three small inventory warehouses located adjacent to the headquarters store in Van Nuys.

Boyd Dameron, who is fifty-two years old, began his retailing career with the Federated Department Store group in 1960. He developed his acumen for the toy industry as a buyer of toys at Federated. In 1964, he left Federated and opened Animator's first store in Van Nuys. Since that time he has served as Animator's chief executive officer. Dameron is well-known throughout California as a long-distance runner, having won over fifty medals and trophies for his age category in state marathons. He is also an avid hot-air ballonist and amateur magician. As Mr. Dameron puts it: "No one has ever accused me of leading a dull life!"

In reviewing sixteen years of operations, Dameron points proudly to a number of business highpoints: adding a second store followed by five others over sixteen years; expanding geographically in southern California; maintaining majority ownership of the company; growing in sales and profits for eleven straight years; steadily expanding the product line to a wider range of age groups; avoiding all long-term debt.

Looking further into the on-rushing decade, Dameron is preoccupied with one large challenge—mall merchandising. "Oh sure," he explains, "there's always the problems of inflation, recession, sales seasonalism, and federal regulation in the toy business, but we've dealt with them fairly capably in recent years. Most industries have been infected with these gremlins. What I'm honestly concerned about for Animator going into the '80s is the nationwide trend to mall merchandising—you know, those giant enclosed developments that are practically a city under one roof.

"More and more retailers with flashy product lines are staking their futures on malls. The more successful toy outlets are certainly no exception. They're closing down existing stores and opening up mall operations right along with the jewelers, specialty apparel shops, department stores, and book mass-merchandisers. I'm worried that if our stores don't jump on the bandwagon soon, our larger national competitors will grab up all of the choice mall slots here in southern California."

Competitive Strategy

"You name it, we've got it! Of course I exaggerate somewhat but Animator stores pride themselves on offering a full-blown product line. No way do I want to hear that customers can't find what they want at one of our stores. If there's one thing I really stress to our store managers it's to keep a full line of stuff in stock. This is our trademark—our competitive edge."

Boyd Dameron elaborates further on Animator's product-line strategy: "We really market a great deal more than toys as people traditionally think of them. We're heavily committed to hobbies, crafts, certainly electronic games. We sell loads of bicycles, scooters, and even some unicycles, believe it or not. We sell numerous items to collectors, from superhero comics and tournament Frisbees to stamp mounting kits and high fashion dolls. We sell leather-tooling items, silk-flower construction packets, decoupage supplies, and modeling clay. When Animator advertises that we are the store for toys, hobbies, and crafts, we definitely mean it."

Dameron estimates that approximately 30 percent of sales go to the adult market, which has more stable demand and fewer fads than the youth market. Dameron cautions, however, not to segment the market into the simple dichotomy of adult versus children toys. In reality, at least seven market segments exist: infant, toddlers, youth, early school age, pre-teen, teen, and adult. Within each segment lies additional stratification as well, including male-female, disposable-durable, and "rough house" versus educational toys. "By no means do we have a simple marketing job," comments Mr. Dameron. "Toys, games, and amusement items appeal to people of all categories. Any way you slice it, there's great demand for what we sell."

Dameron admits he finds it difficult to cope with the concept of target marketing. "For years I struggled with the question of which market segment Animator should really zero in on. Should it be the largest segment of faddist children's toys, or high-profit-margin adult toys, or the hobby-crafts segment? I guess I knew the answer all along—go after all markets large enough to be profitable. This strategy is in keeping with our full product line and extensive inventory. Why should we limit our stores and pass up opportunities to make money? I think our nonspecialized approach separates us from competitors and persuades customers to form a lasting relationship with us."

The Animator stores strive to be competitive in pricing, but Dameron does not endorse the "discounting" approach. Although some items in the product line carry as much as a 50 percent price mark-up, most average about 10 percent. "The whole idea of so-called discount pricing is a bogus concept in retailing today. Discounting from what, the manufacturer's suggested price? That practice has practically disappeared from the scene. It's an anachronism from the 1950s when discount houses in the legitimate sense began mushrooming. But in 1981, price competition is not so simplistic and cut-and-dried. Animator beats K-Mart and Woolco in price on many toys, even though they may have brought in larger volume. They don't necessarily set rock-bottom prices on every item—it's not a part of their overall strategy. Likewise, Animator doesn't jack up the price tag on every item, simply because it isn't our overall strategy to do so."

Dameron explains that price competition is toughest on toys designated as major-line, comprising the most popular and heavily advertised new offerings from the mainline manufacturers (Mattel, Tonka, Fisher-Price, Marx, etc.). "We may not always have the absolute lowest price in town on these items, but Animator is more likely to have them in stock at any given time of the year. Toy departments in many department stores such as Sears and Penney's may carry a full inventory only during the Christmas season. Animator is reliable year round."

In addition to carrying a full product line, Animator offers several other customer services which Dameron feels provide an extra competitive dimension. These include personal sales service, free product layaway, storefront parking, free bicycle assembly, and gift wrapping priced at cost. Dameron feels that Animator enjoys a high percentage of return-customer patronage, even though he has no hard data to prove it.

The Animator stores emphasize image-oriented advertising through radio and newspapers. Television is used only in November and early December. Each store manager handles his own advertising, but all are encouraged by Dameron to stress Animator's wide-ranging product line and mix of services. According to Dameron, the ideal image for Animator is that of the "old fashion" personal service store.

Analysis: Evaluate Animator's marketing strategy. What are the pros and cons of having a "full-blown" product line? Is the company's target market adequately defined?

Store Operations

Each of the seven Animator stores are organized into five profit centers: toys, games, hobby and craft items, bicycles, and books. Exhibit 36-1 summarizes the contribution of each to sales volume. Exhibit 36-2 shows the average profit margin for each general product category.

EXHIBIT 36-1

PROFIT CENTER CONTRIBUTIONS

(by percentage of gross sales volume, 1975-1980)

	Percentages					
	1975	1976	1977	1978	1979	1980
Toys	53%	49%	46%	42%	41%	43%
Games	15	14	17	19	24	23
Hobby/Craft	6	8	9	12	9	8
Bicycles	24	25	24	22	19	18
Books	2	4	4	5	7	8
TOTAL PERCENTAGE	100	100	100	100	100	100

EXHIBIT 36-2

AVERAGE PROFIT MARGIN

(by product category, 1975-1980)

	Percentages					
	1975	1976	1977	1978	1979	1980
Toys	7%	8%	6%	5%	4%	5%
Games	9	7	6	8	8	10
Hobby/Craft	32	32	30	29	28	28
Bicycles	14	14	15	16	14	12
Books	12	10	8	9	10	7

As Exhibit 36-3 testifies, the toy business is highly seasonal. Approximately 60 to 70 percent of annual revenues are generated from October through December. In Dameron's words, "The only person who works harder than we do at Christmas is old Santa himself!"

EXHIBIT 36-3

PERCENTAGE OF ANNUAL SALES VOLUME

(by months of the year)

	Percentages					
	1975	1976	1977	1978	1979	1980
January	1%	1%	2%	1%	1%	2%
February	2	1	1	2	2	3
March	2	2	3	1	3	2
April	4	7	4	5	5	5
May	4	6	5	5	5	4
June	3	3	4	2	3	4
July	3	4	4	3	5	5
August	5	3	4	3	5	3
September	4	3	3	5	3	4
October	22	19	24	20	19	20
November	31	29	32	31	27	30
December	19	22	14	22	22	18
TOTAL PERCENTAGE	100	100	100	100	100	100

Business seasonalism affects not only cash-flow patterns but also purchasing and warehousing. Purchasing is typically done at least six months in advance, oftentimes even more on specialty items. Mr. Dameron attends several toy shows nationally during the spring months and does spot ordering as late in the year as September. Most of the ordered merchandise is inventoried by July or August and in place for the Christmas season.

"Our biggest problem with ordering is associated with cash flow," Dameron explains. "This is to be expected in any seasonal business. Without liberal trade credit to carry us through the summer, we'd be in a fix. Fortunately, manufacturers understand our plight and generally give us November and December dating on orders. In the meantime, we have a whale of a lot tied up in our warehouses."

Animator's inventory warehouses are all located in Van Nuys adjacent to the headquarters store. Forty thousand square feet of inventory space are spread out over a patchwork series of interconnecting warehouses immediately behind the retail showroom. "I guess we're lucky that the warehouses are unobtrusive and don't detract from the store's appearance," observes Dameron. "Rarely can a retailer combine showroom space and warehousing on a single site."

The outlying stores in Glendale, Altadena, Monrovia, and Arcadia are serviced by trucks leased by Animator. The headquarters store in Van Nuys serves as a central distribution center. Dameron feels that a number of operating efficiencies accrue from centralized warehousing, but concedes that it may limit further geographical expansion. "Until Animator grows so large that our stores aren't within easy access by truck, we'll keep the warehouses here in Van Nuys."

The Mall Issue

"Location is Animator's Achilles heel," Dameron candidly admits. "Most of our stores were opened during the late 1960s and early 1970s before the enclosed malls captured retailing. Malls are the wave of the eighties as I see it. Mall merchandising is certainly where our competitors are heading. I don't want Animator to fall by the wayside.

Animator's competition comes from every direction: discount houses, department stores, sporting goods outlets, craft and hobby shops, and toy chains. The latter, both regional and national, are perceived by Dameron to be Animator's strongest future threat. Included among these specialists in various parts of the country are Toys by Roy, Circus World, Kay-Bee Toys, Toys R Us, Kiddie City, and F.A.O. Schwartz.

Dameron elaborates on the perceived threat to Animator: "The national firms, and even several of the regional ones, are well financed and aggressively expanding throughout California. When they enter an area for the first time, they naturally gravitate toward malls. There we sit with a free-standing or strip shopping center store while the customers are going to the malls.

"Don't get me wrong — our seven stores are attractive in appearance and in decent traffic patterns, but none are in malls. Of course, there are a number of business disadvantages to mall retailing, but one has to go where the action is."

Exhibit 36-4 describes the physical facilities of Animator's seven stores.

Animator's three other stockholders are ambivalent about possible relocation of stores in enclosed shopping malls. Burrell Dulany, Animator's treasurer, concurs with Mr. Dameron that malls are currently popular but is reluctant to "mess up the balance sheet" with substantial new capital expenditures stemming from relocation.

Operations superintendent, Chester Wolske, says he's not afraid to "plunge into debt" but has serious reservations about the long-term staying power of malls. He tersely comments, "I'm not at all sure but what they're just another retailing fad."

Alton Ballard, a Van Nuys general practitioner, tends to agree with Boyd

Dameron on the need to "beat our competitors to the draw" on mall expansion. He notes, however, that the existing enclosed malls in Van Nuys, Altadena, and Monrovia are as yet quite small in size and that the Glendale and Arcadia malls are only in the community-planning phases.

All four stockholders are in unanimous agreement on one thing, however: any mall stores opened by Animator should be large enough to accommodate a full product line in keeping with Animator's desired competitive edge. As Mr. Dulany puts it, "We're not about to let mall merchandising cramp our style."

Treasurer Burrell Dulany feels he has "done his homework" adequately in analyzing the pros-and-cons of mall retailing. "There are several factors to be considered about mall operations. By being a free-standing store, we can pretty much call our own shots—the hours we will be open for business and things like that. One of the major disadvantages of being in a mall is that we would have to stay open approximately ten to eleven hours daily, even in the slow season when customer traffic is way off.

"Another disadvantage revolves around the costs of getting into a mall. Rent would certainly double over our present costs, and that's not even considering the two stores we're free and clear on. Utilities would undoubtedly be higher too.

"Another disadvantage concerns the sheer enormity of malls. Many people much prefer a free-standing type store where they can drive right up to the entrance. To get to any particular store in a mall, they may have to walk half a mile.

"One more problem concerns lack of protection against competitive firms coming into the mall right along with us. We'd be behind the eight ball if Circus World or somebody like that were to locate right there under the same roof with us."

Mr. Dulany concedes that his accounting orientation gives him a natural bias against relocation. "I admit that I'm fiscally conservative, but I still don't think Animator needs to be in malls." Boyd Dameron is otherwise persuaded about malls and not reluctant to air his views.

"I have the highest possible respect for Burrell and would be hard pressed to run Animator without his expert guidance. However, I do feel he is being penny-wise and dollar-foolish about the mall issue. I mean, so what if we incur some new operating expenses—most, if not all, of our stores are in a pretty good position to take on heavier lease payments. We've done a darn good job of keeping our expenses down on mortgages. I'd much rather be in a mall, even with its high expenses, if that's where the customers are.

"Neither would I mind having to compete head on against another specialty toy store if they should happen to already be in a mall or move in subsequently. I think we can more than hold our own against the competition."

Dameron concludes, "As the times change, we've got to change right along with them. Marketing is what the toy business is all about. Enclosed malls are with us to stay in retailing."

Towards The Future

"Ideally, I'd like to expand all throughout southern California with Animator stores—maybe add five or ten more by the end of the decade." Dameron thus sums up his future vision for Animator. "We have what I feel is a pretty fair track record so far, so what's to hold us back in the '80s? I wouldn't necessarily be averse to going public so long as I could maintain controlling ownership. The only thing I definitely don't want to do is stand pat with things as they now exist. Stagnation isn't part of my working vocabulary."

Analysis: Recommend policy guideline for the mall expansion issue. What are the inherent risks and opportunities of mall expansion?

EXHIBIT 36-4

ANIMATOR PHYSICAL FACILITIES

Store	Location	Description	Age	Size	Outstanding Mortgage	Monthly Payment
1	Van Nuys	free standing	16 years	3500 sq. ft.	-0-	-0-
2	Glendale	free standing	13 years	3300 sq. ft.	-0-	-0-
3	Monrovia	strip shop. center	12 years	4300 sq. ft.	$12,000	$1,445
4	Arcadia	strip shop. center	12 years	5200 sq. ft.	$14,500	$1,650
5	Glendale	downtown	10 years	6000 sq. ft.	$27,900	$1,898
6	Arcadia	strip shop. center	8 years	5200 sq. ft.	$42,500	$4,150
7	Altadena	free standing	6 years	7850 sq. ft.	$75,450	$8,200

EXHIBIT 36-5

Animator Toys

INCOME STATEMENT

for fiscal years ended December 31, 1975–80

	1975	1976	1977	1978	1979	1980
Sales	$2,123,000	$2,767,000	$3,021,000	$3,769,000	$4,236,000	$5,023,000
Cost of Merchandise Sold	1,523,000	2,019,900	2,200,021	2,749,237	3,092,349	3,645,430
Gross Profit	600,000	747,100	820,979	1,019,763	1,143,763	1,377,570
Less Operating Expense						
Salaries	309,796	356,121	369,076	426,097	501,126	576,050
Interest	15,207	15,093	14,767	14,021	13,769	13,658
Utilities	49,941	58,576	67,943	77,026	89,624	107,623
Supplies	43,966	50,123	58,421	67,978	77,647	89,347
Depreciation	27,500	27,500	27,500	27,500	27,500	27,500
Other	5,948	6,763	7,021	8,031	9,763	11,392
Total Operating Expenses	452,358	514,176	544,728	620,653	719,429	825,570
Net Income After Expenses	147,642	232,924	276,251	399,110	424,222	552,000
Less Income Taxes	28,321	49,978	69,456	100,021	109,003	121,061
NET INCOME	$119,321	$182,946	$206,795	$299,089	$315,219	$430,939

EXHIBIT 36-6

Animator Toys, Inc.

BALANCE SHEET

December 31, 1975-80

Assets	1975	1976	1977	1978	1979	1980
Current Assets						
Cash	$121,075	$123,658	$126,000	$131,796	$133,131	$138,976
Accounts receivable	1,861	2,047	2,369	2,765	3,104	3,693
Inventory	252,348	275,761	305,913	341,768	370,694	410,953
Other	15,076	3,021	3,943	2,694	4,038	1,865
Total current assets	190,360	404,487	438,225	479,023	510,967	555,487
Plant and Equipment						
Building and equipment	500,000	500,000	500,000	500,000	500,000	500,000
Less accumulated depreciation	75,000	102,500	130,000	157,500	185,000	212,500
Total plant and equipment	425,000	397,500	370,000	342,500	315,000	287,500
Total Assets	815,360	801,987	808,225	821,523	825,967	842,987

EXHIBIT 36-6 Continued

Liabilities and Stockholder's Equity						
Current Liabilities						
Trade accounts payable	93,476	103,492	123,941	136,918	147,145	153,619
Other payables	15,937	23,126	23,921	24,615	27,121	24,916
Total current liabilities	109,413	126,618	147,862	161,533	174,266	178,535
Long-Term Debt						
Mortgages payable	198,921	194,003	189,061	184,113	178,496	172,350
Total Liabilities	308,334	320,621	336,923	345,646	352,762	350,885
Stockholder's Equity						
Capital stock	400,000	400,000	400,000	400,000	400,000	400,000
Retained earning	107,026	81,336	71,302	75,877	73,205	92,102
Total stockholder's equity	507,026	481,336	471,302	475,877	473,205	492,102
Total Liabilities and Stockholder's Equity	815,360	801,987	808,225	821,523	825,967	842,987

sicorski and associates

37

Davis Sicorski is managing partner of Sicorski and Associates, a venture capital partnership in San Francisco which specializes in business buy-outs. Over the past nineteen years, Mr. Sicorski has served as consultant in over two hundred buy-outs, earning a reputation as a leading expert in pricing the going concern.

Mr. Sicorski, what methods do you use in determining the worth of a company that is up for sale?

Unfortunately, there is no simple method of evaluation that will satisfy all of the parties involved in a buy-out. After all, the buyer wants to use a method that derives the lowest possible price for a firm. The seller wants the very highest possible price. Then, of course, there are frequently mitigating considerations, such as the buyer's desire for minimum cash involvement and the seller's thoughts of tax avoidance and deferred income.

However, there are four evaluation methods which are used with some frequency: net worth, market value of assets, capitalization of earnings, and available tax loss. Each approach has its advantages and disadvantages depending on the particular situation at hand.

Would you please give us a situational assessment of each evaluation method.

Okay, let's start with the easiest method, net-worth evaluation. All you do here is subtract total liabilities from total assets. Obviously this is a poor technique, because a firm's balance sheet may or may not give a good picture of what the firm is really worth. In most cases, net worth understates the true value.

For example, assets are probably carried at deflated costs from an historical period with a lower inflation rate. The replacement price of those assets may be drastically different than the balance-sheet value.

Depreciation rates also have a large impact on balance-sheet evaluation. The business may have greatly speeded up depreciation for taxation purposes, thus understating the asset's worth.

The evaluator must also bear in mind that many smaller companies do not have audited statements and may not always adhere to generally accepted accounting principles. This can really distort the net-worth estimation.

The second evaluation approach, market value of assets, involves appraising the firm's assets at some market value. Determining what market value to use is the real challenge. Should it be market value in a forced-sale situation, replacement market value, or market value if the assets could be sold gradually over time as buyers are located?

Which market value approach do you favor?

Well, again it depends on the needs and expectations of the parties involved. The forced-sale market value would be logical only if immediate liquidation were anticipated. Under such circumstances, an expert appraiser should be called in.

Market value for replacement generally would favor the seller of the business, since inflation hikes the price of most assets. Market value and replacement value are similar when assets are evaluated on the sold-over-time basis.

If the buyer has some doubts about the firm's capacity to generate a profit immediately, he should certainly strive to attain a good deal on evaluating assets. In particular, he should avoid paying for "goodwill" or what's sometimes referred to as "blue sky." Trying to put a number on a company's image with customers is generally too subjective.

The third evaluation method, earnings capitalization, basically seeks to project future earnings from the company's past performance. If the future earnings of a company were known with certainty, the worth of any business could be determined easily. However, since few of us are clairvoyant, we use the next best approach of capitalizing earnings.

Exactly how is this done, Mr. Sicorski?

It involves solving two problems. First of all, you must determine which past earnings to use. Secondly, you have to gauge at what rate to capitalize, or affix a growth percentage, to those earnings. Let me explain briefly.

Since the profit track-record of a company may be inconsistent, it is no simple matter to determine which historical earnings rate to use in gauging future earnings. Some people merely take an average of three or five past years, and I generally find this acceptable. The evaluator must take great care, however, if he uses recent earnings for the projection. These can easily be distorted by a slick accountant who is dressing the business for sale.

In determining what percentage rate to place on earnings, the buyer should consider how risky the venture is and what alternate investment opportunities he has available. The higher the risk and the more alternatives available, the lower the earnings should be capitalized.

The fourth evaluation method is available tax loss. If the potential purchaser can lower the taxes of his present company by utilizing tax write-offs accumulated from losses of the for-sale firm, even an unhealthy looking firm can be a prudent buy. Of course, the buyer must have confidence that he can turn the company around and quickly nurse it back to financial health.

Is price always the most important consideration in buying or selling a business?

Not always. Sometimes the terms of purchase are far more important to the parties involved than the price. For example, the size of the down payment is often of critical importance to the purchaser. Many entrepreneurs are long on enthusiasm and willingness to work but short on cash. Their primary concern may be simply to get enough after-tax dollars to pay for the business. In fact, to get proper terms, a new entrepreneur should be willing to pay a premium for an established business.

Can you cite some examples of these terms?

Certainly. The seller might accept a relatively small amount down, with the remainder paid out of earnings over a time period long enough to allow a cushion for business fluctuations. Or the buyer might purchase the controlling share of a closely-held corporation and then purchase remaining shares over time.

In one recent deal I was involved with, the seller of a business was surprised to hear the buyer offer 20 percent more than the seller had asked. The buyer was willing to pay the premium in return for prorating payments gradually out of earnings. The seller was happy to close the deal because he was in no particular hurry for the money.

It may also be possible for an entrepreneur to purchase a company while employed by its present owner. If the buyer feels he has skills to more fully tap the company's potential, but he lacks purchasing capital, he might arrange to pay for the firm out of earnings increases he is able to generate while working there.

Since terms are of major importance in a purchase or sale, the prospective buyer should refrain from discussing price until the negotiations have nearly concluded. Too many times the first question asked is "What price do you want for your business?" when, in fact, the opening question should be, "What do you plan to do with the funds that you derive from selling your business?"

Once the buyer understands the seller's intentions, he is in a much better position to discuss terms of purchase. For example, if the seller intends to pay off his home mortgage and take a six-month vacation and then wants to live off interest income derived from selling his business, the buyer can calculate the total costs involved and offer a higher interest rate than the seller could get otherwise. Both parties close the deal amicably.

In other situations where the seller plans to reinvest only a part of the funds derived from selling out, terms can be developed where the cash portion of the payment is staggered to equal the reinvested amount. As I mentioned earlier, the terms of a buy-out may often be more important than the selling price.

In the final analysis, Mr. Sicorski, what is a business worth?

Its ability to produce future earnings.

Analysis: Why would an enterpreneur prefer to purchase an existing business rather than start his or her own?

To what extent is the worth of a business a function of the time value of money?

Besides the things mentioned by Mr. Sicorski, what other factors should the buyer of a business carefully consider?

nardis creations

38

In late 1980, Todd Dodge was at the helm of Nardis Creations, a small greeting-card company headquartered in Long Island, New York. Since 1977, Nardis Creations had been in the red, losing $250,000 in 1980 alone. Former CEO John Carrisi stepped down in April, 1980, to make room for Dodge who had been brought in by the Nardis family to turn the company around by 1982.

Dodge had a well-established reputation as a "turnaround artist," having revitalized two "dog" companies into "stars" in a six-year period. When brought on board Nardis Creations in the summer of 1980, he was given free reign to shake up the company as deemed necessary. The Nardis family wanted the firm to show a profit of $200,000 by the end of 1982, giving Dodge just twenty-four months in which to make the $450,000 turnaround. A lucrative profit-sharing contract was more than adequate motivation for Dodge, who fancied himself as a modern day "gunslinger."

The Nardis Product Line

Hallmark and American Greeting dominated the greeting-card industry. A host of smaller companies competed in the industry, doing business in the $3 million to $10 million range. Nardis, with sales of $5 million, specialized in Christmas cards and distributed a line of stationery and wrapping paper. It had also been experimenting with a gift line.

Nardis Christmas cards sold at the very top of the price range at $40 to $250 per 100 cards. All cards were tailor-made to meet customer specifications. Nardis offered 220 different covers, 187 greetings, 43 distinctive type styles, and 8 colors. Envelopes came in 8 separate colors and were either unlined or lined with gold or silver foil. In 1979 the average card order was $70 per customer.

Nardis added stationery, wrapping paper, and gifts to its line in order to give its sales representatives additional items to offer customers. The gift-wrapping line consisted of $15 and $25 packages containing paper, appliques, and ribbon. Since its introduction in 1975, wrapping sales had been minimal.

The stationery line consisted of twenty-five items ranging in price from $14 to $25 for twenty-five personalized sheets, twenty-five plain sheets, and twenty-five envelopes. Stationery sales volume was about 25 percent of that for cards, but the average stationery order was for only $17 versus $70 for cards. Over the past fourteen months, a rather sizable inventory of discontinued stationery styles had accumulated.

The Nardis line of gifts, initiated in 1977, included jewelry, silver, crystal, and luggage. All pieces were manufactured by prestige companies such as Cartier and St. Croix. Introduced with considerable fanfare and a splashy $50,000 catalog, the gift line enjoyed little financial success. Since 1977, orders have been on a 5 percent annual decline despite a growing per order average. Exhibits 38-1 and 38-2 summarize 1980 sales by product line and greeting-card category.

Operations Problems

Todd Dodge saw a number of internal problem points plaguing Nardis, including cash flow, composition of the card line, sales-force inadequacies, and a disturbing auditing report.

The company's cash-flow problems centered around the burgeoning inventory of stationery, an accumulation of receivables, and difficulties associated with financing finished-goods inventory. Most greeting card customers did not want to take delivery until after Labor Day. Nardis therefore had to keep a sizable quantity of inventory sitting idle during much of the year in anticipation of shipping. Dodge was concerned over poor sales for three entries in the firm's Christmas card line: Old Masters, scenic, and quotations and poems. He was also concerned with the mismatch between the product offering and sales.

The responsibility for designing and marketing cards lay with Jeremy Blake, a 25-year employee of Nardis. When asked by Dodge to state his marketing philosophy, Blake responded that his foremost goal was maintaining the company's 40-year tradition of offering a complete catalog of holiday greetings cards.

Dodge was alarmed over Nardis' nondynamic sales force consisting largely of widowed women over sixty who sold cards strictly on a part-time basis. Although the top representative sold more than $40,000 worth of merchandise annually, the vast majority of the 1,500 representatives sold less than $3,000 per year.

Henry Gladstone, sixty-three years of age, headed-up the sales force. He was responsible for recruiting, determining territories, and training. Since health problems prevented him from traveling, he dealt with the sales force primarily by letter and telephone. Although Gladstone expressed concern over the lackluster performance of much of his sales force, he praised their loyalty and professionalism.

One other "red flag" worrying Dodge was a critical auditing report just issued by Nardis' auditor. The report, excerpted in Exhibit 38-3, questioned a number of the company's current financial and managerial practices.

Working during the Christmas holiday of 1980, Todd Dodge prepared his turnaround plan for 1981 and 1982. He knew he was faced with a formidable challenge but resolved that he would successfully revive Nardis Creations. He had rescued other sinking ships and was not about to lose this one. His reputation was on the line.

Analysis: Develop the 1981 and 1982 turnaround plan for Nardis Creations. Recommend action priorities for the company, implementation guidelines, and organizational changes. Make your plan results-oriented, realistic, and timely.

What difficulties is Todd Dodge likely to encounter in implementing your turnaround plan? What advice would you offer him?

Is a "turnaround artist" a true entrepreneur?

EXHIBIT 38-1

1980 PRODUCT LINE ORDERS

	Cards	Stationery	Gifts	Totals
January	1,115	520	17	1,652
February	650	633	37	1,320
March	416	270	--	686
April	504	235	--	739
May	8,614	534	101	9,249
June	11,336	1,216	237	12,789
July	14,052	4,396	184	18,632
August	8,180	2,853	214	11,247
September	5,033	2,216	215	7,464
October	7,333	2,901	171	10,405
November	5,922	1,225	91	7,238
December	1,185	181	17	1,383
TOTALS	64,340	17,180	1,284	82,804

EXHIBIT 38-2

1980 GREETING CARD SALES

Card Category	Percent of Card in Total Line	Percent of Total Sales
Old Masters	5	10
Santa	15	20
Religious	35	25
Scenic	2.5	10
Lettering	20	15
Quotations and poems	2.5	5
Madonnas	20	15

EXHIBIT 38-3

EXCERPTS FROM NARDIS AUDITING REPORT

1. The financial reporting and accounting requires redesign to facilitate better management decision-making.
2. Internal accounting controls are very weak in the areas of cash, payrolls, and gift sales.
3. Cash-flow forecasting must be greatly improved.
4. Departmental managers request more input into the budgeting process and desire a more comprehensive annual performance review.
5. The processing of orders should be streamlined.
6. Duties and responsibilities of the controller, order entry supervisor, and warehouse supervisor must be clarified.
7. Communication between controller and accounting manager requires immediate improvement.
8. Monthly financial reports must be prepared on time.
9. Inventory controls are nonexistent and must be designed.

EXHIBIT 38-4

Nardis Creations

COMPARATIVE INCOME STATEMENT, 1978-1980

	1980	1979	1978
Net Sales	$4,839,700	$3,864,308	$3,493,858
Cost and Expenses			
Cost of sales and operating expenses	2,317,566	1,880,301	1,784,126
Selling expenses	1,935,880	1,545,723	1,397,543
General and administrative expenses	654,386	400,590	258,199
Interest expense	127,900	107,348	83,491
Total	5,035,732	3,933,962	3,523,359
NET INCOME BEFORE TAXES	($196,032)	($ 69,654)	($ 29,501)

EXHIBIT 38-5

Nardis Creations

COMPARATIVE BALANCE SHEET, 1978-1980

Assets	1980	1979	1978
Current Assets			
Cash	$ 12,257	$ 16,391	$ 296,157
Accounts receivable	245,085	230,867	197,522
Allowance for doubtful accounts	(35,000)	(25,000)	(20,000)
Inventory	758,061	635,711	429,182
Prepaid expenses	31,689	68,420	36,376
Total Current Assets	1,012,092	926,389	939,237
Property and Equipment			
Leasehold improvements	194,647	188,148	182,285
Machinery and equipment	346,376	340,205	234,323
Office furniture and fixtures	85,659	83,871	81,671
Transportation equipment	16,644	13,126	3,366
Total	643,326	625,350	501,645
Less accumulated depreciation	424,234	351,321	311,580
Total Property and Equipment	219,092	274,029	190,065
TOTAL ASSETS	$1,231,184	$1,200,418	$1,129,302

Liabilities	1980	1979	1978
Current Liabilities			
Notes payable to bank	$ 454,874	$ 428,304	$ 348,145
Accounts payable	367,374	313,056	279,667
Accrued liabilities (Salaries, wages, taxes, royalties, commissions)	354,318	277,258	257,290
Advances by customers	10,834	7,254	—
Total Current Liabilities	1,187,400	1,025,872	885,102
Long-term Liabilities	34,200	34,200	34,200
Total Liabilities	1,221,600	1,060,072	919,302
Stockholder's Equity	51,000	51,000	51,000
Net Earnings	(148,195)	47,837	117,491
Additional Paid-in Capital	106,779	41,509	41,509
Total Stockholder's Equity	9,584	140,346	210,000
TOTAL LIABILITIES AND EQUITY	$1,231,184	$1,200,418	$1,129,302

goodbuy grocery

39

"Goodbuy has a new lease on life and I'm going to take full advantage of it. Three months ago, it looked like we were out of business. Today we are blessed with a golden opportunity that can literally put us back on the map. If we play our cards right by making prudent decisions, the future will be much brighter than the past."

Roger Herrington, owner of Goodbuy Grocery, just received a check in the amount of $125,000 from his insurance company. A fire, judged to be accidental, had completely gutted Goodbuy three months earlier. After the usual insurance doubts and delays, Mr. Herrington was awarded the casualty claim. He immediately made plans to rebuild but was giving serious consideration to revamping Goodbuy's sales strategy as well as relocating at a new site in Canton.

In 1967, Herrington built Goodbuy in an older, residential area on Canton's east side. Managing the store with his son Lester, Herrington carved out a neighborhood niche. The store generated a fairly healthy income for the Herringtons from 1967 to 1976 but entered a period of sales deterioration in 1977 and continued to decline throughout 1978 and 1979. The ruinous fire in February of 1980 closed the store.

Comments Herrington, "The fire may have been a blessing in disguise. Kroger was the beginning of the end for Goodbuy. The handwriting was on the wall. With my insurance money, we can put Goodbuy back on the Canton map. A new location and marketing philosophy should give us the fresh start we need."

The No-Frills Store

"As I see it," Herrington observes, "the up-and-coming thing in Canton and across the nation is discount food retailing. More and more stores are switching to the no-frills approach and slashing their prices pretty much across the board."

Discount outlets, often referred to as food warehouses, offer a limited array of products, no shopping bags, and posted prices rather than prices marked on each individual item. Oftentimes products are displayed directly in open boxes. Discount stores typically employ only a skeleton crew, they advertise little and frequently dispense with all expensive food-maintenance equipment, such as refrigerated display cases. Consequently, fresh produce, dairy items, and perishables generally are not stocked. Many items are generically labeled.

In comparison with conventional supermarkets, no-frills stores require less floor space and operate on a much lower investment in fixtures. According to industry statistics, a typical 25,000-square foot conventional supermarket would require $800,000 in fixtures and inventory. A no-frills store would require only $50,000 to start and have one-third to one-half of the floorspace. The no-frills outlet would offer price discounts from 10 to 30 percent on most durable items, such as canned goods, sugar, and flour.

Mr. Herrington expresses unreserved support for the no-frills concept. "Judging from the success of Kroger's no-frills operation near Goodbuy's old site, today's food shopper is keenly conscious of price."

Kroger's Bi-Lo stores pursue a strategy of combining discount pricing with product quality. Kroger ads make the claim that "all Bi-Lo products are not only comparable but often superior to their famous name brand equivalents."

EXHIBIT 39-1

SUPERMARKET COMPETITION IN CANTON

	Houchens	Winn-Dixie	IGA	Kroger*
Number of Stores	2	1	3	2
Years in Canton	16	4	9	6
Average size of store (sq. ft.)	16,000	22,000	14,500	21,000
Location in city	Northwest Southwest	Northwest	Northwest South East	Northwest East
Approximate local market share	21	13	19	25

*Does not include Bi-Lo store

Supermarket Competition in Canton

According to Herrington, the chances of succeeding with a new no-frills store in Canton hinge on two factors: store location and competition. "Kroger has proven to me that the no-frills approach can work in Canton. I think they could have picked a much better location than they did, though. Canton's east side has quit growing. I should know, since I operated there for more than a decade. But their mistake is potentially my gain. There's no reason why I have to rebuild Goodbuy in the old location. I can relocate in the suburbs where all the growth is occurring.

"From the standpoint of local competition, the time is now ripe for opening another discount store. This is especially true for the suburbs, where no-frills competition is absent altogether."

Canton is presently serviced by four supermarkets: Houchens, Winn-Dixie, IGA, and Kroger. Exhibits 39-1 and 39-2 present competitive data about each.

EXHIBIT 39-2

PRICE COMPARISON OF CANTON SUPERMARKETS

	Houchens	Winn-Dixie	IGA	Kroger*
Cheerios (15 oz.)	.95	.95	.89	.98
Sugar (5 lb.)	1.09	1.13	1.09	1.13
Tuna fish (6.5 oz.)	.65	.59	.74	.59
Dog food (14.5 oz.)	.31	.29	.34	.29
Sliced peaches	2.8¢/oz	2.0¢/oz	2.6¢/oz	2.0¢/oz
Vegetable oil	3.7¢/oz	3.7¢/oz	4.2¢/oz	3.7¢/oz
Bar soap (5 oz)	.39	.39	.33	.39
Alka Seltzer	3.2¢/tab	5.8¢/tab	3.2¢/tab	5.8¢/tab
1 gallon whole milk	1.69	N/A	1.95	2.16
1 lb. butter	1.49	N/A	1.39	1.79

*Does not include Bi-Lo store

Exhibit 39-3 presents demographic data for Canton's four dominant residential areas: south, southwest, east, northwest.

A New Lease On Life?

"I have given considerable thought to opening another no-frills venture here in Canton. I've got the capital and experience to do it, and the present competitive situation is giving me the green light. Furthermore," Herrington points out, "I've got a definite competitive strategy in mind.

EXHIBIT 39-3

1980 DEMOGRAPHIC DATA FOR CANTON

(by residential area)

	South	Southwest	East	Northwest
Average home as percent of Canton mean value:	88%	91%	53%	115%
Population as percent of total Canton population	22%	24%	34%	20%
Percent minority group	19%	9%	41%	0%
Percent over 62 years	7%	17%	35%	12%
Percent under 18 years	41%	40%	28%	42%
Annual population growth-rate (1975-1980)	7%	11%	-5%	21%

"I plan to locate in the affluent, mushrooming northwest side with 16,000 square feet. I'll be open seven days a week, sixteen hours a day. We'll carry around six hundred non-perishable items displayed in cut-off boxes, and some refrigerated items. National brands will be carried for some items, as well as regional and private labels. Thirty to forty percent of the canned goods and staples will feature generic labeling only.

"Although the new store definitely will be no-frills, I plan to carry some shopping bags and will allow customers to write checks on local accounts. In my advertising I don't want the store to develop a cheap image, so these services should help.

"My projected earnings look decent enough, particularly in comparison with what they were at the old Goodbuy Grocery. With my son and I doing most of the work, I don't see how the store could fail. Like I said before, it's a new lease on life for us!"

Analysis: Critique Mr. Herrington's transition strategy for Goodbuy. Do you agree with the proposed switch to no-frills merchandising? With the relocation decision? What other promising transition strategies are available to Herrington?

In what ways could Herrington benefit from marketing research before finalizing his transition plans? Suggest guidelines for him to follow in conducting the research.

If Goodbuy does reopen as a no-frills store in Canton, recommend an advertising strategy for Herrington to follow. Be specific.

EXHIBIT 39-4

PRO FORMA STATEMENTS

Projected weekly sales	$30,000	
Cost of Sales	$26,250	
Gross Profit		$3,750
Miscellaneous Income		$ 27
Total Income before Expenses		$3,777
Expenses		
Wages (checkers, stock clerks)	$ 500	
Payroll taxes (checkers, stock clerks	$ 47	
Wages (owner, manager)	$ 400	
Payroll taxes (owner, manager)	$ 25	
Workmen's compensation, group medical	$ 297	
Buying Service Charge	$ 660	
Drayage (trucking charges)	$ 450	
Advertising	$ 50	
Rent	$ 300	
Licenses & Taxes	$ 4	
Insurance	$ 52	
Accounting	$ 30	
Depreciation	$ 77	
Interest	$ 89	
Total Expenses		$2,981
Net Profit before Income Tax		$ 796
Provision for federal & state income tax		$ 255
NET PROFIT		$ 541

EXPERIENCE PHASE IV
the entrepreneurial lifestyle

an entrepreneur's diary

40

Stephen Tanner owns and operates a car-rental agency in Reno, Nevada (RenoRental) and is part-owner of a theater chain in Nevada and Utah (Innertainment Corporation). He has been self-employed since graduating from college in 1957 and conservatively estimates his personal net worth at well over $3 million.

Mr. Tanner describes himself as hard-working, success-motivated, and eternally optimistic. Forty-three years old, he plans to sell out all business interests within seven years and pursue "a life of leisure." He is married and has three teen-age children.

During the month of February, Mr. Tanner agreed to keep a diary of his daily business experiences. At the close of each day, he highlighted his activities and provided personal impressions.

February 2 (Monday)

"Attended three problem-solving meetings today for RenoRental. Met with Dyer and Kennerman [operations manager and controller] to go over the bank's tightened credit line and determine monthly cash needs. The bank is getting awfully tight-fisted. They blame it on the Fed's anti-inflation campaign.

"Met with Ted Aurno [representative for General Motors] to go over possibilities for getting more small car rentals—especially Citation and Chevette. No dice. They're already behind on dealer orders. We'll have to stick with Malibus and the old Chevettes.

"Ate lunch with Lennie [Leonard Stouffer, maintenance supervisor] and authorized the new vacuum. Made a note to order 50 new cases of oil."

February 3 (Tuesday)

"Got a call from a Mr. Brad Rangier who wanted to discuss possibilities of using RenoRental automobiles to host the Miss Reno beauty pageant in April. Sounded promising to me as long as we could get RenoRental's name in print a few times during the pageant. They'd have to supply the chauffeurs though, because we simply don't have the available manpower.

"Spent most of the afternoon helping up front [in the rental agency office] dealing with customers. Diane was sick today."

February 4 (Wednesday)

"Drove to Provo for tomorrow's Board meeting with Innertainment. Motel didn't have my reservation when I got there. Waited ninety minutes until I could get a no-show's room.

"Had dinner with Aaron [Aaron Lange, majority owner of Innertainment] and went over the Palmer Mall option [a six-month option to reserve space for a new theater in Salt Lake City's Palmer shopping mall, projected for construction completion in 1984]. Aaron thinks we should not exercise the option yet. By delaying, we'll have time to run a market study on the mall site to determine if it wouldn't be smarter to locate the theater a quarter of a mile away on cheaper land. We also need to decide whether to go with two screens or four."

February 5 (Thursday)

"Had an unusually long Board meeting. Stayed past supper (another free meal!), cancelling plans to make it back to Reno today. Just as well, because that's some long trek.

"Tovar and Hines [Board members] thought we shouldn't waste the Palmer option. It'll be the largest mall in Salt Lake and supposedly a prime retail drawing-card. Aaron reminded them of the sky-high rental but agreed that Innertainment didn't want to give away the theater rights to GC [General Cinema] or a local yokel.

"I had to agree with Tovar and Hines and encouraged Aaron to exercise the option. I imagine he will, although he was still noncommittal when we closed the meeting."

February 6 (Friday)

"Aaron twisted my arm (!) and convinced me to stay over for a long weekend of skiing. I flew Joanne [Tanner's wife] down, leaving the kids with the Paines [the Tanner's neighbors]. The IRS can treat me to a mini vacation!"

February 9 (Monday)

"A day for brushfires! Had a rental car stolen and dumped in Carson City. It was stripped and virtually a total loss. Spent over two hours on the phone dealing with the police and the insurance guy.

"Spent the better part of the afternoon helping Rick Kennerman trace down a couple of hot-check writers and trying to collect a raft of late receivables from steady corporate customers. Hate to cut them off, but what can you do when they don't pay up?

"Finally got home about 8:25 p.m. A long day for sure!"

February 10 (Tuesday)

"Spent most of the day researching the possibilities of adding single-engine airplanes to our rental fleet. Talked to Vegas Air Service at the airport and learned they would be willing to throw customers my way in return for a piece of the action. The owner of Vegas, Hal Gholson, offered to form a fifty-fifty partnership with me. He's got the planes; I've got the local reputation plus personnel.

"Plan to defer a definite decision until I can look into all of the insurance angles. What would happen if a client were to crash, and so forth?

"The deal does appear to have the smell of money."

February 11 (Wednesday)

"Met with Hank Sylvester [manager of Reno's three Innertainment theaters] in the morning to look at his P&L for December and January. Looks like it's time to raise ticket prices again. The concession prices are about as high as we can go with them.

"Reno's not exactly your typical town—not even a typical tourist stop. The theaters are open all night long, just like the casinos. Getting someone to sell hot buttered popcorn at 3:00 A.M. is easier said than done!

"Got a letter from the mayor's civic committee, asking me to serve on Reno's Tourism Committee. I'm flattered, of course. Talk about a goldmine for business contacts!"

February 12 (Thursday)

"Mostly routine paperwork today—cooped-up in the darn office all day. Signed umpteen insurance forms; authorized the payroll; signed a slew of checks; wrote letters to four prospective rental clients who recently made the Reno scene; sent off my resume to the Tourism Committee; approved several maintenance expenditures.

"I sure am tired. I wonder why, since I haven't accomplished anything of substance all day."

February 13 (Friday)

"The month is flying by. Had coffee with Gholson again today and moved a step closer to firming up some kind of a deal to rent airplanes. I really would like to be the controlling partner from a decision-making point of view, but my knowledge of the air rental market is awfully sketchy.

"Ordered a WATS line today for my calls to Vegas, Provo, and Salt Lake. Kennerman wasn't overly enthusiastic about it, but accountants are like that. Got to spend some money in the short-run to save some over the long-run.

"Had to fire two of our maintenance people today for releasing cars which hadn't been cleaned or checked-out mechanically. Claim they forgot, but it happened to them twice before this month."

February 14 (Saturday)

"Went to the office early (5:30 A.M.) to finish up some loose ends. Met Stu Lambert and two lawyer friends at the golf course at 11:30 for a fast nine holes. To show you how bad they played, I came back $35 richer. Doesn't happen often!

"Went back to the office and helped with customers for a few hours. Almost cleared the lot of cars. Saturdays are something else in Reno."

February 16 (Monday)

"Thought I'd start the week out right by using our new WATS line to drum up some business. Called nine travel agencies in Utah and southern California and made them a pitch about our hourly rental rates. Lots of tourists stay in the Reno airport for a few hours between flights with nothing in particular to do. Why not rent them a car for an hour or two so they can make the casino scene? All but two of the agents said they would mention the service to stop-over clients.

"Gholson must really be serious about wanting the partnership. He dropped by today and offered me free flying lessons! It would be nice not to have to drive any more to Provo for the Innertainment meetings.

"Interviewed three people to replace the two maintenance guys canned last week. Wasn't overly impressed with their looks, but for $5.65 an hour, what can you honestly expect?

"Took a long lunch-hour to attend the first Tourism Committee meeting. Turned out to be more stimulating than anticipated. Made the 10:00 news."

February 17 (Tuesday)

"Devoted the morning to a skull session with Carl Dyer. Had to cull out a number of automobiles from the rental fleet that had outlived their usefulness. Sold them to a local used lot for about 70 percent off original list. Not a bad deal for either of us really.

"Spent the remainder of the day negotiating a new floor-financing loan with GMAC [General Motors Acceptance Corporation]. Got to get some new cars in soon."

February 18 (Wednesday)

"Drove to the U. of Nevada–Las Vegas campus today to guest lecture in a couple of classes. Things have certainly changed a lot since I went to school there. The kids are all smarter, and I'm hopelessly older!"

February 19 (Thursday)

"Tough day today. We got held up. Can you believe it? In broad daylight no less. Some guy doing the ski mask routine hit the small downtown office and made off with $1200. Too bad for him credit card receipts aren't spendable, because we had a lot more than $1200 in them on hand.

"Fortunately my employees cooperated in every way, so no one got hurt.

"Pretty much blew the whole day on this mess. What will take longer, the police reports or the insurance paperwork?"

February 20 (Friday)

"It was the insurance paperwork that took up the most time after the robbery. We'll get our money back though. Police haven't caught the guy yet, however.

"Radio Shack delivered the mini-computer today that we ordered in January. Found a nice spot for it in Dyer's office; he'll be the main person using it. Should really be a boost to our budget-control and inventory-planning. Keeping track of 345 cars takes time!

"Got a call in the afternoon from Metro Marketing [RenoRental's advertising agency]. Will visit with them next week to plan our spring and summer media campaign. Watch out Avis and Hertz!"

February 21 (Saturday)

"Couldn't manage to leave the office any earlier than 5:00 today. Had to get with Dyer to work up some pro formas for the banker. We need a $35,000 three-month loan for financing replacement tires for the fleet. Thank goodness GMAC will finance our rolling stock inventory. No way we could pay the bank's high rates for a loan that large.

"Also made an appointment to talk with Goodrich's rep on Thursday. They really seem to want our business."

February 23 (Monday)

"Drove down to Las Vegas Sunday night for the travel agency convention today. Spent the entire day drumming up new business and making contacts. Ate breakfast twice and lunch three times. I've got this wining and dining down to an art!

"Drove back to Reno at 7:30 P.M. and didn't get home until mighty late."

February 24 (Tuesday)

"Spent the day with Dolph Artis [owner of Metro Marketing] going over our new ad campaign for the warm season. We decided to stick with the same basic theme—'RenoRental is your auto rental alternative'—but to put more of a spotlight on our nonauto rentals. Looks like I definitely may want to cement the airplane deal."

February 25 (Wednesday)

"Had a productive day. Bought out the two Scott theaters in downtown Reno, which Innertainment had been after for five years. Got a good enough price to make our remodeling plans cost-effective. We plan to convert the two old screens into four new ones. Appears to be a good downtown market—especially for revival runs [reshowing of old classic films].

"Also got our bank loan okayed for tire financing. Will put me in a good bargaining position with Goodrich tomorrow."

February 26 (Thursday)

"Closed the Goodrich deal in less than an hour. Decided to go with polyglass instead of steel radials. Saved a bundle.

"Worked with Carl [Dyer] on getting the fleet computerized. Not nearly as much of a hassle as I anticipated."

February 27 (Friday)

"Had a slight cold today, so I stayed home and caught up on some of my reading."

February 28 (Saturday)

"Still under the weather, but had to sign checks at the office. Also worked on a revised fringe-benefit plan for our employees.

"Another month has flown by! I think my business interests are all better off than they were in January. Got a long way to go though."

Analysis: Describe Stephen Tanner's professional lifestyle: how he spends most of his time, his apparent priorities, his problems, his satisfactions, and so on. Is he an entrepreneur?

Why do you think Mr. Tanner continues to work so hard despite being a millionaire?

What do his diary entries indicate about the realities of small business management? What managerial skills are illustrated in the diary entries?

new generation software, inc.

41

New Generation Software, Inc. of Aberdeen, South Dakota, manufactures and distributes software packages for computer systems and a variety of data-processing paper supplies, including printer paper, coding forms, and keypunch-machine ribbons. The company was started in 1975 by Harris Monahan, a black entrepreneur who grew up in East St. Louis, Illinois. In the following interview, Mr. Monahan traces the growth of New Generation Software and assesses his experience as a minority entrepreneur.

Harris, would you please give us an overview description of your company?

I'm proud to say that we're entering our fifth profitable year of operations and it seems certain that we'll go over $500,000 in sales this year. New Generation is a leading producer of EDP software and paper products. We're especially well-known nationally for our software systems relating to medical accounting. More doctor's offices use our software for bookkeeping purposes than all of the other competitive packages put together. New Generation is also a major manufacturer of ink ribbons used in keypunch machines.

We have one production facility located here in Aberdeen. We employ approximately thirty-four people in the plant and use manufacturer's reps for our sales force. I am president and head of R&D.

Fill us in on your personal background.

I grew up in Illinois in East St. Louis, where my father was an entrepreneur of sorts. He operated a small grocery store with my mother and also managed a small piece of land for a farmer. I grew up helping out in the store learning the ABCs of business from my parents.

I attended a college in St. Louis majoring in engineering but quit mid-way through to work for an audio-visual firm. My father had passed away, so I had to lay out of school to assist my mother in selling the grocery store. Before I knew it, I was married and looking for a better paying job. This was in 1973. My education was just going to have to wait.

I signed on with Xerox as a sales rep and was transferred to Rapid City, South Dakota. I worked there for two years or so learning a lot about technical products and marketing.

In late 1974, I got wind of a deal through a client I called on regularly in Rapid City. He knew of a paper-processing plant up in Aberdeen that was going under and about to be liquidated. The owner wanted $139,000 for the plant, lock-stock-and-barrel.

My client, whose name was Rollin Davids, asked me if I knew anything about computer products and if I would be interested in helping him launch a new venture relating to EDP services. It just so happened that I had been taking computer courses in night school and had some ideas for developing software material.

Well, things began to gel and before I knew it, Rollin and I purchased the Aberdeen facility for just $88,500. We struck a mutually beneficial deal with the former owner where he would keep some of the paper-processing equipment and leave us the rest with the building. I personally invested $52,000 in equity, using some money I had saved and borrowing some from my mother's savings.

Rollin, who is also black, and I began New Generation Software in May of 1975, manufacturing paper for computer printers and ribbons for keypunch equipment. As time went on, we successfully developed over a dozen software packages pertaining to medical bookkeeping. Thus we have been able to attain a blend of manufacturing and R&D work in our company.

Rollin sold out his interest to me in February 1980, so I am currently the sole owner of New Generation. He still stays in close touch with the business, however, and throws a lot of new customers our way.

Harris, how conscious are you of being a minority entrepreneur?

This may sound odd, but the only time I'm really conscious of my racial background is when others bring it up. I consider myself a businessman competing in the market with a useful product. Certainly I'm proud of my black heritage, but my business is really no different from any other.

To what extent do you strive to do business with other minority-owned companies?

It's tough to find many minority-owned firms that purchase EDP products. Most of my sales come from the majority community. I do go out of my way, however, to purchase raw material supplies from minority firms.

To what extent have you relied upon government assistance in your growth?

As little as possible. Certainly no more than any other small business. I've had a couple of SBA loans and a few governmental agencies for customers, but that's the extent of it. What people hear about government assistance for minority business is mostly myth. Lucrative government ties are very difficult to come by and most of the time not worth the extraordinary hassle involved.

I'm firmly convinced that most small companies, minority or majority, would be much better off spending their time seeking out private sector rather than public sector business. So much time and paperwork is involved with public sector stuff, not to mention uncertainty and unpredictability. The government can help minority firms out basically in the same way it can help out majority firms: cut taxes and regulations and control inflation.

Do you feel minority firms face any unique problems or challenges?

Oh sure, there's no getting around the realities of occasional racial discrimination. But I would again mention that the key to any business is the bottom line. Minority businessmen face all of the same operating problems as anyone else. It takes a good product or service backed up by skilled management to run any business. That's where the real challenge always is.

I guess the primary race-related problem faced by minority companies is how we are perceived by white customers and clients. Fortunately, the days of blatant discrimination are mostly history. However, a sensitivity to affirmative-action mandates does exist.

By that I mean that many majority-owned companies have the feeling that we have sought them out solely on the hope that they would want to play ball with a minority company. In other words, some white business people believe that black firms want special treatment. That notion is nearly always erroneous.

New Generation Software hustles business aggressively all of the time. We don't expect to be treated differently because of race. We want our products to be the focus of attention. I'm sure most other black entrepreneurs feel the same way.

Sometimes a funny thing happens because of our society's obsession with affirmative-action statistics. Occasionally one of our customers who does not know me personally will learn that New Generation is minority owned. They will then become disgruntled because they weren't able to report their deal with us as being supportive of an affirmative-action effort. To us, it was simply a straight business proposition. It would have been to them too, except for the federal government!

If you were to start New Generation Software over again, what would you do differently?

I would prepare myself more diligently. I would gain more financial expertise, read up more on management techniques, and develop a detailed business plan to help launch the business.

I also would control the company's growth better, slowing it down somewhat. I would have sought-out more outside advice and consultation—especially from other entrepreneurs who had traveled down the same road before me.

What advice would you pass on to other minority-group individuals about to launch a new venture?

First, I would advise them to start out working for some other company in the industry they would like to operate in. Learn the tricks of the trade and become familiar with the terrain while you're getting paid for it.

Secondly, I would strongly recommend getting a good formal education. Unlike me, finish school and soak up as much general knowledge as possible.

Third, don't expect others to do you special favors—especially the government. It's hard to overcome the temptation to depend on government loans and contracts. Just remember that over the long run, you will have to make it on your own.

Finally, and most importantly, I would advise minority entrepreneurs to remember that, first and foremost, they are businessmen not blacks or whatever. They should be proud of their heritage but also proud of their managerial ability. Business people of any race or color who can't make a profit are ultimately a drain on society.

Analysis: Do you feel Harris Monahan's views are typical of other black business owners? Do any of his statements surprise you?

In what ways has the federal government sought to promote minority capitalism? What else do you feel should be done in this regard?

In what ways can the white business community lend support to minority firms?

mcgowan realty

42

Meredith McGowan, majority partner of McGowan Realty in Pensacola, Florida, has been one of the nation's top-producing realtors since 1973. In that year, she was Pensacola's "Rookie of the Year" real-estate award-winner. In subsequent years she has won numerous other performance and civic awards. Meredith is a graduate of the Realtor's Institute and is a Certified Residential Specialist. She has been married seventeen years and has four children.

Meredith, tell us a little about your company McGowan Realty.

In 1973 and 1974, I worked for Milam Real Estate here in Pensacola learning my way around in the profession. I quickly established my reputation in town and began to develop a client following. My income in 1974 was just under $37,000—not bad for a gal with no college, and with previous business experience only in waiting tables and driving a rural school bus.

Although I very much enjoyed working with the folks at Milam, I really wasn't all that thrilled with turning over half of my commissions to the agency. So, with my husband's encouragement, I left Milam and worked for a year in a small partnership.

That got old quick, because I sorely missed the staff support provided by an agency—an office, telephone, Xerox machine, and so forth. I was having to work out of my house. That was no way to succeed. It kept interfering with my family's home life, and they made things a lot more hectic for me.

It finally became obvious that I needed to set up an office away from home where I could do my own thing without causing family problems. Given my distaste for sharing commissions, my only real option was to start my own agency. So I did. I already was licensed and had selling experience.

I rented and renovated an old office near Pensacola's fastest growing residential area and hired-away two other top performing gals from Milam. We had always liked one another and knew how to work together. We formed a three-way partnership with me taking the lead. This was in September of 1976.

Since then, the agency has added a dozen more reps and three full-time staff people. We're the third largest agency in Pensacola and rising fast. Our reps are highly productive and make better than average money. We have a successful operation because we're customer-oriented, knowledgeable, professional—and darn hard working.

What roles do you and your two partners have in the agency?

They manage and I sell. Both Marjorie and June like to manage. They handle the administrative paperwork, coordinate our sales force, and stay in touch with the accountant. They both still find time to do some selling, but it's not their main thrust.

As for me, I like to put maximum distance between me and the management routine. Don't get me wrong; I appreciate what Marjorie and June do, but I'm motivated by selling and meeting new people. I was born in June and I guess I'm a typical Gemini—I like people and a fast pace.

I think I set a good example for our other sales agents. They respect me because I perform, and I can help them troubleshoot problems because I'm a fellow agent. We work together well in the agency because everyone pretty-much gets to do what they enjoy most and are successful at. We're all working so hard that we don't have much time to create internal problems.

Tell us what a typical day is like for you, Meredith.

In my business, there's no such thing as a typical day. If variety is the spice of life, then I lead a very spicy existence!

My job revolves around people. I meet at least two or three people every day. Every time I strike up a new relationship, my professional reputation is on the line. After all, the only thing I have to sell is service—my knowledge of real estate and my professionalism. In the final analysis, results are all that count. If a realtor can't produce, she can't do anything.

Selling real estate is hardly an 8:00 to 5:00 job with Saturday and Sunday off. No matter what I'm doing, it seems like I always end up taking care of some business. If I go to the beauty shop, I usually wind up talking real estate with someone. Same thing at church and even the grocery store. I make a point never to bring it up outside the office, but people I meet always want to talk real estate. I'm generally more than happy to oblige them!

I work seven days a week averaging eight to fourteen hours a day except for Sundays. On Sunday I work in the afternoon after church.

Could you work less if you wanted to?

Somewhat; but people who think real estate can be done part-time are just fooling themselves. In order to win the confidence of clients, I have to exert myself to the fullest. And that takes time. I have to look at houses, get to know my clients personally, keep up with new legislation, and stay in reasonably close touch with my partners and the agency. You can't do all this on just a few hours a day.

You know, success does indeed breed success. The more buyers and sellers I come through for, the more people call on me for my services. I can hardly turn away new business when it's brought to me practically on a silver platter. So, I stay busy. But I wouldn't have it any other way, at least for the time being.

Meredith, what are the primary joys and frustrations of your job?

People. I can't think of a more people-oriented career than mine. So, naturally, people make up both the high points and low points of my work. Let me give you an example of a low point.

One time I had this little couple who had three preschoolers. We had been out all day in the hot summer looking at homes. We must have looked at every listing in Pensacola twice! But nothing was good enough. So we called it a day and started back to the office. I stopped by a place and got snowcones for the kids. Before I knew what hit me, one kid deliberately dumped his down my back while I'm driving. Did I belt him like I would have my own kid? Hardly, I just had to stay cool, which wasn't easy to do even with the ice down my back!

But most of the time I enjoy my contacts with people and get a real "charge" out of helping them. Buying or selling a house can be a traumatic experience for many people, especially when they're being uprooted in the process. Knowing that I can be of help to them is a gratifying part of my job—and of my life.

Other things I don't particularly love about my job revolve around managing the agency. Even though my partners carry the load here, I still have to get involved in more ways than I care to. Things like committee meetings, paying bills, tax decisions. They're no fun, but they come with the territory. You just have to learn to take the bad along with the good.

I guess one other joy I would mention involves the constant feeling of accomplishment. To put it indelicately, I love to "score" on the job—to successfully buy and sell homes for my clients. There's no doubt about when you've done your job: a customer smiles, a contract is signed, and a commission is made. You've scored a touchdown.

You've made it no secret that you dislike management work. Why is this, Meredith?

It's not so much that I dislike management, it's just that I like to let others do it! Seriously, though, I've asked myself the same question more than once. I guess the reason is that, in my profession, managing gets in the way of performing—scoring touchdowns as I said before. The more time I spend pouring over budgets, making personnel decisions, and so forth, the less time I have for buying and selling homes. That's the way I look at it.

Selling and meeting people is what I enjoy and excel at. It would be a disservice to the agency to stick me behind a desk. Even though the agency does carry my name, there's no reason I have to be the most active manager. Let me represent the agency out in the field.

What impact does your job have on your family life?

Plenty, but we've managed to handle it okay. My husband and four kids have backed my career all the way and therefore deserve most of the credit for whatever success I've attained. They put up with my long hours and fragmented schedule. They answer the phone for me and take messages at least a dozen times daily. They really are jewels.

My husband is a warehouse superintendent. Fortunately, he has a steady, predictable schedule and is able to be here every evening and on weekends. He's the source of stability every family has to have.

My kids are proud of my success and wouldn't have my life any other way. Although I must admit that problems do occasionally arise. Like the time I missed my oldest daughter's junior-high graduation because I was closing a deal. That definitely hurt her feelings.

Is your job a stressful one, Meredith?

Much of the time it is. I think I've adjusted to the stress pretty well, but nonetheless it is there. I'm under stress simply because my clients are under stress when they need my services.

People hardly ever buy or sell a home under relaxed circumstances. Most of the time they're under pressure to make the transition. Maybe a relative just died, and the house has to be disposed of. Or maybe the husband has been transferred suddenly, and he needs to get out from under two house payments. The emotions run high, and I'm right in the middle trying to make things work out.

Besides this constant pressure to perform, there's the stress that comes from a work schedule ruled by interruptions. The phone rings for me at the office and at home all day and night. You hardly sit down to dinner but what some hot prospect is in town for a few hours and needs your services immediately.

Also, there's the pressure from my agency affiliation. Meetings to attend, the banker to wine and dine, occasional personnel squabbles. My two managing partners certainly can't handle everything by themselves.

Don't let me create an overly pessimistic picture in my comments. Without some stress, I'm afraid my job would stagnate and become boring. Also, some stress is necessary if I'm to perform up to my fullest potential. I don't view stress as my friend, but it certainly isn't my arch enemy either.

Why have you been so successful in your job?

Hard work, discipline, family support, love of meeting people, and perseverance. Also some luck and good breaks. You know, it's only in retrospect that I notice myself having attained some measure of success. I've never really thought of myself as anything other than a hard-working gal—certainly not as a success story. I've always been too wrapped-up in my daily activities to think about establishing some sort of a glamorous track record. My career and job are constantly being renewed and revitalized. What I've done in the past hasn't been in my consciousness much. To me, success has always been one step ahead in the future. I'm constantly working toward it rather than contemplating having attained it.

What are your long-term goals?

To retire with my husband within six years. The nest will be empty then and Joel and I can start a new life. We'd both love to travel extensively and have a lot of time to ourselves. We've paid our dues.

What advice do you have to offer others who would like to launch a business of their own?

Work hard. Be supremely committed and dedicated to excellence. Set attainable goals that stretch you just a bit. View money strictly as a by-product of excellent performance, not as the reason to perform. Uphold honesty and integrity at all times. Learn how to like people for who they are not just for what they can do for you. Don't take yourself too seriously. Do your own thing in your own way.

Analysis: In what ways does Meredith McGowan fit the profile of a typical entrepreneur?

Is her lifestyle representative of other entrepreneurs?

Are you surprised at all by her long-term goal?

Would you trade places with her professionally?

the keys to entrepreneurial success: a roundtable discussion

43

In December 1980, four business professionals collaborated for a roundtable discussion centering on the keys to entrepreneurial success. Participating were: Coy Hamphill, a small business consultant from Chicago; Erik Sawyer, a new venture banker from Miami; Gloria Cisneros, who manages a public accounting firm in New Orleans; and Orson McCord, a venture capitalist from New York City.

The panel addressed itself to four questions:

1. What are the most common mistakes made by entrepreneurs and small business managers?
2. What is the profile of a successful entrepreneur?
3. What are the most difficult problems and challenges faced by entrepreneurs and small business owners today?
4. What advice would you offer to someone seriously contemplating starting a new business?

Coy Hamphill describes himself as a self-made millionaire who thrives on assisting others in accomplishing the same feat. He developed one of Chicago's largest warehousing cooperatives during the 1960s, selling out in 1968. Since that time he has operated his own consulting firm, Midwest Ventures, specializing in consulting support to new retail ventures.

Erik Sawyer heads up a prospering bank in Miami which caters to new and small businesses. He previously owned and operated an import firm, with manufacturing facilities in Haiti, which was expropriated by the Haitian government in 1972. He holds a doctorate in liberal arts from Emory University.

Gloria Cisneros is managing partner of Cisneros Public Accounting in San Diego. Since opening as a limited bookkeeping service in 1974, the firm has grown into one of the largest independently operated public accounting offices in California. Ms. Cisneros is also part-owner of three other local companies and on the boards of four firms. Born in Mexico City, she is a naturalized American citizen.

Orson McCord is senior partner of McCord, Alexander, and Purcell, a venture-capital partnership in New York City. He received his C.P.A. in 1962 and worked for twelve years in an investment brokerage firm. In 1975, he formed his present venture-capital firm which caters to high-technology products.

What are the most common mistakes made by entrepreneurs and small business managers?

Coy Hamphill—I suppose the most common mistake I've personally observed involves the entrepreneur who gets so wrapped-up in the new-venture idea that he doesn't adequately investigate the very real start-up problems soon to be faced: cash-flow paralysis, partner hassles, and things like that. I've found that too many entrepreneurs fail to have contingency funds on hand during the first year of operation to use in overcoming unforeseen problems and emergencies. They make the mistake of planning for the first year as though it were something stable and routine. Nothing could be further from the truth.

Erik Sawyer—There are a couple of blunders that I see commonly repeated from my vantage point as a banker for new ventures. One I will term the tunnel vision syndrome. Entrepreneurs typically have single vision—their attention is focused on the new-venture idea to the exclusion of practically everything else. In their single-mindedness, they overlook the essential support mechanisms of business, money in particular. They act as though funding will automatically flow in just as sure as tomorrow morning's sunrise.

The second recurring mistake is insensitivity to people. Entrepreneurs are notorious for being impatient and hard-driving, and my banking experience bears this out. In their haste to make things work out right, entrepreneurs frequently chew up a lot of people, including their own families sometimes. Entrepreneurs tend to be autocratic managers, poor listeners, and always on the move. The potential for people problems is obviously high.

Gloria Cisneros—I must echo the finance theme. New ventures that are undercapitalized are almost doomed to failure. The reason for this is fundamental; the more you're under financed, the fewer mistakes you can get away with. Thus, only superbly-managed firms can readily overcome patchy financing.

I guess one other mistake I see frequently involves poor business location. Many entrepreneurs give only scant consideration to where they open up, only to later discover many better-suited locations. By then the investment is already sunk and irretrievable. Also, many entrepreneurs never consider opening their venture in another city altogether. Every community has a need for certain types of businesses—especially mundane ones—but these businesses are not always evenly distributed geographically.

Orson McCord—I concur that undercapitalization is the most common shortcoming of new ventures. The entrepreneur fashions an elaborate, detailed business plan and subsequently fails to obtain all of the financing the plan calls for. What does he do? He attempts to implement the plan as originally put together but with less capital than anticipated. Pretty soon the entrepreneur is having to cut corners to hold the plan together. Before much longer, it begins to fall through completely.

One other mistake my partners and I often see involves the entrepreneur who has not developed his or her business plan to the fullest. An incomplete planning document is an obvious red flag for a venture capitalist.

What is the profile of a successful entrepreneur?

Coy Hamphill—That's mighty tough to distill into a brief summary, but I'll give it a try. Most successful entrepreneurs I know have a seemingly boundless store of energy, drive, and determination. They work hard and show results for it. Successful entrepreneurs have to be generalists capable of dabbling in all phases of their business. This is especially true in dealing with external technical consultants such as lawyers and accountants. Consultants too easily get off track if you can't follow what they're doing.

To be successful, it is essential to be a good judge of character. Entrepreneurs deal with so many key people who must be trustworthy. Success also hinges on being able to define and solve problems efficiently by cutting through all the garbage. Finally, I too would mention that successful entrepreneurs know how to work with other people. If you're dependent on others, you certainly had better be able to work with them daily.

Erik Sawyer—I have spent a great deal of time pondering the question of what makes one entrepreneur a success and another a failure. Certainly there is no simplistic answer to such a tough question; if there were, I'd be the best loan maker that ever graced a financial institution!

There is one thing, however, that I've observed of every successful business owner I know, and that is perseverance. Successful people in all walks of life are consumed with what they're doing—totally committed and dedicated. This is frequently the only thing that keeps them going and rebounding from setbacks. People who desperately want to succeed at one thing usually do.

Gloria Cisneros—Successful entrepreneurs are self-starters—internally motivated. They do lots of routine, behind-the scenes work and generally are willing to put in however many hours are necessary to get the job done right.

The successful entrepreneur generally has plenty of insight and awareness. He or she knows his or her own strengths and weaknesses, capabilities and limitations. I refer to this as having a mellow attitude—a sense of perspective and confidence.

I would also say that successful business operators make decisions based on the total picture. The long-run welfare of the entire company is considered the first priority. The entrepreneur is willing to make short-run sacrifices for long-run prosperity.

Orson McCord—From a venture capitalist's point of view, I can tell you that I look at an entrepreneur's personality and character before I look at his pro formas. There are several personality characteristics that really turn me off in an entrepreneur wanting financial backing. I like to refer to these as the four "Cs": cuties, Cadillacs, cruisers, and credit cards.

A cutie is a male entrepreneur who obviously lavishes a lot of money on girl friends. We don't want him buying diamonds and furs with our money. A Cadillac is an entrepreneur who spends lots of bucks on luxury automobiles. Cruisers spend big on yachts. Credit cards are entrepreneurs who finance all of the above on credit! I won't deal with one of these characters even for one minute because their profligate lifestyle simply isn't conducive to success.

The one other personality characteristic that is deadly to entrepreneurial success is lack of commitment. There are darn few people around who became millionaires with a part-time job. If a client of mine is not willing to commit himself life, body, and soul to his business, I want nothing to do with him.

What are the most difficult problems and challenges faced by entrepreneurs and small business owners today?

Coy Hamphill—The three toughest problems I know of are interrelated: cash flow, budgeting, and time. To put it succinctly, to control cash flow properly requires constant budgeting and that requires time. Most small business operators say they never find enough time to budget and control cash flow. No wonder! You have to make time for these—first things first!

Erik Sawyer—I see three additional, horrible problems victimizing entrepreneurs today: government regulation, inflation, and energy. These are all external forces which no business person can directly influence. Problems beyond your direct control are always the most frightening to deal with, and especially for entrepreneurs who pride themselves on their independence and self-sufficiency.

Big business often can absorb these external problems through passing on costs to the consumer, but few small firms enjoy such a luxury. Day-to-day survival can be very tenuous for the small guy today.

Gloria Cisneros—Besides the financial problems already alluded to, entrepreneurs have a devil of a time today finding qualified employees who will stay with the company through thick and thin. Almost every business manager I've talked to in recent years is concerned about this problem, and they have no easy solutions.

Orson McCord—Besides lack of capital, I think the biggest problem faced by many entrepreneurs is too much optimism. I see too many hot shots who think they're going to become millionaires overnight simply because they think they've got some grand scheme or idea. They proceed to spend money like a millionaire, painting themselves into a corner. I guess what I'm really saying is that too many entrepreneurs are their own worst enemy—they make problems for themselves.

What advice would you offer someone seriously comtemplating starting a new business?

Coy Hamphill—I would highlight two things. First of all, concentrate heavily on good day-to-day planning and surround yourself with qualified people capable of executing the plans. Secondly, make absolutely certain that you have enough cash to sustain you through the initial twelve to eighteen months. Do these two things, and you will be able to stay on top of problems on a daily basis. That's where long-run survival and prosperity will come from.

Erik Sawyer—Once again, I'll echo the theme of commitment. I'd tell the prospective entrepreneur that he or she must want the business so badly as to be willing to sacrifice practically everything for it. They should have the itch so deep that it can't be scratched. If the individual has a lot of other interests or values, they had better work for someone else.

Gloria Cisneros—First of all, I would advise the entrepreneur to make absolutely certain that he or she had a minimum of three professionals backing up the venture team: a CPA, a lawyer, and a banker. Not just any old CPA, lawyer, or banker but ones who will give the business a decent priority. Shop around and find some good professionals. Don't settle for mediocre consultants.

Also shop around for financing. Banks differ a lot more on interest rates and loan demands than most people suspect. Some banks want to play games with you; others genuinely want to go the extra mile for you.

One final piece of advice concerns premature growth. Far too many small companies get intoxicated with their first smell of success and immediately expand—sometimes too far too fast. Uncontrolled growth is usually worse than no growth at all.

Orson McCord—The first thing I would tell someone is to make sure you're serious about wanting to go into business for yourself. Without incredible dedication, you won't be able to pay the dues required.

Secondly, I would advise someone to make certain that they have thought through the business well on paper. The time to make mistakes is on paper, not when you've already spent a bundle. Look before you leap!

Analysis: Based on the roundtable discussion, develop your own integrated analysis of the keys to entrepreneurial success.

What is your own profile of the successful entrepreneur?

---

damon electric

44

Damon McIver is president and sole owner of Damon Electric Corporation in Seattle, Washington. Mr. McIver founded the company in 1977 for the purpose of repairing large electrical equipment such as transformers and generators. After graduating from the University of California in 1966 with a double major in math and physics, Mr. McIver worked in a series of marketing positions for several large industrial companies, including a leading electric contractor. He received an M.B.A. in finance from St. Louis University in 1975.

Damon, describe your business for us in general terms and give us the story of your start-up.

We repair large pieces of electrical equipment, such as transformers, generators, motors, and switch gear. I've got a 13,000-square-foot building and nine full-time employees. In 1980 the business grossed $150,000.

I got the idea for Damon Electric in 1977 when I noticed that only two major companies were in the business of repairing large electrical equipment for the likes of General Electric, Westinghouse, and Siemens. There were a lot of small mom and pop outfits that specialized in repairs for selected pieces of equipment, but only two companies covered the waterfront. I figured surely there was room for a third major repair company.

I had no desire to lead the way in pioneering some new kind of business never before in existence. I might be what could be called a conservative entrepreneur, if such an animal exists. Getting into a large market with limited competition was enough opportunity for me.

Once I clarified the basic nature of Damon Electric, my next challenge, besides physically locating somewhere, was to establish credibility with the large electric companies. General Electric or Westinghouse will not hire just anyone to fix a $50,000 transformer. I knew I had to come up with a strategic plan that would encourage GE and friends to accept me.

My approach was simple: build credibility through hiring creditable people. I became Morgan the Pirate and began stealing away the cream of the crop from my former employer. I hired away one guy who had been in the power-transformer business for 22 years, a shop foreman with 15 years of power-transformer experience, and four engineers with production-shop backgrounds.

The next thing I needed was a facility—one large enough for a crane capable of lifting up to 25 tons. Finding the right layout at a price that wouldn't immediately bankrupt me was not going to be easy—at least so I thought.

I was playing handball one day at a local club in Seattle when I ran into an old buddy I hadn't seen in years. He asked me what I was up to these days and I said, "I'm looking for a high bar crane." To my utter surprise, my friend responded, "Come see me tomorrow. I think I've got just what you're looking for." And sure enough he did. He worked for an engineering firm which had recently purchased a fabrication business with excess facilities. What was excess to them was made to order for me. What luck!

Analysis: Do you feel "luck" plays an important part in the success of many new ventures? Cite several illustrative examples.

To what extent do you feel entrepreneurs often "make their own breaks"? Again, cite illustrative examples.

Tell us how you got Damon Electric off the ground.

Well, there I was with a lot of fixed costs, $2,500 monthly for the building and over four grand a month for employee salaries. I needed some business fast. I managed to scare up a list of 2,300 companies across the country who potentially needed electrical repair work. I developed a series of mailings promoting Damon's services and sent them out on four successive weeks.

My aggressive merchandising worked. Within six weeks we had enough jobs to keep our small crew working overtime. From November of 1977 to September of 1978 we continued to expand rapidly—so much so that we outgrew our facility and contracted for additional space.

In October 1977 I made an even more aggressive expansion decision, purchasing another plant facility in Grand Island, Nebraska. I got 9,000 square feet for

$173,000. Now I had a Midwest facility to balance out the Northwest site. The company's ability to serve national customers was greatly enhanced. Damon Electric was definitely beginning to establish a solid reputation as a first-class competitor in the electrical maintenance industry.

What were your toughest problems at this stage of the game?

Cash flow and generating growth capital. Fortunately, I have part interests in two other businesses, both Kelly Girl-type operations. I have siphoned out funds consistently from both to put into Damon Electric. They have been excellent cash cows thus far. Other than this, Damon has been financed on debt—mostly short-term.

The electrical repair business is actually very self-sustaining, with about 20 percent net profit on sales after taxes. The need for large amounts of long-term capital is therefore fairly manageable.

Is Damon Electric, with its two locations, becoming too large for you to handle singlehandedly?

It's not quite there yet but well on the way. A professional manager will soon be needed, not just because of the size but also because of my personal need to constantly pursue new business ideas. No mature business can really tolerate an entrepreneur in the driver's seat for very long. Both growth and stability would be threatened.

Analysis: Why does Damon McIver state that no business can be successfully guided by an entrepreneur over the long run? Do you agree with him?

How can an entrepreneur determine when the time is ripe for turning over daily business operations to a professional manager?

Damon, have you always thought of yourself as an entrepreneur?

Not necessarily. When I was a corporate manager several years ago, I was quite content working within organizational constraints. At least when I got to do things my own way. Maybe that was the entrepreneur coming out in me after all!

If you were content working for others, why did you decide to go it alone?

Had to—I was fired. In 1976 my employer decided it couldn't put up with my wheeling and dealing in their repair division. I was too successful, ironically.

The company had me in charge of their maintenance services located in St. Louis. I was supposed to oversee technical operations and keep my nose clean. In six months or so the technical stuff was old hat to me, so I challenged myself by hustling up new clients for them. They didn't appreciate the entrepreneurial spirit from an operations manager.

In March 1977 I got a telegram at home: "Effective tomorrow you are terminated." I had been on vacation. They had decided to extend it indefinitely you might say! My wife Stacy told me that getting fired was the best thing that could have happened to me because it helped me figure out what I was really cut out for. I guess she was right.

If you had not been fired, do you think you would have ever started your own company?

I honestly can't say. I like to think that eventually I would have, but I sure was comfortable with my $50,000 annual income. The future had seemed fairly bright too. But not as bright as it seems now!

Analysis: Why exactly do you think Damon was fired?

In what ways can entrepreneurs be disruptive to companies? What actions can a large company take to accommodate entrepreneurs successfully in its personnel ranks?

Damon, have you ever regretted the decision to go it alone in your own venture?

Let's just say I've had to fight off pessimistic moods numerous times. I don't know that I've ever really second guessed myself, but I periodically become depressed over the wrenching challenge of keeping the company perking.

The mental and physical energy required is horribly draining at times, especially in the wee hours of the morning when I'm all alone at the office. The aloneness and darkness can have a depressive effect on even the most ebullient optimist.

But the low-lows produce high-highs. I can't tell you how much lasting satisfaction I derive from doing my own thing, as the cliche goes. Owning your own business gives you a real sense of purpose in life. It is your life. When my time comes, I fully intend to die sitting behind my desk!

Is the company your foremost priority in life coming before family and other pursuits?

My wife is first even though I spend more time on the business than with her. Stacy is my life-support system. In no way does she resent my dedication to the company because she knows that family also plays an important role in my life.

Do you know of many other wives who would call losing a $50,000 job the best thing that had ever happened to her husband? Stacy and I are a unified team with single-minded purpose.

Sure, I'd love to spend more time with Stacy and my two daughters. But if doing so meant abandoning my independent, achieving lifestyle, I'm convinced that the family would lose out in the long-run. Stacy and I would lose a dream. I would lose self-fulfillment. We'd all be losers. The vitality would be taken from our lives.

Analysis: Do entrepreneurs have to be "workaholics"? Can business success come any way other than through all-out personal commitment and dedication?

Do you personally feel you would be better off staying single if you intended to start your own business venture?

The following is an interview conducted with Damon's wife, Stacy McIver:

Stacy, describe Damon's entrepreneurial lifestyle from your own personal point of view.

Although I'm not involved in running the business in any direct way, I keep in fairly close touch with daily events. That Damon works hard is undeniably true, but he sincerely loves what he's doing. He thrives on it.

He usually gets home each evening around 8:00, although twice last week he stayed at the office past midnight. His schedule is hardly what you would call predictable, although he is home most nights. Work is his life and he is my life. Therefore, I don't mind being flexible and supportive in whatever way I can.

I suppose, ideally, I would like Damon to have a more traditional 8:00 to 5:00 schedule, but not if it prevented him from enjoying his work. I'm more interested in the quality of time I spend with him than the quantity.

I've always seen the desire in him to be his own boss and to call the shots in his own company. He's very well-adjusted in his job and successful. How many people can really say that?

I knew when I first met Damon that he had different qualities from most people. He's always had so much confidence and aggressiveness. His nervous energy propels him from one idea to the next, and he can hardly wait to put them into action.

Damon calls you his life-support system. Explain what he means by this.

Well, that's very flattering for him to say. I'm sure he's referring to the fact that I don't have any qualms or reservations about giving his career all-out support. We both have dedicated our lives to making Damon Electric successful.

It's not really a matter of putting his interests ahead of mine, because his interests are my interests. I have never had a desire to strike out on a career of my own. I'm fulfilled through Damon's success and the lives of my children.

I know that all sounds trite and old-fashioned, especially in light of today's E.R.A. trends, but it's the way I feel. I don't see how any entrepreneur could be very successful early in his career without strong family support.

Analysis: Did you agree with Stacy McIver that few entrepreneurs could establish themselves without strong family support?

What sacrifices do you feel an entrepreneur's spouse and children have to make?

What advice would you have for the wives of other entrepreneurs?

I really hesitate to hand out any general advice for others because I realize that not all women are like me. I certainly don't begrudge any woman the opportunity to pursue her own career. I just ask them not to put me down because I have chosen to support my husband's work. Entrepreneurs require freedom and flexibility. Hopefully the entrepreneur's family will not impede that freedom to any significant extent. The business owner has enough work-related problems without also having to fight domestic battles. Something has to give.

There's great satisfaction in teaming up with your spouse on a project that is truly meaningful to you both. That's what marriage is supposed to be all about, isn't it?

Analysis: Besides family support and encouragement, what other external factors must be right before an entrepreneur can successfully launch a new venture? Cite illustrative examples.

If you had a viable venture idea you wanted to pursue, would these external factors give you the "green light" or "red light"? What would have to change in your life before you could successfully initiate a new business venture?

what's your entrepreneurial potential?

45

There is no questionnaire, or assessment instrument, that can predict with absolute accuracy your chances of achieving entrepreneurial success. Success in the real world eludes simple formulas. However, a growing body of empirical research is making it increasingly clear that individuals with certain personal characteristics and behavior patterns are more likely to initiate business ventures and to establish successful performance track records.

The following questionnaire is designed to help you assess your own entrepreneurial potential more intelligently. By no stretch of the imagination is the questionnaire foolproof as a predictive instrument. But that's not its purpose. The sole purpose of the questionnaire is to stimulate your own thinking about the personal dynamics of entrepreneurship. Hopefully, the questionnaire will help you to better "know thyself."

Scoring instructions: Respond to each of the statements below. Put *A* in the answer blank if you basically agree with the statement; place a *D* in the blank if you basically disagree.

It is important that you reflect on the statement a few moments before you respond. Avoid "shooting from the hip" in your responses. For questions concerning interpersonal situations, it might help you to seek out the opinions and perspective of close acquaintances. In some areas of your behavior, other people may know you better than you know yourself!

_____ 1. Mistakes prevent success.
_____ 2. I am willing to take risks in order to meet my goals.

_____ 3. I generally like to do things exactly my way.
_____ 4. Nothing ventured, nothing gained!
_____ 5. I can be relied on to get the job done.
_____ 6. People sometimes tell me to slow down and not work so hard.
_____ 7. I feel guilty when I have a lot of free time on my hands.
_____ 8. I don't hesitate to make my opinions known to others.
_____ 9. Ultimately the best measure of success is money.
_____ 10. It generally takes strong external pressure to really get me working.
_____ 11. I value my security more than my freedom.
_____ 12. I tend to do most things like other people do.
_____ 13. I feel good after an unusually busy day.
_____ 14. Illness is no stranger to me.
_____ 15. Luck and factors beyond my immediate control have determined much of my life.
_____ 16. I tend to let other people set the standards; I strive to attain them.
_____ 17. I have more energy and pep then most of my friends.
_____ 18. I am frequently conscious of being different from other people.
_____ 19. I see most situations in life as opportunities for competition.
_____ 20. I am what I do.
_____ 21. I would rather work by myself than with other people.
_____ 22. I get sick and run down more often than most people.
_____ 23. I am conscious of setting goals for myself everyday.
_____ 24. People rarely take advantage of me.
_____ 25. I generally know about what time it is.
_____ 26. Wealth should be distributed to everyone equally.
_____ 27. I have been fairly successful in most of my past undertakings.
_____ 28. I am in control of my life.
_____ 29. Conformists usually get ahead.
_____ 30. Money is a poor measure of success.
_____ 31. I often doubt my ability.
_____ 32. Losers make more mistakes than winners.
_____ 33. I value status above accomplishment.
_____ 34. I fear failure.
_____ 35. What others think of me is more important than what I think.
_____ 36. If you want something done right, do it yourself!
_____ 37. The best teacher is experience.
_____ 38. People seldom misunderstand me.
_____ 39. I frequently duck problems hoping they will eventually go away.
_____ 40. I set high, but attainable, standards for myself.
_____ 41. I enjoy leisure activities more than work.
_____ 42. Money is very important to me.
_____ 43. Being fired from a job represents an opportunity rather than a failure.
_____ 44. I am a tougher competitor than most people I know.
_____ 45. Efficiency is still a virtue.
_____ 46. Competition is healthy.
_____ 47. Children should be required to earn part of their allowance.
_____ 48. I have little desire to get something for nothing.
_____ 49. Fate plays a large role in the lives of many people.
_____ 50. I know what I'm going to do tomorrow.

210719